Engraved by J. C. Buttre

FRANCIS WAYLAND.

From a bust executed in 1860
by Thomas Ball of Boston.

A MEMOIR

OF THE

LIFE AND LABORS

OF

FRANCIS WAYLAND, D.D., LL.D.,

LATE PRESIDENT OF BROWN UNIVERSITY.

INCLUDING

SELECTIONS FROM HIS PERSONAL REMINISCENCES
AND CORRESPONDENCE.

BY HIS SONS,

FRANCIS WAYLAND AND H. L. WAYLAND.

VOLUME II.

NEW YORK:
SHELDON AND COMPANY.
1867.

Stereotyped at the Boston Stereotype Foundry,
No. 4 Spring Lane.

CONTENTS

OF THE SECOND VOLUME.

CHAPTER I.

CHAPTER II.

CHAPTER III.

CHAPTER IV.

CHAPTER V.

CHAPTER VI.

CHAPTER VII.

CHAPTER VIII.

CHAPTER IX.

CHAPTER X.

CHAPTER XI.

CHAPTER XII.

CHAPTER XIII.

CHAPTER XIV.

CHAPTER XV.

LIFE

OF

FRANCIS WAYLAND.

CHAPTER I.

VOYAGE. — LIVERPOOL. — BIRMINGHAM.— PARTY SPIRIT. — BASSINGHAM. — LINCOLN CATHEDRAL. — FRANCE. — PARIS. — OBSEQUIES OF NAPOLEON. — LOUVRE. — HOTEL DES INVALIDES. — LOUIS XIV. — LONGING FOR HOME. — VERSAILLES. — JARDIN DES PLANTES. — IMPRESSIONS OF FRANCE. — LONDON. — THE QUEEN. — COURTS OF LAW. — LEARNED SOCIETIES. — UNIVERSITY OF LONDON. — WESTMINSTER ABBEY. — CAMBRIDGE. — J. J. GURNEY. — MRS. OPIE. — EDINBURGH. — OXFORD. — JOHN FOSTER. — HOME. — REMINISCENCES OF COLONEL DAVIS.

DR. WAYLAND had long desired to enlarge his knowledge of the most approved modes and systems of instruction by visiting the world-renowned seats of education. In 1840 the corporation voted him leave of absence for the purpose of visiting Europe, and requested Professor Caswell to discharge temporarily the duties of the presidency.

Professor Stuart, in a note accompanying a letter of introduction, remarks, —

"I need not say to you that a voyage to Europe has made a dunce of many an American who had some sense before he went. I believe it will not influence you in that manner. You do not go to see the *lions*, but to know more about men, and to advance your own resources. Peace be with you and yours.

"Glad should I be to hear from you when in England or Scotland, if you find any literary or religious phenomenon that will interest me, as no doubt you will. *Vive et vale.* The God who rules the seas protect and guide your way."

Atlantic steam navigation was then an experiment; and probably this consideration, combined with a hope of gaining in health from a prolonged voyage, led him to embark in a sailing packet. The voyage was long, rough, and every way unpropitious. He suffered greatly from sea-sickness; his digestion became deranged, and the physical and consequent mental depression seemed to cling to him during almost his entire absence.

To his father and sisters he writes, —

"... A more uncomfortable twenty-three days I have rarely experienced. A sea life is anything but agreeable, let them say what they may. It was peculiarly otherwise to me, in consequence of the absence of all religious society. Still I hope that it was not wholly unprofitable. I never was thrown so much on my Bible and on God. Never have I so much felt the excellence of prayer, and I trust also so many answers to it. I could not but believe that the prayers of my friends were on various occasions answered in my behalf."

During his journey Dr. Wayland maintained a somewhat full correspondence with his home, and also kept a diary for Mrs. Wayland. From these materials we shall make a few extracts that peculiarly illustrate his character, or explain his subsequent views. But for the most part the letters and the diary are either entirely of a personal nature, or have been robbed of their interest by the lapse of twenty-seven years, and by the vastly increased travel between America and Europe.

"*Liverpool, November* 1, *Sabbath.* Attended Dr. Raffles' church. The singing was more general throughout the house than with us; it was softer, but seemed to me rather careless. In prayer Dr. R. was delightful; devotional, calm, earnest, but solemn; particular, but not familiar. It raised the souls of the people to God, and kept them near to the throne. His voice is soft and musical, though not of great compass; his manner animated, yet not boisterous; his diction chaste, and sometimes ornate. He is, by the tone of his thought as well as his voice, rather calculated to produce admiration than conviction; to awaken feeling and gratify taste rather than to arouse the conscience and subdue the heart. On the whole, I was greatly pleased. I was never so much melted in any services of the sanctuary, unless it may have been at some communion seasons. The contrast between this and my last three Sabbaths, the voice of praise from the assembled multitude of Christian worshippers, the united prayers and thanksgivings from so many who loved the Lord Jesus, all came on my spirit with thrilling effect; and when the stanza, 'My God, how excellent thy grace!' was sung (a stanza which I have always greatly admired), and when I remembered the preservations of the voyage just closed, the answers to prayers still fresh in my recollection, my heart, in the language of Fisher Ames, 'grew liquid' while I sung, and I 'could pour it out like water.' . . ."

"I find it to be the common impression that the Tory interest is strengthened. I am told that when the reform bill passed, many of the reformers, elated by their success, determined to make it merely the commencement of a much more extensive and radical change. They declared at once for a dissolution of the connection between church and state. This had the twofold effect of arousing the dormant but enormous power of the Establishment, and of cooling the ardor of many of the most judicious reformers, who were satisfied with what they had gained, at least until they should see how it would work. By this means the Tory and Church party have gained, and are at this moment more powerful than they have been for many years.

"*Monday Evening*. I took tea at Dr. Raffles', in company with the dissenting ministers of Liverpool, who meet at each other's houses in succession on the first Monday of the month, and go from thence to the monthly concert. They were generally young, and seemed greatly oppressed by secular religious business. Every charity is governed by a committee, and these ministers form the committee, — a very time-consuming arrangement.

"I am struck with the great difference between an old and a new country. Here everything is fenced around by precedents; you cannot move without infringing on vested rights. If you attempt any reform, you are called upon to consider how it will affect the landed interest, or the aristocracy, or the church. It is taken for granted that everything must remain as it is, in so far as the powerful and the men of rank are concerned, and then, what is left may be managed for the good of the lower classes, provided you will give all the management into the hands of those whom 'God has made responsible for power.' I may be wrong. This is a first impression, and I so record it, that I may compare it with my subsequent views. With us everything stands on its own merits. There are no constitutional embarrassments. And in another respect there is a vast difference. I had no idea of the variety of grades and degrees which are marked below zero in the social scale. In addition to the various grades of titled rank, there are, below these, the rich and independent, the independent though not rich, the various ranks of retailers and artisans, the laborers and servants, and all those who are able by ordinary effort to procure food and clothing. This is with us as low as the scale usually goes. But here, I fear, there are many lower grades down to absolute starvation; and these grades comprise so large a portion of the population, that a benevolent mind shudders to think of it. It seems to be conceded that there is necessarily so much poverty, that the idea of doing away with it is not to be even entertained. I presume it is so to a very considerable extent in the large cities of our own country. But such is not, I think, the feeling of our people. We have much stronger confidence in social perfectibility.

"*Friday*. Made calls and dined at 'Green Bank' with Mr. Rathbone. The cottage, as it is called here, is of stone, beautifully built and delightfully situated. I do not know of anything of the kind in America — all the conveniences of a city, all the luxuries of living, all the elegances of literature, combined with the retirement of the country. There were present Mr. and Mrs. Rathbone,

Mr. Roscoe (son of the historian) and his wife, Mr. Booth, a gentleman distinguished for knowledge of mechanics, and manager of the B. and M. Railroad, Mr. Smith, Mr. Heady, Dr. Raffles, Mr. and Mrs. Thom, the latter a daughter of Mr. Rathbone. Conversation turned on phrenology, animal magnetism, politics, &c. It was free, perfectly good-natured, and animated. The party separated at about ten o'clock.

"Mr. R. accompanied me to my bedroom, and we talked, standing before the fireplace, for nearly an hour. He is a delightful man, very quiet, very intelligent, and guileless as a child. He reminds me in social intercourse of Dr. Bowditch, more than any other person whom I remember. He has the same love of justice, the same impulsiveness, the same gleefulness. Mrs. R. is a very intelligent woman. Mr. R. quoted a remark of Jeffrey: 'He did not object to blue stockings, provided the petticoats covered them.' I apprehend the remark could be applied to but few persons with more justice than to Mrs. R.

"*November* 7. Took the train to Birmingham. The road passes through a very level country; the soil, in general, a stiff clay, at present saturated with water. The hedges, of which we hear so much, were very often broken down, and the hawthorns straggled and interrupted. The climate is so moist that the brick and stone soon become dark-colored, and the roofs in a few years are covered with green moss. Everything looks old. The fields are small and well cultivated, of course, since the price of land renders this indispensable. The cattle are better than ours, but I did not see one cow equal to mine. The grass is still green. There has been no black frost, and the cattle are yet in the fields. They have rain instead of cold.

"This railroad is smoother than is common with us. The journey (ninety-eight miles) is made in four and a half hours. Saturday evening arrived at Birmingham, where my friend Rev. Dr. Hoby lives in a very pleasant style, and preaches the gospel without compensation. I have received from Dr. and Mrs. Hoby the utmost Christian hospitality.

"*Sabbath Morning*. Dr. Hoby's chapel. Was unwell, and did not hear to advantage. Preached in the evening, still unwell.

"*Monday.* Went out with Dr. Hoby. Bible meeting. The king's printer receives ten thousand pounds a year from the printing of the Scriptures — a shocking monopoly, which to this amount, for no reason whatever, increases the price of the holy oracles. Rev. J. A. James visited us, and took tea. All the talk about abolition, &c. It is amazing to perceive how this question seems to absorb every other among the dissenters, and to what extent they carry out their notions. A man who does not adopt their opinions is, it would seem, excommunicated from church and society. I have already had some reason to observe this. May God grant me grace to act like a Christian, and the more abundantly to love them the less I be loved. I respect their motives and their love of freedom, although I have small sympathy with their modes of expression. I have suffered intolerably from low spirits. I apprehend that this arises partly from ill health. I pray God to restore me to health, and to enable me diligently to employ the time which he has allotted to me here, that I may be the means of promoting the cause of education, and of doing good to my country and to the church of God.

"Birmingham has been remarkable for the strength, I may say bitterness, of its political animosities. Here Dr. Priestley's house was torn down by a mob. Here was formed the famous union which drew together two hundred thousand people to petition for reform. It is still the centre, to a considerable degree, of all radical political action. The same temper seems to be carried into religious, and even into benevolent, associations. Here, at present, all is in agitation and ferment among the dissenters about abolition. It is assumed that these gentlemen are to decide not only whether slavery be right or wrong, but also in what manner it is to be abolished, and that they have a right to treat as they will whosoever does not, under all circumstances, do as they see fit. They decide what is the duty of the northern states and of every citizen thereof, and they excommunicate, without reserve, every one who does not agree with them to the utmost. Here, then, we see in dissenters the admission of the very principles which they abhor when put in practice by the Establishment. It is an assumption of the power and right to inflict disabilities or exclusions on those who differ from them in points on which every man may justly claim to entertain an opinion of his own. They know not, as it seems to me, what manner of spirit they are of. And, besides, this spirit of exclusion, let it exist where it will, is anti-social. If the claim on which it is founded be allowed, where is it to end? One party excludes another for disagreement in respect to the slavery question. By the same principle they should proceed to exclude each other for disagreement on the question of temperance, or of peace, or of woman's rights. Thus exclusion begets exclusion *ad infinitum.* The result is party spirit, bickerings, seclusion from each other, and all its natural attendants — the indulgence and the cultivation of the evil passions of the human heart. Is it a wonder, then, that the best — and these are always the peace-loving — are attracted to the Establishment, where such feuds are less known, and where, at least, this exclusive tendency is, from the nature of the church, unable to take effect? Is it strange, then, that, with all the errors, and faults, and weaknesses of the church, and even in spite of the false position in which it is placed, it should not only maintain its ground, but even make head against its opponents? . . ."

We quote from the reminiscences of Dr. Stow: —

"When I was in England the following summer, I was informed of an incident which I could well understand. Dr. Wayland, in the course of his visits to the English institutions of learning, called to see the Baptist Academy in ——, where many eminent Baptist ministers had been educated. The principal, who was also the preacher at —— Chapel, after giving Dr. Wayland all facilities for examining the institution, said, 'Sir, I am sorry that I cannot invite you to occupy my pulpit next Sabbath. Personally, I have no objection; but some doctrines in your treatise on "The Limitations of Human Responsibility" have rendered you unpopular in England, and, were I to do it, I should incur reprehension.' Dr. Wayland replied in one sentence: 'Sir, when I ask for your pulpit, it will be time enough for you to refuse it.'

"Several times, while I was in England, I heard that story related, and the severity of the rebuke justified. In a few other places he encountered supercilious treatment from small men, and several of his replies to discourteous words were quoted as proofs of his power of disposing effectually of such annoyances."

From Birmingham he went to Bassingham, where he was a welcome guest in the accomplished and cultivated family of his uncle, Rev. Daniel S. Wayland, rector of Bassingham. His acquaintance with this gentleman, which was subsequently maintained by correspondence, and by the interchange of frequent kind offices, was one of the most pleasing incidents of his journey. There was something not a little remarkable in the mutual attachment subsisting between two men, of whom one was an Englishman, thoroughly loyal to church and state, the other the sturdiest of republicans; one a conservative in religion and politics, the other in the front rank of progressives; one an Episcopalian, the other an Independent and a Baptist. But a common appreciation of all that is excellent in the world of letters, and a common loyalty to the Redeemer, afforded them a broad ground of sympathy, a strong bond of attachment.

From Bassingham he proceeded to Lincoln.

"Until I had seen Lincoln Cathedral I had no conception of the power of architecture. As you survey its exterior, you are struck with its vast size. Yet, owing to the perfect proportions, the great height, the profusion of ornaments (ornaments, however, so light and graceful, so in keeping, that all seems precisely in the right place, and never too much nor too little), you forget its magnitude in admiration of its beauty. The great tower is immensely high, and is the most impressive part of the exterior. It looks like the work of fairy hands. You would not believe that stone could ever assume a form so fragile, much less that it could retain that form unhurt for centuries.

"But all this impression is deepened when you enter the building and look up the nave of two hundred and eighty feet. Here you see the power of the Gothic pillar and arch. You pass to the transept, and gaze upon the painted windows, the stone compartments of which look as though cut out of paper. You proceed to the choir, and examine the carved work which adorns it so profusely on every side. You visit the chancel, where repose the ashes of the builder, the bishops of the Cathedral, and other eminent dead. You walk through the side aisles; you gaze upon the arch supporting, with infinite ease, the mighty mass of the central tower; and at every step you are filled with wonder, which you strive in vain to express. It is the epic of architecture. It is certainly one of the most wonderful efforts of human talent. I do not remember ever to have seen any work of art which impressed me so powerfully. Grecian architecture — a simple, beautiful, and sublime conception, but all external — fades away before it. The greatest power of the Gothic is within. The sense of beauty is in the highest degree gratified in both, but in Gothic the effect is more various and more inexhaustible, with a vastly deeper tinge of sublimity. It accomplishes its purpose — a more difficult one — with greater skill, and more perfectly. The Grecian merely suggests to you that this was the work of man. The Gothic is all so light, so strong, so flexible, so rich in ornament, and yet so consistent with itself, that the idea which constantly presents itself to you is, that it grew; that it is the work of nature, and not of art; and yet, when you reflect that this is all the work of man, that man designed, conceived, and planned it, knew the difficulties, and how to overcome them, and did actually overcome them, you are overwhelmed at his genius, and cannot fail to perceive that he must have been one of the most able men of any age.

"The Roman Arch is remarkable for its associations. What events have transpired since it was erected! What generations have passed away! Lincoln was once an important Roman station. Here works were erected to keep in check the hordes of barbarians whom Rome was subduing to her sway. And now those barbarians are able to cope with the world in arms, and Rome, 'lone mother of dead empires' — what is she? . . ."

After crossing the Channel, he writes, —

"Everywhere in France we found soldiers in great numbers. The milita are detailed to serve in the army, I believe, from nineteen to twenty-six. Thus the flower of the nation, at an age in which character is forming, are obliged to learn the habits of the camp and barracks.

Such a shocking waste of human beings I had never conceived. The soldiers whom we saw were all young, and seemed to have nothing to do, with one exception. At St. Omers we saw a detachment returning from work with shovels on their shoulders. But this was merely military labor. It added nothing to the means of human subsistence or human happiness. These men were taken from the plough, the workshop, and the mart of business. I do not, however, blame the government. What could they do better? Such a government is infinitely better than anarchy. Yet why will man not learn that self-control is wiser than force? that religion is cheaper than muskets? that the proper cure for human evils must begin with the heart? O God, send forth thy light and thy truth, and illumine with the rays of the Sun of Righteousness the dark places of the earth, and reclaim this world, which the Savior has purchased with his blood! Never before did I realize the necessity of strong faith, and never before did I conceive of the immensity of power which is involved in the fulfilment of the promises of God. Look at this nation, advanced in civilization, bowing down in form to the Romish ceremonial, yet without God in the world. 'By whom shall Jacob arise?' How shall this kingdom be subdued unto Christ? we ask; but we can make no reply. Faith alone looks to the promises of God, and, relying upon them, knows that what God has spoken he will certainly fulfil. But this is one of the nations denominated *Christian;* what are we, then, to say of the millions and hundreds of millions of Heathendom and Mohammedanism? How great is the work which is to be accomplished before Jesus Christ takes to himself his power, and reigns King of nations! Hasten it, O God, in thy time, and let me, though most unworthy, in some manner conduce to the good of thy chosen, the prosperity of thy heritage!

"Every step and every moment impress me more strongly with the fact that Americans know not their own mercies, nor how to conceive of them. The blessings of true religion, of equal rights, of being each one allowed to take care of himself, of not being over-governed, — all throng upon an American abroad with a depth of meaning of which at home he knew nothing.

"*Friday*, *December* 11, *Paris.* Visited the preparations making for the reception of the remains of Napoleon. It is said the ceremony will be the most imposing that modern times have witnessed.

"... Nature and art have united to grace with their loveliest offerings this city of taste. Much of this is owing to Napoleon. He intended to make Paris the centre of the civilized world. In part he has succeeded, but only in part. No city or nation can be central to the world without surpassing all others in wealth and mental energy. These can only exist under free government, enlightened by universal education, and by the religion of the gospel, with its benign and ennobling effects. Of these he had no conception. He aimed at results which physical means could not accomplish, and thus he signally failed.

"I expect, during this week, to behold more of the glory of man than ever before. Grant me, O God, a wise and holy temper! Enable me to survey everything in a kindly spirit, willing, nay, desirous to be pleased, yet as a Christian and as an heir of immortality. Grant me health, if it may please thee, that I may accomplish something for myself, and especially for the cause of education and of religion. May I be seriously in earnest. May my faculties be aroused, my observation awakened, and may I thus obtain knowledge which shall be of permanent use to me. May I never forget the lessons which thou art teaching me. May I be strengthened to confide in thee, and may I, by every vicissitude through which I pass, be enabled the better to glorify thee both here and hereafter. All this I ask for Jesus Christ's sake. Amen.

"*Monday*, *December* 14. The whole city seems in motion. Every part is crowded. A vast number of strangers is said to be present. Yet I saw nothing that looked like disaffection or unkindness to the government. All seemed pleased and satisfied. There were no knots of persons consulting or criticising. I apprehend the fears of an outbreak are groundless.

"In the afternoon returned and wrote to friends at home. After dinner attended the conversazione of M. Coquerel, a distinguished Socinian Protestant preacher, and one of the most effective pulpit orators in France. He is also a voluminous writer. He seemed exceedingly quick, learned, eloquent in conversation, and polite. He is strongly impressed with the belief that Protestant sentiments are gaining ground in France. His church — an established Protestant church — is crowded. Many of his hearers are distinguished men; among them is Guizot. Whence his hopes arise I know not. He thinks that a reformation will proceed from the Catholic clergy themselves. I learn from him that all the lectures here by the most eminent men are gratuitous. He said that, no matter what might be the subject, be it science, or the arts, or languages, you would find it taught gratuitously. Yet among the people in general education is at a low ebb.

"*Tuesday*, *December* 15. The pageant is over. I presume that from fifty to one hundred thousand troops were present. Besides these the crowd was immense. Everything seemed well conducted. The houses were deserted, the shops shut, and all was in motion; yet I have not heard that any accident occurred. The pageant in line of motion, aside from the car and the personages immediately near it, was not impressive; there was almost nothing except the body of troops, and from a single station you could see but little of the long line. It was very cold, and a sheltered situation was worth a great deal, and, I may add, cost a great deal. The people seemed but little affected. They cheered when the car approached, but nothing was funereal; and, upon the whole, the impression on my mind is that of a splendid, vain show. Such is human glory!

"Americans say — and 'The Guide to Paris' seems not to deny it — that the people of Paris are totally devoid of honesty to foreigners. Such, however, might be expected to be the condition of a country without God. Yet, with all this, there is intense love of knowledge among scientific men, great self-sacrifice in advancing it, and an intense love of truth, that is, scientific truth. The ardor in this cause is such as we have no conception of in our country. All catch the enthusiasm; but then it is remarkable that it is but slightly connected with benevolence. Men study diagnosis, and are willing to do anything to diagnose; but whether a patient live or die is almost a matter of indifference. I say *almost*, but this is hardly true. They rather prefer that the patient should die, as this enables them to determine the truth of the diagnosis.

"Visited the Louvre again, and walked through the gallery of Spanish pictures purchased lately by the present king. The number is very considerable, but I should think the value could not be great. I saw few that struck me pleasantly but Murillo's. These were almost universally fine. A picture of Joseph and the Savior was, I think, the best picture I have seen in Paris. The others seemed hard and dry, the outline fixed, and the coloring a dead level, without relief or any gentleness of shading. I have a very clear idea of what I mean, but I know not how to express it. I have not the language of the art, and hence, if my meaning cannot be guessed, it will probably be unknown.

" *Saturday*. Hotel des Invalides. The chapel and the approach to it are hung with black cloth studded with bees in silver paper, and lighted with innumerable chandeliers. In the centre is the catafalque, an immense gilded structure, containing various emblematical figures, and bearing on its top the black marble coffin, in which are the remains of the emperor. Its appearance is imposing, but everything has been done for parade and in a hurry, and already the frail fabric begins to show signs of decay. Such is human grandeur! O God, why should we fix our affections on earth? It is all deceitful, vain, and more fleeting than a shadow. Suppose we add to this, what is infinitely better, the pure affection of upright souls; still what is this to thy love, to the consciousness of thy favor, to the indwelling of thy Spirit! Whom have I in heaven but thee, and there is none upon earth that I would desire in comparison with thee. Reveal thyself to me, O God. Make thy face to shine upon me. Fill me with humble and adoring views of thy character and work; and may I here and everywhere, and through time and eternity, glorify thee in my body and spirit, which are thine.

" *Wednesday*, *December* 23. Visited the gallery of modern sculpture, at the Louvre. Louis XIV. is a great favorite with the genius of France. His likeness is seen everywhere in stone or on canvas. His praises have been sung by poets, and his deeds recorded by historians. Men and women — I had almost said kingdoms — bowed before him. And yet, when weighed in the balance of justice and truth, what was Louis XIV.?

" Sunday morning I spent at home, afternoon preached at Chapel Thaibout, from Rom. viii. 1. I felt it a privilege to be permitted to lift up my voice for God in the midst of this city. May the Holy Spirit render it a blessing to some immortal soul.

Monday. Attended the Chamber of Deputies. The speakers were animated, but monotonous; the attention about as good as in our House. Rather more were present; fewer were engaged in writing, more in talking, and there seemed more noise. The speaker was frequently employed in rapping on the desk with the handle of his paper-knife, and in ringing his bell. This occasioned a little variety, but I did not perceive that it had any effect in diminishing the rattling of tongues. The representatives are, in general, an intelligent company of men.

"*Monday Evening.* Went to Monsieur J.'s soiree at the Royal Library. It was numerously attended. Moderate refreshments, coffee, some sort of spirits and water, hot, in small glasses, and little pastries and tea, made up all that I saw of the material part of the entertainment. Mr. J.'s rooms, three in number, lined with books, engravings, and curiosities, were open, and the visitors looked at the one, read the other, or talked together, as suited them, without restraint, and came and went as they pleased. Mr. J. was dressed as usual, having a green shade over his eyes, and seemed a happy, cheerful old gentleman. He was with Napoleon, attached to the scientific corps in Egypt, and is the last survivor of that body. It is the custom in France for gentlemen whose society is at all sought after, to have an evening which they appropriate in this way to the reception of company. They send to their friends a general invitation. In this manner various parties and numerous individuals are brought together, and the social bond is strengthened throughout all the walks of literary and well-bred society. It could, I think, be well introduced into our country.

"Last evening I went to General Cass', to see Marshal Soult. I arrived, through the indolence and stupidity of the coachman, just as he had left. Such is the fate of a traveller. You traverse thousands of miles to see persons and places, you have but a fixed time to devote to each, and some accident occurs which puts it wholly out of your power to accomplish your purpose.

"*Friday, January* 1. Mr. S. proposes to accompany me to Italy if I will go. I am strongly tempted. I know that many of my friends will expect me to go. I know there is much to be seen there, and I should be pleased to travel with Mr. S. But, after all, I am a husband and a father. I am under the obligation of these relations. I doubt my right to spend this time in pleasure. Besides, I am no longer young. My time, to the church and the world, ought to be valuable. I doubt whether I have a right to spend it in this manner. Life is too short to devote much of it to sight-seeing.

"I have been here a month. I have not been idle, and yet how very little have I gained or learned which I did not know before! and of what small value is that which I have learned! A man who does not speak the language of the country in which he is, can see nothing but buildings, trees, &c., the mere external forms; and these in winter are not very beautiful or very attractive. Besides, several matters in my own country seem to demand my attention — the Convention, at which I might possibly be of use, the meeting of my brethren in May, where I hope to be present. Indeed, I feel more than ever the importance of laboring for Christ while it is day. This sort of life does not suit me, and I had better return, as soon as Providence permits, to my labors. My conscience intimates to me that this is the path of duty, and my feelings unite in the decision."

To Deacon Lincoln he writes, —

"... I hope by the blessing of God, and in answer to your prayers and those of my brethren in America, to return in April. I have seen enough of the Old World, its church and state, its blessings and its curses, to make me long inexpressibly for home. I feel as I never felt before the utter vanity of everything earthly, and the supreme desirableness of living at all times and in all places for God. Never before did the church of Christ seem half so precious, or the communion of saints half so lovely. Never before did I so clearly recognize the importance of laboring to spread the gospel at home, or desire so strongly to live for Christ alone. I want to be at home at the meeting of the Convention, to say to my brethren, 'Love one another,' and to strive with them to keep the unity of the Spirit in the bonds of peace. You cannot imagine the advantages we enjoy until you see the condition of others. Our country, bad as it may be, is simple, virtuous, moral, and religious, in comparison with other countries. God bless her, and lift her up forever. . . ."

To another friend he writes, —

"You well know how sweet to the travelling exile is the package of letters from the land of his fathers. One thing, however, you do not know, and that is how delightful it is to hear from that land, of the welfare of wife and children, from whom you have been absent. May you never be thus separated. No one who has not made the trial can be at all aware of the pain which it involves and the care through which it leads. All London would not tempt me to repeat the experiment."

"*Monday*. Jardin des Plantes. This magnificent establishment, nearly two hundred years old, is upon a scale more grand than I had conceived. I learn that travelling professors are continually exploring every corner of the globe, and sending home, from time to time, all that they can collect of whatever has not yet been treasured up in the Garden of Plants. Lectures, on an average of four a day, are delivered by the most eminent men in France or the world, on all subjects of natural science. And all this is open to the public in the freest sense. Any one who chooses may avail himself of these advantages. It is difficult to imagine a more attractive mode of recommending science to an intelligent community. Here is one of the most delightful spots to be seen on earth, possessing everything that can gratify the eye or please the taste, and all this devoted to science and made to minister to knowledge.

"*Saturday*. Visited Versailles. The gardens form the most remarkable feature of this place. The whole gave me a conception, such as I had never before formed, of royal magnificence. It also raised my conception of the talent of Louis XIV.

"But it cost, as is supposed, forty millions sterling. This sum would have constructed thirteen canals, each as expensive as the Erie Canal, and would before this time have doubled or trebled the wealth of France. I am well satisfied to be without such monuments, and specially without the power in a government to make such a use of the money of the people.

"I hear my countrymen sometimes lament that we have

no monuments to taste and the arts, no palaces like those which we see in Europe. I do not participate in their lamentations. It may be said that these things foster love of country. But what is love of country? Is it the admiration of splendid palaces, of magnificent paintings, of gilded domes, of lofty columns, of spacious gardens, of powerful fleets, and numerous armies? These may tend to exaggerate what is called the love of glory, the love of national supremacy, but it is far different from what I call love of country. I love the cities, and far more the fields, the woods, the rivers, the waterfalls, the clear blue sky, the interminable horizon of my native land. And I love them, I trust, as sincerely as a Frenchman loves his old chateaux or his splendid Paris.

"But more, far more, I love her free institutions, her universal education, her spiritual liberty and her religious observances, her moral purity and her simple manners, the perfect freedom with which mind is there suffered to develop, and the means afforded to foster that development. These are the attributes which awaken my love of country.

"I see that here no revolution would be produced by enlarging or abridging either the means of education, or by increasing or diminishing religious freedom. But I presume a serious murmur would arise if the sums appropriated to the theatres and operas were restricted, or if the public squares were allowed to decay. I believe in the beauty of public places. I believe in sacrificing to taste as much as taste is worth. But supposing a given amount of money is raised, in what proportion shall it be devoted to the intellectual cultivation of a people, to improving their condition physically and mentally, and what proportion to buildings, palaces, and splendid but useless edifices. I must say I go for the useful. Palace after palace has been raised in Paris, million upon million has been expended in adorning the capital, but there is no railroad yet from Paris to the sea, nor any railroad in the kingdom, except from Paris to Versailles — a railroad to see a show. I am more and more a Puritan. I love simple manners, simple tastes, a simple government, which has very little to do, which leaves everything possible to be done by the individual, and which stimulates talent of every kind, not by patronage, but by giving talent free exercise, and leaving it to its own resources; a government of which the constitution may remain firm as adamant, while the men who administer it may be changed every year by the popular will. This is the country for me, and may it be the country for my children; and may it please God that such a country long may be the United States of America.

"Here are books, libraries, lecturers, all the means for learning, and here is learning itself. We have neither books, libraries, nor learning. But we have institutions which develop mind, which unfold and invigorate the faculties, and give action and energy to whatever knowledge we possess. This, at least in some degree, counterbalances the defect in learning. An American mind of the same native strength is, I apprehend, a match for a European. Learning does not give a European the same advantage when compared with us, that it does when compared with his own countrymen. We are benefited by our training, he is not. So, at least, it seems to me. It may be nothing but Yankee prejudice; but this is my opinion, and there is the end of it.

"On Thursday left Paris in the diligence for Boulogne. We had taken passage in a particular line, because we were informed that it was fitted up expressly for winter. It was cushioned in some peculiar way to promote the passengers' comfort, and warmed by vessels of hot water placed under the floor. When I looked at the coach, and inquired for the warm water, I was told that this day was so warm that it would be uncomfortable. When Mr. B. inquired of the agent, he was told that they were out of repair, and would not be used at this time. When we had proceeded half the journey, we asked the conductor about it, and he laughed at our credulity. The whole story was a humbug. The consequence was, that one of our party suffered most severely from cold. From first to last, all my dealing with Frenchmen has shown me more and more their disposition to lying and dishonesty. I left Paris without a single regret, nay, with a feeling allied to exultation. Why it was so I can scarcely say. I had seen many interesting things there; I had learned something of men and manners; I had experienced in some cases hospitality, and in one or two cases, especially, the most devoted friendship. But I was glad to be out of a city without a God, a city of frivolity, of heartless gayety, of thorough selfishness, and of sensual appetites and savage passions. I know that all this is glossed over by much that is attractive, and much that is fascinating. There is in Paris an unusual degree of taste, rather than refinement, of civility, if not of politeness. But there seems to be among the people at large no moral basis. Their feeling seems no deeper than a shrug of the shoulders. But I had better stop here. I like them not, and may be prejudiced against them. They treat Americans better than they do Englishmen. The one they cheat kindly, the other surlily; but both are considered, I think, in the nature of victims."

Dr. Stow favors us with the following: —

"When I first entered Paris with my wife and Mr. and Mrs. G., while on our way to our hotel, we met Dr. Wayland, and were welcomed by him with warm cordiality. He was often at our rooms, appearing greatly to enjoy the society of those whom he knew, and who could speak English. He was suffering from depression of spirits, occasioned partly by the physical effects of an uncomfortable sea voyage, and partly by a feeling of loneliness among a people of whose character he had not a high estimate. At different interviews he made remarks expressive of his state of mind, such as, 'This crossing the Atlantic is no joke.' 'This visiting Europe is not what it is cracked up to be.' 'You have come here for your health: that is well enough; but I do not think any minister has a right to spend six months for the mere purpose of sight-seeing. All the talk about mental improvement is the merest fudge. Life is too short to justify the waste of such a fraction of it. If I live to return, I shall set my face against the practice as wicked.' One Sabbath evening he came in deeply affected by what he had seen of the desecration of the day, and expressed a desire to join with us in some religious service. After tea he gave us a rich exposition of Romans viii., and then offered prayer — such a prayer as only he could make, and such as seldom ascends from that city of frivolity and sin. That evening was one of the greenest spots in our tour.

"While he was in Paris, General Cass, then our minister at the French court, made arrangements to 'present' a number of Americans to the royal family. In that number Dr. Wayland and the Hon. Isaac Davis, of Worcester, were included. When the company was collected and duly arranged in the audience-room at the Tuileries, they had to wait some time, standing in a semicircle for an introduction to his majesty. The doctor was ill at ease, and at length expressed his regret that he had suffered himself to be placed in such a position, and made strong remarks indicative of a feeling of humiliation. Subsequently he declared to me his conviction, that such homage to a man, mortal like himself, was 'unworthy of an ambassador of the King of Kings.'"

Returning to England, he writes, —

"*Saturday*, *London*. Breakfasted with Sir R. H. Inglis.

"At breakfast Sir R. and Lady Inglis, Lady Raffles, and two gentlemen. Sir Robert is a fine specimen of an old English baronet, intelligent, straightforward, with firmly fixed opinions, yet tolerant, frank, and I should think very consistent and religious. It was a very pleasant occasion. Lady Raffles is a most interesting woman, subdued with grief, yet cheering up in conversation.

"In the evening, dined at Mr. Bates'. There were there Dr. Milman, prebendary of Westminster (the poet), and his wife, Mr. and Mrs. P. Butler (Miss Kemble), Mr. Baring, &c. Dr. Milman is not externally very much of a poet. His appearance is heavy, and his manner slow. In conversation he evinces good taste and much kindness of manner.

"*Evening*. Dined at Mr. J. Parkes', a distinguished barrister. Conversation on state of country, political and religious. Mr. Parkes is, I think, the most remarkable man I have ever seen in England — cool, sagacious, unruffled, bold, determined, yet willing to bide his time. He will rise to eminence, and if ever trouble comes, he will be a man to be looked up to.

"*Monday*. Called to see Miss Edgeworth, with Mrs. Sigourney. Miss Edgeworth is a woman far advanced, small, not handsome, affable, but with nothing that would betoken the authoress. She has evidently all the kindness which ordinarily attends high and successful intellectual accomplishments.

"Dined at Sir R. H. Inglis'. There were there Hallam

(Middle Ages), the Dean of Chichester, Mr. Palmer (a distinguished Cambridge scholar and barrister), Lady Raffles, Sir Demetrius Balsamachi and his wife, and the late Bishop Heber's widow. I had much conversation, principally on religious subjects, with Lady Raffles. She is a very intelligent, pious, and lovely woman.

"*Thursday*, *January* 26. The queen opened Parliament, and through the kindness of Mr. Bates I was furnished with a ticket. This merely gave me access to the gallery or corridor along which the royal *cortége* and the peers and peeresses passed. There were present the guard, a common looking troop, the yeomen of the guard, and the beefeaters, dressed like harlequins. The peeresses and peers' daughters were passing me for an hour and a half. They are not so fine looking an assembly of ladies as I had expected. I saw no one whose bearing was as noble as that of Lady Raffles. I saw none of that baronial aspect of command, none of that bewitching charm of loveliness, or that majestic self-reliance, which we have been taught to expect in the descendants of ancient families. They acted just as our own women would have acted. They felt as awkwardly in awkward positions, and presented as great a variety of manners and behavior, as well-bred women among us. None of them were strikingly handsome. The queen, preceded by the chancellor, prime minister, and high officers of the crown, passed close by me. Prince Albert led her by the hand. Her robe was borne by two ladies, followed by two gentlemen and four pages. She is a small, pale, girlish-looking young woman, with nothing peculiar in her countenance, at least under the circumstances in which I saw it. Prince Albert is a moderate-looking young person. I could not perceive any marked indication in him, though this could hardly be expected for the moment I saw him. Both he and the queen really looked like persons who were thinking of something else (as was probably the fact), and made you suppose that they were two young and innocent persons who were unable to comprehend the nature of the transactions that were going on around them.

"I know not how it is, but all I see renders me more doggedly a Democrat and a Puritan. I say this wholly without unkindness. I have no objection to these forms, for those at least who like them. I had supposed that such spectacles would be impressive, and would convey some feeling of awe or reverence to my mind or to that of the people. But I confess such was not the fact. It seemed to produce no impression upon anybody, and appears on reflection to be merely a matter of puppet-show. It is nothing but acting, and the mind falls off from it. The peers, if they intend to keep up the thing, should themselves pay more attention to it. If they mean to impress the nation by a spectacle, everything must conduce towards it. If they treat it as a slip-shod matter, it will soon lose all respect among the people, and they may as well give it up altogether. Such, at any rate, is my impression. I am new in these matters, but I believe little in the effect of such things upon the human mind, and I return with more and more complacency to our plain manner of doing things.

"I forgot to say that, before the arrival of the Queen, I went, in company with R. Ingham, Esq., M. P., a Serjeant of Queen's Bench, to visit the several courts. We called at the Chancellor's and Vice-Chancellor's Courts, the Court of Exchequer, the Court of Common Pleas, and Court of Queen's Bench. It was a thing remarkable to look at. I do not now speak of the robes, &c. In the pictures these seem far more august than in the reality. I saw all these in passing from one court to another, and before I had seen them all, I hardly observed them, so readily does the mind lose all power of being impressed with what is merely a matter of form. I say, this did not look particularly venerable. But when I remembered that before me, on every bench, were men who were the lights of the world, men whose authority on any question of law or justice would be respected to the remotest limits of Christendom, and that these men were there devoting themselves, with the full power of their faculties, to the administration of justice throughout this realm,— this, I must say, impressed me. Here I beheld the majesty of law. Here I saw a temple erected for the habitation of Justice. Here I saw a barrier to the encroachments of aristocracy, and a rampart against the waves of popular fury. I felt that the voice of law uttered there was heard and obeyed throughout the land, and I knew that I was in a region of civilization, of justice, nay, of Christianity; for out of the limits of Christendom, where shall all of this or any of it be found?

"I was much pleased to perceive with what freedom the counsel addressed the bench on a point of law. The judge and the counsel differed, and the counsel pushed his lordship as closely and as freely, though with entire respect, as he would have done one of his brethren, and, as it seemed, without offence.

"The whole bearing of the assembly was that of several men of eminent talent and learning, striving, to the best of their abilities, to arrive at law and justice, in the cases submitted to their jurisdiction. It was a more impressive sight, I must say, than the scarlet robes of the peers, the ermine of the bishops, the crown of state, the robe of her majesty, or all the pomp and circumstance which I witnessed an hour or two afterwards.

"*Wednesday.* Breakfasted with N. W. Senior, Esq., a gentleman well known as a writer on political economy, and the author of the present poor law system. He was formerly professor of political economy in Oxford. Two other gentlemen were present.

"*Thursday Evening.* Met, at Mr. Kenyon's, Mr. Rogers, the poet, and his sister, Sir George Staunton, and many others. Mr. Rogers is a rather stout-built old gentleman, with a very short neck, somewhat stooping, and looking as though a mistake had been made in setting his head on his shoulders.

"*Friday.* Went to Stepney, to Dr. Murch's, to dine. Here I met Rev. Messrs. Dyer, Cox, Angus, Stovel, Crow, Steane, and Greene, and possibly some others. They are all Baptist clergymen, and seem intelligent men. They are generally rather young, a good deal interested in abolition, but good-natured in all their intercourse with me. I was pleased with the interview. We had some conversation on slavery, on the Bible question, the condition of dissenters, and the manner of organizing congregations. I believe that not a word was said that gave any offence, and the whole thing passed off very pleasantly. Mr. ——, who had been represented to me as the most bitter, as I presume he is, after a good deal of conversation, walked with me to the omnibus, and evinced a very pleasant and candid temper of mind.

"*Saturday.* Dined at Sir James Clarke's. There were present Sir J. Lubbock, a banker, and president of the Royal Society, a very able mathematician, Dr. Arnott,

Dr. Key, Professor Wheatstone, Professor Madden, Dr. Forbes, and some others, all men of science. Their dress and manners were plain. I believe I was as much dressed as any of them, which rarely occurs when I am in company. Sir J. Clarke lives in a plain and not very commodious house, not richly furnished, and seems to bear his elevation with the utmost meekness and the most unassuming good nature. It is delightful to observe a man basking, as he is known to do, in the sunshine of royal favor, carry so little of the appearance of it in his outward bearing. His dress and manners are plain, and I presume royalty has rarely had so respectable and worthy a medical adviser to rely upon. It would be interesting to know how it happened that so unpretending a man — not at all an old man; not over fifty, as I should suppose — has attained to a station, and an influence in that station, which it is commonly believed can be arrived at only by the possession of very different qualities.

"*Sunday.* Heard Rev. B. W. Noel, text Matthew xxv. 24, seq. The whole discourse was pervaded by a lovely Christian spirit, good taste, good sense, absence of all exaggerations, and a winning ease of manners, that could not but interest all that heard it. After service I conversed with Mr. N. He is a tall, slender man, with light hair and a lively expression of countenance. From all I learn, he must be an excellent pastor and exemplary Christian. He preaches in the church where preached Cecil, Pratt, and Daniel Wilson (now Bishop of Calcutta).

"*Monday.* Spent the greater part of the day at London University. With Professor Madden, professor of Greek and Latin, I visited the preparatory school, and was present at the recitations in Latin, geography, French, and mathematics. These were similar to those with us, in the main. The geography the boys studied from a map, and the master examined them from a large skeleton map — a very excellent plan. In mathematics, I observed the master drew the figure; this seemed to me a mistake. In the French class, the boys were correcting exercises which had been handed to the master previously. One of them wrote the corrected exercise on the blackboard, and the others corrected theirs from it: the peculiarity was, that they in no case had their own exercise, but each one that of another: this secured accuracy. I noticed that the boys all took places for excellence, and that one common reason for change of places was the better choice of an English word by which to render the Latin or Greek. I did not perceive that the master made it a point to construe the lesson after his boys. I next attended Professor Madden. First the Juniors or Freshmen in Xenophon's Cyropædia, and second the Seniors in Thucydides. The manner of doing it was essentially the same as with us, only the instructor lectured more extensively on every point of difficulty, and analyzed words, and phrases, with much greater accuracy. In order to do the same, we want nothing but men able and willing to adopt this plan."

"*Wednesday*. Dined with the club of the Geological Society, on invitation of R. Ingham, Esq., M. P., to whom I am indebted for a succession of favors for which I shall ever be grateful. Nothing could exceed his thoughtfulness or his kindness. At the club meeting were Dr. Buckland, Professor Whewell, Colonel Mudge, and several others well known to fame. The dinner was good, the company in excellent spirits, and all seemed well pleased with each other. In fact, a delightful temper prevailed. After dinner, attended the meeting of the society. There were present Mr. Lyell, Mr. De la Bouche, Mr. Murchison, Professor Sedgwick, besides those before named. Dr. Buckland was in the chair. A member, Mr. Hopkins, delivered a discourse on the *modus* of the formation of the hills in the south of England, with reference to a general theory of such formations, where the crust of the earth has been for a large district heaved up. After the discourse, Mr. Lyell, De la Bouche, Sedgwick, and Buckland, all spoke in respect to particular parts of the discourse, some offering objections, and others confirming its doctrines. A love of truth seemed to pervade every speaker, and no one appeared to consider anything personal, how far soever it might oppose anything which he had advanced.

"*Thursday*. Westminster Abbey. I followed the beadle around, and heard him describe the various groups of statuary, with which the interior of the building is lined. The Abbey is incomparably superior to anything and everything in it. The sculpture is but moderate; much of it in bad taste, and much of it in no taste at all. The statues of Watt, Canning, Sir S. Raffles, Wilberforce, and some others, struck me pleasantly; but few of the rest gave me any satisfaction. But how impressive is all this from its mere failure! This is human glory. This is sublunary immortality. Nelson said before one of his battles, 'Victory, or Westminster Abbey.' He had both, in effect; and what are they? To have a stone or marble image of yourself put up to be looked at and criticised after your name has been forgotten, or, if not forgotten, in fact unheeded, — this is the whole. Such is the object for which men consider life, honor, virtue, the cheap reward. O, what madness is in their hearts! O God, impress this lesson on my mind! May I never ask for any record of my actions but the record of thy remembrance, and seek for no other reward but thy favor, which is life, and thy loving kindness, which is better than life.

"*Friday.* Dined with the Political Economy Club, on invitation from Mr. Senior. There were present Mr. Senior, Colonel Torrens, Mr. Tooke, Lord Monteagle (Spring Rice), and others. After dinner, when the fruit was brought on, the questions for discussion (printed) were handed round the table. The discussion was opened by Colonel Torrens, and continued until ten o'clock, when I came away.

"*Saturday.* Went to Camberwell, to the residence of Mr. Gurney, a leading Baptist, and short-hand writer to the House of Lords. Mr. Gurney mentioned to me a singular fact in his own history, worth recording in a metaphysical point of view. He was engaged in taking minutes of evidence on one occasion from four P. M. to four A. M. It was on the inquiry relating to the Walcheren expedition. At two o'clock he fell asleep, and was aroused by some one asking the reporter to read the evidence of the last witness. It was the evidence of Sir James Erskine, and was a description of the fortifications of Flushing. Mr. G. said to the witness, who was standing near him, 'Sir James, I fear I have not written it all.' 'Never mind,' said the other; 'begin, and I will help you out.' The evidence consisted of nearly two pages of shorthand, and Mr. G. read it through, recognizing perfectly all of it but the last four lines, of which, after a particular sentence, he had no recollection whatever. These last lines were written to the full as legibly as the rest, and he read them without any difficulty. When he ceased, he turned to Sir James, and said, 'Sir James, that is all I have.' 'That,' replied the other, 'is the whole of it.' While asleep, he had continued writing as steadily and correctly as before.

"*Monday*. Dined with Rev. Dr. Harris (author of Mammon, and The Great Teacher) at the Spread Eagle Tavern. Present, Dr. Styles, author of Essay on the Stage, Mr. Jenkyn, author of a work on the Atonement, Mr. Belcher, and Mr. Ward, publisher. They all seemed sensible and good men. The conversation was in many respects profitable. The habits of the English are more convivial than ours. I saw no effect whatever of wine, yet more was used on this occasion than as many New England ministers would drink at a dozen dinners, if, indeed, they drank any. Dr. Harris is, I should suppose, between thirty and thirty-five years old, small, of a good countenance, evidencing strong determination, decision, and quickness. He appeared well, and in everything acted like a Christian and a gentleman. Mr. Jenkyn is a very sound, serious, and sensible man. He is the principal of the college which was formerly Dr. Doddridge's Theological School.

"*Tuesday*, *February* 9. Dined at Mr. Kenyon's. Present, Rev. Mr. Raymond, Mr. Hawthorne, Mr. Robinson, Captain Jones, R. N., Professor Babbage, and others. Mr. Babbage is a man about medium size, or rather less, compactly and firmly built, yet constructed for great activity. His head is remarkable for size, and, I should think, for symmetrical development; his eye deep-seated; nose aquiline, and rather crooked; mouth large and determined; and whole face indicative of strong feeling, easily excited. The eye, however, is the most remarkable feature in his face. It has a vividness that is almost scorching. It is restless, changing, yet always intense. It has the effect upon you of the eye of insanity. Indeed, that intensity of mental action is commonly nearly allied to insanity, and frequently is, for a while, on its very brink. The evening was very pleasant; I came away at a few minutes after eleven o'clock.

"*February* 11, *Thursday*. Dined with Sir J. Clarke, and went with him to Dr. Forbes', to the meeting of the Royal Society. The meeting was full, all the seats in the room being occupied, and several members standing. The Marquis of Northampton in the chair. Sir J. Lubbock proposed Sir H. Vivian, Master of Ordnance, as a member, and moved that according to the custom of the society in cases of persons of distinguished rank, he be balloted for without the usual period of nomination. He was elected immediately. I was informed that in the case of noblemen, bishops, privy councillors, &c., this rule is always adopted. Presently Mr. C. was proposed, and the names read of those who had recommended him at a previous meeting. He was balloted for and elected. I learned that this gentleman was a dentist, in large business. To me, I must confess, all this looks odd. I have nothing to say about hereditary legislators. I enter no protest against an aristocracy of rank. This may be a question of taste. Let those who like such a form of society establish it and maintain it. But I do not see why it should not be restrained within its own limits. Why should it invade the aristocracy of science or of talent? Why should not each be independent within its own sphere? Why should the aristocracy of talent bow down before that of rank? Why should not a peer be treated, in matters of science, like any other man? Why should science assume that its respectability must be supported by rank? These may be useless queries, but to me they seem very natural. It may be said, that, in this manner, the benefits are shared by both parties. I think not quite so. The peerage does not extend its rank to the philosopher. All England would stand aghast were a man to be raised to the peerage on account of scientific merit. Why then should the peerage of intellect be conferred on a lord, on account of his rank? Let both parties blend in social intercourse, where those courtesies may be reciprocal, but let each rank stand for its own order.

"*Sunday*. Dr. Leifchild; a good sermon. Afternoon at home, reading Scriptures, and hymns, and prayer. I have generally spent the afternoon thus, since I have been abroad, and find it, I think, more profitable than the public service.

"15*th*, *Monday*. Purchased various articles for ——, and others. Nothing has seemed to bring home nearer than this occupation. I know not when I have enjoyed any time more.

"*Friday*. Anniversary dinner of the Geological Society. I attended as a guest of Mr. Murchison, the newly elected president. There were present about one hundred persons. The dinner table is set in the room next to that in which the company is assembled. Before dinner every one goes in and ascertains where is to be his place. This is known by his name on a card placed opposite his plate. There were present the Russian ambassador, Baron B.; Marquis of Northampton, president of Royal Society; Bishop of Norwich, president of Linnæan Society; Bishop of Litchfield; and Earl of Selkirk. After dinner, the Queen, royal family, &c., were toasted; the Geological Society and Dr. Buckland, late president; the Royal Society and Lord Northampton; the Linnæan Society and Bishop of Norwich; the Zoölogical Society; the Astronomical Society; the British Institution and President Whewell. The speeches and replies were all good, and some very happy. I observed that the fellowship of science was thus admirably cultivated. Every one who had done anything in any department felt that he was a member of the fraternity, and that his claims were recognized. We need something of this sort very much among us. Our lights are not very brilliant, but if collected in a focus, they would make a much better figure, and throw abroad a much wider illumination, than now.

"*Monday*. To Cambridge with Professor Whewell.

"Evening at Cambridge. Philosophical Society. Professor Whewell explained the principle on which oblique arches should be constructed, and read a paper to prove that all matter must have weight. I confess that I could not see the force of his argument. He evidently took for granted some principles which did not seem to me self-evident; but this was probably my ignorance of the higher mathematics. With the reasons, however, I have not so much to do. I only record the fact. I was not convinced, nor am I now.

"*Tuesday*, 22*d*. Breakfasted with Mr. Carus, Dean of Trinity, a pious and excellent man, the successor of Simeon, of whom he mentioned several anecdotes. Mr. S. was, when he first entered the university, vain, thoughtless, and wicked. He was required to take the sacrament. His unworthiness roused him to reflection, and for weeks he was miserable almost to despair, until he obtained a view of the atoning sacrifice of Christ; and then he began anew to live. He became fellow of the college and rector of a church in the city. At first he was bitterly persecuted. His church doors were nailed up. Dead cats and dogs were thrown at him in the streets. Every one avoided him as though he were infected with the plague. One day, as he was passing through the college grounds, a student touched his cap to him. This act of kindness so affected him that he went directly to his room, and poured out his soul to God, with thanks and tears, at the thought that there was one person who did not despise him. The story of his opening to the passage, 'They found one named Simon, and him they compelled to bear his cross, &c.,' is confirmed by Mr. Carus; only it occurred in his room as he rose from prayer.

"I attended Professor Whewell's lecture. About sixty or seventy persons, most of them graduates, were present. It was on the character and doctrines of Hobbes. It was well done. The points were brought out clearly, and the view given was lucid and distinct. He traced Hobbes' doctrines to the ancient Greeks, and I was surprised that he did not refer to Plato's notion of a republic, which seems to me very analogous to Hobbes' Leviathan.

"*Friday.* At one o'clock, to Dr. Whewell's lecture on the writers that opposed Hobbes. It was well done, but scarcely as interesting as the preceding.

"From Cambridge to Earlham, near Norwich. I was received with the greatest friendship by my friend and the friend of all good men, J. J. Gurney. I immediately felt that I was at home, and this little period has been an oasis in my wilderness of journeyings.

"The governing principle of this family is love. Mr. Gurney is loved most devotedly, and he as devotedly loves and seeks the happiness of all. It is the most delightful Christian family that I have ever seen. The house of our friend is situated on the side of a gentle slope, commanding quite an extensive view in this generally flat country. It is flanked on both sides by a grove and walks. In front and rear, a vista is opened to the country beyond. The house is quite ancient, the oldest part being about three hundred years old, and a newer part two hundred. The entrance-hall is lined with specimens in natural history, in fine preservation. Similar ornaments are seen throughout the stairway, and upper halls and galleries. The rooms are almost everywhere covered with books, to the number of about eight thousand. Mr. G.'s study is filled with books, principally theological; among them are some of the most valuable and rare of the Fathers, some of the best Lexicons in Greek and Hebrew, and many of the best commentators in various languages. The house, the place, the books, the ornaments, are such as express the idea of an English literary Christian gentleman. When I arrived, it was nearly nine o'clock in the evening. I was ushered into the drawing-room, where I was introduced to the family. Tea and coffee, and other refreshments, were ordered; and, as I was not quite well, every attention was paid to my comfort. After hearing the arrangements for the next day, I retired.

"*Saturday*. I arose much better for my night's repose. At half past seven the bell rings for rising, at half past eight for reading the Scriptures. Mr. G., Jr., reads from the New Testament or Book of Psalms; then some remarks or a prayer is offered. Mr. G., while the breakfast is coming, takes a turn round the garden. After breakfast each seems to retire to his or her own business for the day. Mr. G. proceeds with his literary work, or what may require his attention, until he goes to town. The carriage was ordered for me, and with Mr. Taylor, a young friend of the family, I went to Norwich. In the carriage I found a copy of the Holy Scriptures, which, I presume, is always kept there. I called on Rev. Mr. Alexander and Rev. Mr. Brock, the former the Independent, and the latter the Baptist clergyman. Both received me with great kindness. From them I learned whatever was to be known of my mother's relations. We returned in the carriage with Mrs. Opie, the authoress, an intimate friend of the family of Mr. G. She is one of the most remarkable persons I have ever seen. Though now more than seventy years of age, she appears only forty or fifty, with the activity of a girl. Her mental energy seems not in the least diminished. Her conversation is as rapid, her apprehension as quick, and her wit as brilliant, as ever. She has a full recollection of almost all the great men of the time of Pitt and Fox. She was the intimate friend of Lafayette, of whom she entertains the highest opinion. She once had a very good view of Napoleon, reviewing his troops. She gazed on him as long as it was possible, in a sort of amazement. As she returned through the garden of the Tuileries, such was her emotion that she burst into a flood of tears. She said, 'It seemed as if I should die if I could not thus give way to my feelings.' It was a feeling of dread, of indefinable awe, mixed with the conviction that she should never witness such a sight again.

"*Sunday.* Rode into town; heard Mr. Brock. 'I can do all things through Christ, which strengtheneth me.' It was an excellent sermon, showing that Christ knows all our conditions internally, all our circumstances externally, has all power to order everything for our good, and has promised that he will do so. Grant, blessed Redeemer, that I may be enabled thus to rely upon thy strength, and confide in thy power, and be made perfect by thy righteousness. Lunched with Mrs. Opie, and attended worship at the Friends' meeting in the afternoon. Mr. G. spoke briefly and prayed. An aunt of his, a most excellent lady, eighty-four years of age, had died during the week, after a short illness. It affected the whole assembly, and the meeting was for the most part spent in silence. This is the twenty-first Sabbath from home. After six more, if it pleases my God, I hope to see my native country. In the evening at about eight o'clock the servants and immediate neighbors assemble in the dining-room, and Mr. G. reads the Scriptures, with remarks on what has been read. On this occasion the portion was the first three chapters of Ephesians, and his remarks were pious, judicious, and pertinent.

"At breakfast, Monday, we were joined by Mr. Alexander and Mr. Brock, who staid until noon. They are very sensible and religious men, and our intercourse on subjects connected with the ministry, &c., was instructive.

"*Tuesday.* An ordination occurred to-day in Norwich. Mr. A. Reid, son of the Rev. Dr. A. Reid, was to be ordained over the oldest dissenting church here. I had just set out to walk, when Mr. Brock met me in a gig, which he had brought out to take me to Norwich. Mr. Alexander delivered a discourse on the nature of a Christian church. The candidate was asked several questions touching his personal evidence of religion, call to the ministry, views of doctrine, &c., to which he replied by reading from a manuscript in full. This was nearly an hour's exercise. The father then preached from the text, 'He that goeth forth and weepeth,' &c. The subject of the discourse was an analogy between the work of the husbandman and that of the preacher. It was exceedingly well done. The address to his son at the close was very touching, and the assembly was generally moved. I was invited to close the exercises by prayer. It was a very interesting occasion, though too long. It occupied from half past ten till nearly three."

In Edinburgh Dr. Wayland visited the lecture-rooms of many eminent men, with some of whom he enjoyed agreeable interviews. No portion, probably, of his journey afforded him more pleasure than the time spent in this city. He remarks, —

"Everywhere we perceive a strong feeling of kindness towards America, and a dread of war, which is truly delightful to every Christian sentiment."

Of Dr. Chalmers he writes, —

"Dr. C. entered at once into the subject of non-intrusion, and we had a very interesting discussion. If I mistake not, he will soon relinquish his sentiments on religious establishments, and become essentially an Independent. He seems to me now, within a step of it. Dr. C. is a stout, strongly-built man, of middle height, with a very large cerebral development, rather passing into years, but of vigorous and active mind, buoyant with hope, full of benevolence, and, I should think, remarkable for candor and ingenuousness of mind. He walked with us to the Botanical Garden, and we had an hour of animated discussion.

"On Monday we proceeded to the university, where we attended Dr. Chalmers' lecture. The room was well filled by students, of the age and appearance, in general, of our theological students. The doctor wore the gown of a doctor in divinity. He lectures from a pulpit, and the lecture-room contains a gallery for occasional attendants. He commenced with prayer; after this was the calling of the roll, and then the lecture. The subject was the divinity of Christ, proved from the various texts with which we are familiar. He insisted strongly on the following point. The first Christians were originally idolaters. The worship of Christ, if he be not God, is idolatry. The apostles would have guarded their disciples with peculiar care against this idolatry, if it were idolatry. This idea presents the passages in a stronger light than they could otherwise have. His manner is earnest, but his accent was the broadest Scotch I almost ever heard. He seems to have no idea of any distinction in vowel sounds, and frequently the same word will be sounded in several different ways. Yet his earnestness bears him on, and carries you along with him. I was strongly impressed with the opinion that the pulpit is his proper place, and that he erred in leaving it. We dined at Dr. Abercrombie's, so well known by his works on intellectual and moral philosophy. He is a stout, well-built man, with a pleasant, benevolent face, though it has something the appearance of a Jew, using the word in its good sense. It was a delightful visit. We went with him to the meeting of the Royal Society of Edinburgh, Dr. A. in the chair. The papers were mostly controversial, for which the secretary apologized, and assured us that such was not their usual character.

"The meeting was well attended, and much more interest was shown than in the Royal Society of London.

"The papers were by Sir T. Dickland on the parallel roads of Glen Roy, and by Dr. Forbes on his discoveries in the polarization of light. After meeting there was tea, as in the Royal Society of London. We closed the evening by supper at Sir W. Hamilton's. The conversation was interesting, and it was one o'clock before we arrived at our lodgings.

"*Tuesday Morning*. Breakfast with Dr. Chalmers. None but his family and sons-in-law present. Conversation on the voluntary system, non-intrusion, &c. It is a delightful family. It was cheering to see a good man so happy in his domestic circle. From Dr. Chalmers' we hastened to town, and took stage for Glasgow. In the coach were several intelligent people, and I found the topic of universal interest was the non-intrusion doctrines. I am strongly of opinion that the voluntary principle will yet become the doctrine of the non-intrusionists. It would almost be so now, but for the erroneous statements which have been made by Dr. B. and others respecting our country."

Returning from Scotland, Dr. Wayland again visited Liverpool, and at the house of Mr. Rathbone met Rev. J. Blanco White. His interview with this remarkable man made a deep impression upon him, and was often referred to in subsequent years.

From Liverpool he proceeded to Oxford, taking on his way Kenilworth and Stratford-on-Avon. At Oxford he visited the leading objects of interest, and was indebted to the eminent scholars of the university for many courteous attentions. He writes, —

"Of Oxford, what shall I say? Its buildings are magnificent, the surroundings beautiful beyond description. Its foundations are princely. Its colleges are palaces, its grounds all that the eye could desire. The officers are, so far as I saw, thorough-bred gentlemen, highly intelligent, and, I presume, finely educated. It is a place where you would love to dwell, and about which you cannot but wish to linger. But when one reflects on the immense wealth of its establishment, and remembers that this was designed to promote the prosecution of science and the advancement of learning, and not for the cultivation of luxurious ease; when one remembers that it was for the education of the people of England, and not a part of them, and that it is now used for the good of a part, and is the avenue to all social and professional standing, I cannot think of it with unmixed respect. It seems to me a monstrous perversion. I do not speak of the present incumbents, — I know not how far they are responsible, — but of the system. Of this I can hardly speak in terms of too great disapprobation. It is in the main the same as Cambridge, though in detail it is more restrictive, and is more inclined to theology. It seemed to me to be cultivating narrowness rather than expansiveness of mind, and to be conferring rather a fragment of education than an enlarged view of human knowledge. Authority appeared to be the *ultima ratio;* and hence they must, I think, continue year after year to proceed in interminable discussions, without ever making any satisfactory progress.

I may judge them severely, but I must say that I think them too rich, too close a borough, and too much interested in the social system of England, to do anything valuable for the cause of science, or at least anything that shall correspond to their great advantages.

"From Oxford to Frome. Frome is an old town, formerly the seat of extensive wool manufactories. These have migrated to the coal districts, where machinery has taken the place of hand-loom weaving, and Frome is a place of minor consequence.

"We were entertained at Mr. John Shepherd's, a distant connection of mine, a gentleman of leisure, a writer, and a poet. We were treated with great hospitality, and saw much of the environs, which are very beautiful. The country is assuming the dress of spring. The meadows are greener than any I ever saw, and the trees are budding as ours are in May. I saw the house of my father's parents, and traced out some of his relations.

"From Frome to Bristol; and thence to Stapleton, to visit John Foster. He is now an aged man. He wears an old gray surtout, yellow bandanna neckerchief, and old shoes. He talks with all the vivacity of youth, is a most ardent friend of civil and religious liberty, and is better acquainted with America than any man whom I have seen in England. He is oppressed with the infirmities of age. His teeth are almost gone; he wears a wig; and everything reminds you that this, the last Baptist light of England, is at no distant day to be extinguished."

We find no record of his visit to Rugby, nor of his interview with Dr. Arnold.

Dr. Wayland returned to America in April, 1841. Not long afterwards he writes Colonel Stone, —

"As to my coming home too soon, &c., I am well aware that it may seem a mistake; but the fact is, my health was so poor that I was unable to travel until the time for visiting the south of Europe had passed. I had scarcely a well day, a day free from fever, until March. During almost the entire period of my residence in Paris, my pulse was above ninety, and my whole system was very much disordered. Travelling under such circumstances was utterly useless to me."

Undoubtedly Dr. Wayland shared the not uncommon experience of tourists in the feeling that it is very pleasant to *have travelled*. Upon the knowledge acquired while absent he was accustomed to put a low estimate, perhaps lower than was justified by the facts. Probably his observation of the institutions of the old world, alike social, political, educational, and religious, emancipated him from any undue and superstitious veneration. He became convinced that, in common with his countrymen, he was as likely to attain success by cherishing his own conceptions, and by applying his independent judgment to the means of reaching results, as were the men of the old world by worshipping the wisdom of the past. To have learned this was worth a voyage across the Atlantic. If there were other results, if there were, in addition, valued acquaintances and friendships acquired, these were clear gain.

At this point we take pleasure in introducing the following interesting reminiscences, for which we are indebted to Hon. Isaac Davis, LL. D., of Worcester, Mass.: —

"In February, 1841, I returned from the Continent to London, where I met Dr. Wayland. He was unwell and much depressed in spirits, longing to return to his home and family. I had then completed my travels in Europe, and made my arrangements to take the next steamer for America. He urged me to accompany him to Scotland and some parts of England, and to postpone my return to America for two months. After some hesitation I consented, and we left London for Edinburgh, stopping, however, on our way thither to visit his uncle, Rev. D. S. Wayland, who resided at Bassingham. He was a clergyman of the Established church, a ripe scholar, and a Christian gentleman. His household realized my ideal of an English home circle. I have seldom known a family of greater mental culture or more genial social qualities.

"During our journey I took the whole charge of our arrangements, and, so far as was practicable, relieved Dr. Wayland of all care and annoyance. His health soon improved, and his enjoyment of travel increased proportionally.

"When we arrived in Edinburgh, one of the first places which we visited was the university. Dr. Wayland was at once received with marked attention by Dr. Chalmers, Sir William Hamilton, Professor Wilson, Dr. Abercrombie, of the Royal Philosophical Society, Lord Murray, and other distinguished men. The officers of the university very courteously afforded him every facility for examining all its departments.

"We next visited Glasgow. Here, as was natural, the university was the earliest object of attention. The president and professors were unwearied in their courtesies, assisting him in every way to understand the practical workings of their system of education.

"In Liverpool we remained several days. The mayor was very courteous in showing us all places of interest in and around the city. I well remember that Dr. Wayland had more invitations to dine with distinguished men in Liverpool than it was possible for him to accept. Dr. Raffles was especially attentive.

"From thence we went to Oxford. Here he was most cordially welcomed by the magnates of the university. I need not tell you with how eager an interest he visited the chapels, libraries, and printing establishments of this ancient university, or with what patient attention he examined the discipline, courses of study, and educational advantages thus fully open for his inspection. More than a week was most profitably spent in this city of colleges.

"From Oxford we went to Frome, stopping at intermediate places which contained objects of interest. Frome was the birthplace of the father of Dr. Wayland. We were received with great kindness by Mr. Shepherd of that place, and invited to his house. We found him a most estimable man, a lay preacher, 'going about doing good,' like his Lord and Master. He was a distant relative, I believe, of the Wayland family, and a Baptist.

"At Frome there was a Baptist church, where the senior Wayland had worshipped. It was pleasant to discover that he was remembered by several citizens. In this church Dr. Wayland preached. The congregation listened to him with attention, and were more than once moved to tears.

"From Frome we went to Bristol, visited the Baptist Theological Institution in that city, and the Broadmead Chapel, of which Robert Hall was once the pastor. Many interesting reminiscences were collected of that great man from those who had heard him preach, and were on terms of intimacy with him.

"We passed a day with John Foster, at Stapleton, near Bristol. In a letter which I received from Mr. Foster after my return to America he alludes to that day as the most interesting he had spent for many years with friendly strangers. For Dr. Wayland's purity and simplicity of character, as well as for his talents and acquirements, Mr. Foster expressed his most profound respect.

"From the time I met Dr. Wayland in London, until I parted from him in New York, several elements of his character particularly attracted my attention. His humility in all cases and under all circumstances, whether he was among the common people or in the most literary and polished society, his wisdom and learning, were discovered rather than displayed. His benevolence was wide as the world. He pitied all whom he saw in distress, and did all in his power to relieve their wants, often giving indeed more than he could well afford.

"His religious character stood out in bold relief, on all occasions. However late at night before we retired, a portion of Scripture was always read, and prayer offered. So also every morning before commencing the labors of the day. When we had opportunities for being present at any exhibition or place of entertainment, he would say, 'Davis, if Christ were on earth, and present here, would he attend this exhibition?' If he believed Christ would not, he would not. He tested duty ever in this way. Christ-like and striving to obey all the commands of the Master, he lost no opportunity to labor for his Savior and in his cause. Withal, he was cheerful, relishing timely flashes of wit, and enjoying refined merriment. In his interviews with the learned men of England he exhibited a good command of nervous English, and was remarkable for the lucidity of his explanations."

CHAPTER II.

DISCOURSE ON NICHOLAS BROWN. — DEATH OF COLONEL STONE. — PROFESSOR GODDARD. — DEATH OF REV. F. WAYLAND, SENIOR. — RHODE ISLAND REBELLION. — DEBTS OF THE STATES. — ANNEXATION OF TEXAS. — MEXICAN WAR. — "DUTY OF OBEDIENCE TO THE CIVIL MAGISTRATE." — FULLER AND WAYLAND ON SLAVERY. — IRISH FAMINE. — DR. JUDSON. — MISSIONARY UNION. — UNIVERSITY SERMONS. — REVIVAL IN COLLEGE. — PRAYER MEETINGS. — PARENTAL AUTHORITY IN RELIGIOUS AFFAIRS. — "THOUGHTS ON THE COLLEGIATE SYSTEM." — TOWN LIBRARY SYSTEM.

RETURNING to his home, President Wayland resumed his labors, not only cheerfully, but eagerly. He was weary of the pursuit of relaxation, and to be again at work was rest.

The first duty of a public nature to which he was called was the Discourse on the Life and Character of Nicholas Brown, delivered November 3, 1841. While sharing, alike on public and on personal grounds, in the general grief at an event which had dried up a fountain of charity, he willingly undertook, at the request of the authorities of the university, the task of exhibiting before the citizens of Providence an example of boundless benevolence, tender sympathy, and enlarged public spirit. In one passage of the eulogy it is not difficult to trace the influence of his recent journey: —

"If such be the relation which this life sustains to another, and if such be the influence which we must exert over those that come after us, it is manifest that we can accomplish in no signal degree the purposes of our being, unless we act for posterity. We can associate our names with succeeding ages only by deeds or by thoughts which they will not willingly forget. And thus it is that everywhere man seeks to attain to a sublunary immortality. The crumbling tombstone and the gorgeous mausoleum, the sculptured marble and the venerable cathedral, all bear witness to the instinctive desire within us to be remembered by coming generations. But how short-lived is the immortality which the works of our hands can confer! The noblest monuments of art that the world has ever seen are covered with the soil of twenty centuries. The works of the age of Pericles lie at the foot of the Acropolis in indiscriminate ruin. The ploughshare turns up the marble which the hand of Phidias had chiselled into beauty, and the Mussulman has folded his flock beneath the falling columns of the Temple of Minerva. But even the works of our hands too frequently survive the memory of those who have created them. And were it otherwise, could we thus carry down to distant ages the recollection of our existence, it were surely childish to waste the energies of an immortal spirit in the effort to make it known to other times that a being whose name was written with certain letters of the alphabet once lived, and flourished, and died. Neither sculptured marble nor stately column can reveal to other ages the lineaments of the spirit; and these alone can embalm our memory in the hearts of a grateful posterity. As the stranger stands beneath the dome of St. Paul's, or treads, with religious awe, the silent aisles of Westminster Abbey, the sentiment which is breathed from every object around him is the utter emptiness of sublunary glory. The most magnificent nation that the world has ever seen has here exhausted every effort to render illustrious her sons who have done worthily. The fine arts, obedient to private affection or public gratitude, have embodied in every form the finest conceptions of which their age was capable. In years long gone by, each one of these monuments has been watered by the tears of the widow, the orphan, or the patriot. But generations have passed away, and mourners and mourned have sunk together into forgetfulness. The aged crone, or the smooth-tongued beadle, as now he hurries you through aisle and chapel, utters, with measured cadence and unmeaning tone, for the thousandth time, the name and lineage of the once-honored dead, and then gladly dismisses you, to repeat again his well-conned lesson to another group of idle passers-by. Such, in its most august form, is all the immortality that matter can confer. Impressive and venerable though it be, it is the impressiveness of a solemn and mortifying failure. It is by what we ourselves have done, and not by what others have done for us, that we shall be remembered in after ages. It is by thought that has aroused my intellect from its slumbers, which has 'given lustre to virtue, and dignity to truth,' or by those examples which have inflamed my soul with the love of goodness, and not by means of sculptured marble, that I hold communion with Shakspeare and Milton, with Johnson and Burke, with Howard and Wilberforce."

To his sister: —

"... I am glad that you liked the discourse on Nicholas Brown. It gave me a great deal of trouble, and I feared that it might seem stiff and formal. What you say of the paragraph about Westminster Abbey is certainly true. Everything in an old country reminds you of the past, of its changes, and of the shortness of human life. Here everything looks towards the future. In a country that bears the marks of two thousand years, an individual or a race appears exceedingly insignificant, and one is continually reminded of the instability of everything but religion. I felt it constantly."

Dr. Wayland had now reached that period of life at which he must expect, if he himself survived, often to lament the removal of the friends of his youth and the counsellors of his manhood. In the summer of 1844, in the decease of his brother-in-law, Colonel Stone, he experienced one of the severest bereavements of his life. For nearly thirty years the strongest affection and the freest intercourse had subsisted between them, conjoined with the unity in essentials and the diversity in non-essentials, that rendered such intercourse in the highest degree pleasing and profitable. They had discussed in the fullest manner every topic that could interest either of them, whether in the field of education, politics, or morality. And for many years their sympathy had been rendered more absolute than before by an entire agreement of sentiment in regard to the realities of religion.

To Mrs. Stone: —

"August 18, 1844.

"My very dear Sister: Amidst your overwhelming sorrow I scarcely know how to address you. I am too well aware of what you have lost, I feel too deeply my own bereavement, not to understand that at such a moment almost any voice must seem intrusive. Earthly consolations, I know, can offer but little comfort. At such a time 'the proud helpers do stoop under us,' and our only hope is derived from taking hold of things unseen.

"For the greater part of my life I had known your dear husband intimately; more intimately, indeed, than any one of my own brothers. During all this time not a word of unkindness ever passed between us. His temper was so sweet, his affections were so generous and lively, his desire for the happiness of others was so active and untiring, that we soon became intimate, and have always continued so. I feel that a brother at my right hand has been stricken down, and I am left alone.

"And it has, at last, been unexpected. Only by the papers have we learned the mournful event. I had always persuaded myself that he would recover. Everything had seemed to be gradually tending to his restoration. But God has destroyed our hopes, and has recalled our treasure to himself.

"But herein, my dear sister, is our only consolation — God, God in Christ has done it. It could only have been done at his bidding. 'As for our Rock, his way is perfect.' Nothing could be added that would render what he has done wiser, better, or more holy. Nothing could be altered. 'What we see not now, we shall see hereafter.' He will yet teach us that all is right, and that he has in faithfulness afflicted us."

To the same: —

"December 8, 1844.

"I have thought much of you for some weeks past. The change of the seasons, the Thanksgiving last week, all brought home to me recollections of which I would say to any other member of the family, but dare not to you. It would only open afresh those sources of sorrow that bleed sufficiently without being probed. It is very, very sad, and nothing will explain it, but 'even so, Father, for so it seemed good in thy sight.' This is our only support. When we look at home or abroad, at the daily or the literary press, at politics or the history of our country, it seems as if a chasm had been made that could never be filled. At every turn I am reminded that one has left my side with whom I had walked in sweet converse for nearly thirty years, with whom I could always advise, and who would always look at my interest as though it were his own. What, however, is this to your loss? But I will not go on. Such, my dear sister, is this world of sin. 'In the world we must have tribulation;' it is in Christ alone that we can have peace. What a blessed book the Bible is to a bereaved and crushed spirit. Did it ever occur to you to reflect, what affliction and bereavement must have been to the heathen, to whom the grave was a starless midnight? Their affections were, as we know, frequently as strong as ours; and when every hope was destroyed, and every support stricken down, where did the crushed soul look for consolation? It was all the darkness of despair. What do we owe to Him who by the sacrifice of himself brought life and immortality to light! He not only revealed to us the unseen world, but gave himself to render it possible that the world should be heaven, instead of hell, to us. I pray that you may be enabled to stay yourself on God; and even in your sorrow may your peace be as a river, and your righteousness as the waves of the sea. I hope that you will not allow yourself to look back upon second causes. I do not believe that you have the remotest reason to refer to them with pain. I do not know, if the past could be recalled, how we could do better or differently. If dear brother could, six months or a year before, have been taken off from all business, this might have produced, with the blessing of God, a different result. But in this respect it pleased our heavenly Father to spread a veil before the eyes of all of us. We thought that with some modification of labor he might improve; but the veil was the thickest over the eyes of the dear sufferer himself. Yet it was God who did it, and this was his chosen way of accomplishing his purposes."

After Mr. Stone, there was perhaps no one with whom the president held more intimate relations than with Professor Goddard. This gentleman (who was but two years the senior in age) was the first member of the Faculty with whom Dr. Wayland became acquainted, and the friendship continued to grow in strength until the sudden death of Professor Goddard, in 1846. At the request of the Faculty of the university, Dr. Wayland delivered a discourse, afterwards published, upon the character of his deceased friend, in which he paid a generous, or more properly, a truthful tribute to the memory of a man of singularly elegant taste, rare scholarship, and high character.

Three years later, in the spring of 1849, Rev. Francis Wayland, Senior, was removed by death, bequeathing to his children a priceless legacy. The event was not indeed unexpected, for he was within three years of fourscore. But it brought the end of life nearer at hand, and made his son feel that the outposts were driven in, and that none now stood between himself and the advance of death.

To Deacon Lincoln: —

". . . My dear father's end was most blessed. I arrived twenty-four hours after his decease. During his whole sickness his soul was filled with joy. He always spoke of death as 'going home,' and said he had 'a desire to depart and to be with Christ, which was far better.' 'Yes,' added he, 'a thousand times better.' Mr. K., who was with him, said that if he had spoken two minutes before his death, he would have spoken as calmly as at any hour of his life. May God give us grace to follow in his steps. I think I can truly say, that I would prefer the heritage of his life and death to that of all the honors this world could confer. I cannot conceive of any comparison between being the son of such parents and being the son of any whom the world calls great or noble." *

To his brother-in-law, Rev. Dr. Bartol: —

"There is in the death of friends who have on earth realized something of heaven, a remarkable power to draw the mind upward, and teach it communion with eternal things. We seem to be looking through a veil which has been made transparent. The joys that we saw on earth seem merely continued in eternity. The one appears to be a sort of measure of the other. It was thus, in a peculiar manner, with my father. His sickness was one continual longing to depart and be with Christ."

The following letter of Dr. Wayland was written to a niece who was then suffering from illness, which soon proved fatal.

"My very dear Niece: We had been waiting for many days, in great anxiety, for a letter from the Springs. We had heard that you were unwell, and daily remembered you in our prayers, but we knew not the extent of your illness. The letter which we have received to-day has awakened our serious apprehensions. I lose not a moment in writing to you.

"I need not assure you, my dear child, how deeply we are grieved at such accounts of your sickness. You have been a great comfort to us all, and we all feel towards you the affection which belongs to a daughter or a sister. We have tenderly loved you for your gentleness, your disinterestedness, your self-sacrifice, and your undeviating yet mild conscientiousness. I do not say these things simply to praise you, but I want you to feel how much you are beloved, and to know that we all have appreciated your constant desire to render those around you happy.

---

* "My boast is not that I deduce my birth
From loins enthroned and rulers of the earth;
But higher far my proud pretensions rise —
The child of parents passed into the skies."

"These things make us lovely, my dear child, in the eyes of men; but you know, as well as I can tell you, that they form no ground of acceptance with God. In his eyes we are all sinners, under just and solemn condemnation. Judged by his law, we are wholly without excuse. But, blessed be his name, our helpless sinfulness is no ground for despair. 'God so loved the world that he gave his only begotten Son, that whosoever believeth in him should not perish, but have everlasting life.' The gate of heaven is thrown wide open through the atoning mercy of Christ. 'Whosoever cometh unto him he will in no wise cast out.' 'This is a faithful saying, and worthy of all acceptation, that Christ Jesus came into the world to save sinners.' All this is the simple truth. The blessed Savior says precisely and exactly what he means; only, human language cannot reveal the extent of his love.

"Strive, then, my dear child, to go in simplicity of heart to the Savior. Suffer nothing to interpose between him and your soul. If any objection arises in your mind, take the objection to him, and lay it at his feet. Look to him to strengthen you in weakness, to raise your eyes that you may look up to him, and to direct your hands, that they may take hold on him. Endeavor to cast aside everything, and ask him to help you to do so. Lie down at his feet, and touch the hem of his garment. May his grace assist you!

"Your aunt and I are very desirous to do everything for you which is in our power. Should you become able to leave your home, we shall be delighted to have you come to us. I do not expect you to write. I know you are too feeble for this. But let me hear from you, and tell me as much of your feelings as you are willing to dictate. . . ."

In the letters of Dr. Wayland, written during years of intense political excitement, the reader has probably noticed but few allusions to the party strife then dividing the country. Whether one set of men or another should occupy the offices of government, was a matter to which he was indifferent. He frequently urged his friends not to become too much absorbed in questions which did not turn on great principles. In his correspondence with gentlemen largely interested in politics, he sought to assuage the violence and rancor of party strife, and to urge the cultivation of friendly and fraternal feelings.

But he did not seek to withdraw into a literary seclusion or clerical neutrality when the country was imperilled. In the year 1842, the State of Rhode Island was the scene of profound and painful agitation. A portion of the inhabitants, becoming dissatisfied with the restrictions upon the right of suffrage imposed by the existing charter of the state, attempted to overthrow the government by force of arms, and, in the attempt, resorted to means that were as abhorrent to morality as their purpose was subversive of social order. Upon the Sabbath following the suppression of the first outbreak, and again upon the day of Thanksgiving appointed by the state authorities after the final restoration of order, Dr. Wayland preached two discourses (afterwards published), in which he unfolded the true principles of constitutional government, and exhibited the duty of the citizen to the commonwealth. As he incurred unmeasured abuse at the time for these utterances, and as attempts have been sedulously made to misrepresent the question at issue, it seems proper to remark that the question was not in the least whether the privilege of suffrage should or should not be extended, but rather whether a company of men, without the semblance of law, could overthrow all social order, and put the property and the life of every citizen at the disposal of an armed and irresponsible mob.

Two years later, when some of the states were repudiating their obligations, he wrote two articles, for the North American Review and for the Christian Review, upon the Debts of the States, urging, with all the power of argument and appeal of which he was capable, an adherence to the dictates of honesty and national honor.

It needs scarcely be said that he was profoundly hostile to the annexation of Texas; regarding it as a measure utterly needless to a nation already possessed of more territory than it could profitably occupy, calculated to involve us in war, and, above all, tending to increase the extent and power of slavery. At the election of 1844 he voted for Mr. Clay, designing by this act to protest against the annexation scheme.

The Mexican war he regarded with unfeigned abhorrence, and never ceased, in public and in private, to urge the cessation of a wicked invasion, and to pray for those whom we were, by cruel hands, reducing to widowhood and orphanage. In 1847 he preached, in the chapel, three sermons upon "The Duty of Obedience to the Civil Magistrate," * suggested by the events of the war then transpiring. The citizen, in his view, is under obligation to obey the voice of the magistrate, so long as the commands are such as he can obey without a violation of conscience. But if the state directs the citizen to do a wrong act, if it bids him go forth, causelessly and needlessly, to murder his innocent fellow-men, then the obligation to obedience has ceased; the citizen may not at its command engage in an iniquitous war, nor may he derive profit from any complicity in the wrong-doing.

To Rev. Dr. Cutting (then editor of the New York Recorder) he writes, —

"I read your article on the war, in the main, with pleasure; but I thought that it did not take high ground enough. The whole war is so bad, that arguing on the conduct of it is a compliment, take what view you please. It is, *ab origine*, wicked, infamous, unconstitutional in design, and stupid and shockingly depraved in its management. Were I you, I would have a few short articles, setting forth, first, the causes in their naked deformity; second, the cost of the war in blood and money; third, the guilt of it as resting on the nation."

* Afterwards published in "University Sermons," and in "Salvation by Christ."

To his sister: —

"December 16, 1847.

"It is a long time since I wrote to you; but I am not wholly without excuse. The fact is, I cannot use my eyes in the evening (I am now transgressing the law). I have been at work for the press as fast as I was able. The results you have seen. I had written the introduction to the 'Recollections'* in the vacation, but was dissatisfied with it, and wrote it again. The sermons I had preached long since; but they required re-writing. In the mean time rheumatism came on, and broke me up for three weeks. I grew cold in my affections towards the sermons, and the more so, as I was obliged to work by snatches, as I could. However, after much delay, they at last reached the press. At first I apprehended that they were destined to blush unseen; but within a day or two their chance of obtaining a hearing has somewhat improved. I never felt more anxious about anything I have published; not, I trust, on my own account (for necessity was laid upon me, and I could not but bear my testimony), but on account of my country. I see not what is to be the result if the moral sentiment of the nation cannot be awakened. I should rejoice to see my sermons die and be forgotten, if this would arouse some one to undertake the task who is better fitted for its accomplishment."

---

* We have seen how agreeable an episode, in his experience of foreign travel, was his visit to Bassingham Rectory, the residence of his uncle, Rev. D. S. Wayland. His aunt, to whom he was strongly attached, died December 22, 1846. In 1847, a collection of reminiscences of incidents in a country parish, prepared by her at his solicitation, was published in America, under the title of "Recollections of Real Life in England," with an introduction by Dr. Wayland. This little volume was designed to illustrate the condition of the laboring classes in an agricultural district, and especially the relation which exists in more favored instances between these classes and the parochial clergy.

The graphic description which Dr. Wayland gives of English rural life under its most attractive aspects, and his vivid and truthful picture of the varied and invaluable labors of a faithful clergyman and his family, occasion a feeling of regret that he could not find time for a more extended narrative of his observations in England.

In 1844, Rev. Richard Fuller, D. D., then of Beaufort, S. C., had addressed a letter to the editor of the Christian Reflector in reply to arguments that had been urged against slavery. In the course of his letter he appealed for confirmation of his sentiments to some of the principles laid down in the Elements of Moral Science. The circumstances seemed not only to invite, but almost to demand some reply from Dr. Wayland. And he was more than willing to embrace the opportunity afforded him. He had long felt that he had a testimony to bear in behalf of his brethren who were in slavery, as well as a duty to discharge towards those who were holding in bondage the little ones of Christ. In an interview with his pastor, Rev. Dr. Granger, Dr. Wayland entreated him to pray that he might be so guided by wisdom from above as not to say anything at variance with the spirit of the gospel, and that the discussion might tend to the promotion of piety and the interests of humanity.

In a series of letters addressed to Dr. Fuller, Dr. Wayland exposed the fallacy of the arguments that had been drawn from the Scriptures in defence of domestic slavery. These letters, together with those of Dr. Fuller in reply, were collected in a volume, and published under the title "Domestic Slavery considered as a Scriptural Institution." The arguments of Dr. Wayland, weighty in themselves, derived additional force from the temperateness and courtesy with which they were urged. The letters tended to form and confirm the Christian public sentiment that twenty years later was to remove slavery from the nation. How far the correspondence circulated at the south we are not informed. We have no knowledge, however, of its having changed the opinions of any who, from interest or education, were defenders of slavery. The time for that had passed, and everything was hastening the inevitable and final appeal. Yet whatever the reception of his words, it never ceased to be, on his part, a cause of gratitude to God, that he had been permitted to lift his voice in behalf of human liberty.

Holding the views which he did, there could be little room for doubt as to Dr. Wayland's action, when the question arose upon the admission of slavery into the territories of the United States. He favored the adoption of the Wilmot proviso, and voted in 1848 for the candidates of the Buffalo Convention.

But while a citizen of America, Dr. Wayland was no less a citizen of the world, and his sympathies, though intense, were not narrow. Upon the breaking out of the Irish famine, he was among the first to urge the people of Providence to exhibit their wonted liberality towards a suffering nation. As a member of the soliciting committee, he labored personally in collecting money, and at his suggestion the means which were raised were transmitted for distribution to his friend William Rathbone, Esq., of Liverpool, whose personal kindness, practical wisdom, and enlarged benevolence had deeply impressed Dr. Wayland while visiting him in 1840. It may with confidence be asserted, that no portion of the contributions forwarded from America were more productive of good, than were the moneys intrusted to Mr. Rathbone.

Dr. Wayland writes to his sister, —

"... This morning I have been out in behalf of the Irish. In less than two hours we raised here sixteen hundred dollars. We hope to increase it to seven thousand dollars, and send it by the next steamer. The amount received by Great Britain from this country will be large, and I hope will set a new example of national intercourse. It is noble to see such efforts in behalf of humanity, for the sake of Christ, and even for the sake of general benevolence. It shows that the gospel of Christ is influencing nations. It is a bright spot in the darkness that in many directions seems so closely to envelop us."

We have alluded in a previous chapter to the part which Dr. Wayland took in the reorganization of the Triennial

Convention in 1826, and the success which attended the missionary operations of the Baptist denomination for a number of years after the changes there inaugurated. Gradually, however, it became evident that other modifications were needed, and that a new impulse must be imparted to the work of missions. The withdrawal of the Baptists of the Southern States seemed to render prompt action needful, and in November, 1845, a special meeting of the Convention was called, for the purpose of effecting such changes in the constitution of the body as were demanded by the exigencies of the times.

Peculiar interest was imparted to this meeting by the presence of Dr. Judson, who, after more than thirty years' absence, had been compelled, by his own declining health and that of his family, to return to America. Dr. Wayland had invited Dr. Judson to visit Providence, the scene of his collegiate education, on his way to the meeting of the Convention in New York. It is needless to repeat the account of this visit, as the narrative is fully given in the Memoir of the missionary, the author of which has recorded the profound impression made on him by the apostle to Burmah; but we quote the following from Dr. Wayland to his sister: —

". . . We had a pleasant visit from Dr. Judson: he staid with us from Saturday to Monday evening, and accompanied us to New York. He is a most modest, meek, and heavenly-minded man. He is, to all appearance, wholly unmoved by the adulation he receives, and seems to wonder, with unfeigned *naïveté*, why any one should be so much interested in him. I went to Boston to accompany him here. I met him there, and he asked me when I should return to Providence. I told him, whenever he was ready, as I came to accompany him. His simple reply was, lifting up his hands, 'Why, I am ashamed.' I really think that this is a specimen of his feelings and temper. It is most delightful and edifying to see a man on whom the eyes of the whole country are turned, so entirely destitute of self-consciousness. When he was at our church, a large congregation was present, for the purpose of seeing him. He did not rise during the services, and almost every one was disappointed. You never saw anything so remarkable as the veneration in which he seems to be held. It was a difficult matter to get him out of the church, such was the press to shake hands with him."

Dr. Wayland presided at the meeting of the Convention (having been elected its president in 1844), and introduced the honored missionary to the body, with the memorable words, "Brethren, I present to you 'Jesus Christ's man.'" The address of Dr. Wayland on this occasion, with other interesting proceedings at the Convention, are found in the Memoir, which is undoubtedly in the hands of all who will read these pages.

In reference to the changes in the constitution of the Convention, which were proposed and adopted at the meeting, we are happy in being able to quote the words of Dr. Stow.

"In 1845, after the disruption of the General Convention by the secession of the southern wing, a committee of nine, of which Dr. Wayland was one, was appointed to prepare a new constitution for the body, to be submitted at a special session. As the members of the committee were widely scattered, and could not conveniently meet, it was agreed that Dr. Cone should draw up one, and Dr. Wayland another, and that a Boston member should, as secretary, construct one out of the two, for final consideration. The two forms prepared by Drs. Cone and Wayland, and their letters to the secretary, are now in my possession, and contain materials for a chapter, showing an equal fervor of interest in the missionary enterprise, but a wide diversity of opinions as to the shape of the organization for carrying it forward, the views of Dr. Cone being eminently democratic, those of Dr. Wayland insisting on greater power in the executive agency. As the instrument was finally adopted, it embraced all that Dr. Wayland regarded as essential in preserving the organization from harm by any sudden irruptions of popular excitement. In the compromise effected between Drs. Cone and Wayland, on that occasion, there was a beautiful exhibition of their strong elements of Christian character.

"In the debate upon the constitution, one member was apprehensive lest the door was not sufficiently closed against the admission of slaveholders, and reflected with some severity upon the motives of the committee in leaving thus unguarded the entrance to membership. Dr. Wayland, then presiding over the body, felt keenly the insinuation, and made some remarks, repelling it with a force which none who were present can have forgotten. His words were few, but they were crushing, and showed a manly indignation, that made impossible a repetition of the offence."

Alike under the old organization of the Convention, and the new organization of the Missionary Union, Dr. Wayland was frequently present at the anniversaries. He had studied the whole subject of missions thoroughly; he read every missionary biography or narrative of interest, that appeared; he was familiar with the geography of the regions which were the scene of these self-denying labors for Christ. When he spoke, there was little of rhetorical ornament. But there were a sincerity, a clearness, a moral earnestness, an unselfish devotion to the object in view, and, mingled with all, a courtesy and a freedom from personality, that commanded attention, and rendered his presence a power. At this point we may with propriety again quote from Dr. Stow.

"In 1848 there was a conference at the mission-rooms in Boston, to adjust some difficulties that had arisen between the executive committee and prominent individuals outside, respecting some questions of missionary policy. The difference of views had generated considerable personal feeling, and the parties came together under a heavy burden of solicitude. Dr. Wayland was requested to open the conference with prayer. As he knelt, the first sentences were uttered with a solemnity that was impressive, almost awful — 'O God of eternity, this is not our cause; it is thine. We are nothing. Thou art all.' That prayer gave the key-note to all that followed, and the final result was favorable to harmony and earnest coöperation."

But amid all these public labors for the regeneration of the world, he did not forget that his first duties were to the college, and peculiarly to the moral welfare of its members. He sought to avoid the ground of self-accusation, found in the recollection, "My own vineyard have I not kept." The series of Sabbath afternoon sermons, which had been for a few years intermitted, was resumed in 1845. A portion of these discourses were published in 1848, under the title of "University Sermons," although, as has before been intimated, the contents of this volume give but an inadequate idea of the tenderness, the yearning of heart, the personal wrestling of soul with soul, which often characterized the services in Manning Hall.

The work alluded to provoked criticism from theologians. By some persons there was thought to be too much latitudinarianism in the Sermon on the Unity of the Church. Others were of opinion that disproportionate stress was laid on the obedience and holiness of Christ, as a part of the work of the Messiah, and they could have wished a stronger presentation of the sufferings of Christ, as an equivalent for the merited punishment of mankind. Others, still, were dissatisfied with his view of human sinfulness, and thought that his definition of depravity did not answer the demands of the symbols. But, on the whole, the book met an exceedingly favorable reception, and its circulation (which, including the edition subsequently published, as "Salvation by Christ," reached four thousand copies) was much larger than is usually accorded to a volume of sermons.

To Rev. Dr. Bartol: —

"December 25, 1848.

". . . I am greatly obliged to you for reading my sermons through, and am gratified to learn that they impress you favorably. Newspaper notices I have no confidence in. They are usually written without looking at the book beyond the title page, and are considered a remuneration for sending the book and advertising in the paper. When a person capable of judging correctly reads a book through, his opinion counts. In any case of this kind I seek for the opinions of a few persons, each representing a class, and from them, taken together, make up my own mind. When this has been done, I let the matter rest, and think but little more about it. Until I have got so far, I am always a little solicitous, for all this is a matter of experiment, and no one can pretend to be a judge of his own work; and I am not so much of an old stager, as to look upon failure and success with perfect indifference.

"You say that my views are preferable to Calvinism. I am glad of it; but I did not know that they differed from it. I have never read any of Calvin's works, or anything on controversial theology. . . . A *happy* Christmas to you. I cannot say *merry;* if Christmas means anything, *merry* does not seem the epithet that belongs to it."

He was far from feeling that he discharged his whole duty to the souls of his pupils by delivering these discourses. No means of moral influence were left untried. Nor were his cares always fruitless. Early in the winter term of 1847, it became known to the president that a student, a young man of fine abilities and scholarship, hitherto prone to scepticism, had become anxious about his soul.

The gentleman to whom we refer says, —

"The president met me, and desired me to call at his study the next Sabbath morning at nine o'clock. I went very unwillingly, for I did not care to have any one know how I felt. He talked with me most kindly, and cited several passages of Scripture very apposite to my condition. Then he said, 'I should like to pray with you before you go.' He knelt down near me, while I, looking at him, really lost all apprehension of what he was saying, so struck was I with the moral beauty of his appearance, his profound humility, mingled with dignity. That was the first of many interviews. His wisdom was as great as his kindness. I was at first troubled about the evidences of Christianity. So I got from the library Paley, and Chalmers, and Butler, and pored over them until my head was weary. The president said to me, 'You had better go and take a walk. Now, to-morrow is Saturday. Go off and walk. Be in the air all day.' This was the wisest advice that he could have given me, and I found the benefit of it. It was not long before every doubt and difficulty was removed, and I was rejoicing in a Christian hope."

Meanwhile, a few students, each unaware of the feelings of the other, were agitating the questions that deal with eternal realities. In no long time religion took precedence of all else within the walls of the university. The annual Fast-day deepened and extended the prevalent seriousness. The president spent almost the entire time, not demanded by his prescribed duties, in his study, conversing with young men who desired to open their hearts to him. Carrying the spirit of these personal and familiar interviews into the prayer meetings, he seemed to speak to each heart while he was addressing a hundred. Fearing lest his presence should prove an embarrassment, he usually did not enter until half the time of the meeting had expired. The heart seemed aware of his coming before the eye or ear had discovered it. He occupied always the same seat. His tone was familiar and conversational; his words were with power from above. We give an incident — though it is already familiar, and though it belonged, chronologically, to an earlier period.

A member of the class of 1839 has related, that, in one of these meetings, the president said, in substance, "Do not, young gentlemen, throw away your souls without trying to save them. Make *one honest effort* for their salvation. Even if you are lost, it will be something *to have tried.*" Profoundly impressed with these words, the young man went to his room, determined that he would follow the advice which he had heard. Soon he was rejoicing in the forgiveness of sin. He subsequently became a clergyman of eminent usefulness in the Baptist church.* A brief and touching narrative of his conversion, written by himself, after appearing in the columns of the American Messenger, was published as a tract by the American Tract Society, and widely circulated. A few months since, in an account of a revival which took place in the parish of Rev. T. L. Cuyler, of Brooklyn, particular mention was made of the good which was accomplished by the tract, "One Honest Effort."

Of course among the young men who resorted to the university were the members of families holding a wide diversity of religious opinions. The question will naturally arise, on what principles did President Wayland proceed in giving religious instruction to the representatives of these varying faiths. While believing with the fullest conviction in the truths of evangelical Christianity, and in the distinctive doctrines of his own communion, he yet recognized the right of every man to follow the dictates of his own conscience, and the right of every parent to choose what religious instruction shall be given to his children, so long as he is charged with their support, and intrusted with their management.

In 1842, in the court of Lycoming County, Pennsylvania, Hon. Ellis Lewis, president judge, and more recently chief justice of the state, delivered a decision in which he upheld the right of a parent to control the religious instruction which should be imparted to his minor children. In the course of his decision, he cited a passage from the Elements of Moral Science, and in doing so, paid a high tribute to its author. A copy of the opinion having been sent to Dr. Wayland, he wrote to Judge Lewis as follows: —

* It is an interesting fact that this gentleman is the son of the clergyman who, as we have seen, at an early period in Dr. Wayland's history, proffered him generous aid in the prosecution of his studies.

October 14, 1842.

"My dear Judge Lewis: I received and read, with great pleasure and attention, your decision in the case of the Commonwealth *vs.* Armstrong. It was my intention to write you immediately, but I have been prevented by ill health. I seize the earliest opportunity of performing this agreeable duty, and of thanking you for your letter, which a day or two since came to hand.

"I thank you for your decision upon one of the most delicate and important questions which has ever come before a court. I believe it to be correct in principle, impartial in spirit, and lucid in statement; and I rejoice to see truths of so much importance thus set forth by so high authority. I presume that we should not differ upon any point of it. That we may compare our views with the greater certainty, I write for your consideration such thoughts as have occurred to me on the subject. I do this with the greater pleasure, inasmuch as I know you will correct me if I err.

"The Creator has established it as the law of our being, that the parent must be an adult. This law was manifestly established in order that the child may receive the benefit to be derived from the experience and wisdom of the parent, directed by strong natural affection. But this wisdom and experience would be useless to the child, unless there were conferred upon the parent the authority to enforce his decision. This authority continues during the period of the child's minority, and no longer. When the reason for the authority terminates, the authority terminates with it.

"The next question which arises is, Does religious instruction come within this rule? I think that on this point there can be no diversity of opinion. If the parent is bound to care for the soul of his child, he is bound to superintend its religious education; and he must possess all the authority necessary to the carrying on of that superintendence. This I understand the law to give him.

"But it sometimes happens in the education of children, that the child comes to entertain different religious sentiments from the parent. The parent conscientiously requires the child to do, or to abstain from doing, and the child's conscience forbids it to obey. Now, inasmuch as both parties, in the absence of evidence to the contrary, are to be supposed equally conscientious, the question cannot be decided upon this ground. It must, therefore, be decided by the general principle above stated; and as the parent is older and wiser, the law would confer the authority upon him, and give him reasonable means of enforcing obedience. In this case, since the law at the period of the child's majority relinquishes its power, it acts merely to postpone an action, which in a few years, at most, may be done without offence.

"While, however, I suppose this to be the legal right of the parent, I by no means would assert that it is always wise or just to enforce it. When a child has arrived at such maturity that it is able to judge of its duty by reading the Scriptures for itself, and has thus formed its opinion on questions of religious duty, it is very difficult to decide in how far the parent is morally bound to interfere, provided it be a *bona fide* case of religious belief. He should doubtless advise, and teach, and persuade. He may use his authority to oblige his child to reflect maturely on the subject, and decide without the interference of interested persons. But having done this, I think that he should allow the child to obey the honest dictates of its own conscience.

"But suppose the parent were disposed to press the subject further, and command a child to do what it could not, without, as it believed, disobeying God, or the contrary. What in such a case is the child to do? This is a most trying case, and would be decided by a variety of circumstances. The parent has the legal right to control the child, but if the child, from an honest sense of duty, disobeys, and meekly suffers the consequences, I do not know that we could blame it.

"But another question arises. How far does the law undertake to protect the parent in the exercise of his authority? It certainly gives him the right to teach his child at home, to direct the reading which it shall pursue, and the person who shall visit it. No one has a right to interfere with these parental privileges. But suppose a parent allows his child to mingle in society, to go where it pleases, how far does his authority then extend? Is every person bound to ask a parent on what subject he may talk with his child? And again: suppose the child honestly desires religious instruction, and comes to me to ask for it.

I may not go to the parent's house to proffer it; I may not in any manner obtrude it upon his child; but if the child come to me and ask for it, am I obliged, or at liberty, to refuse to impart it? I think not. Or suppose a child of a full age for religious responsibility came to me for my professional assistance, to enable it to perform a service which it supposed commanded by God, am I at liberty to refuse? I should urge upon the child to delay — to set the reasons of the act before the parent. The law gives the parent the power of prevention if he choose to use it; but if he does not use it, and the child comes to me to perform this religious service, I do not know that I am at liberty to refuse. Nor has the parent, that I see, any ground of complaint against me, provided I have acted on the principles above specified. Were it otherwise, every religious teacher, and every other man, would be almost forbidden to speak; and if I were preaching, and a child came in, whose parents were of a different opinion from my own, I must stop, and in fact I must perform an ordinance of religion not according to the will of the subject, but of its parents. In fact, if every parent has the power of dictating to every person what he shall say to his child, all conversation must cease, for in a mixed company you could say nothing that would not offend somebody.

"This is the way in which it strikes me. I wish very much to know how far you agree with me; I am ashamed to be giving opinions of this kind to a learned and experienced jurist; but I know that you will forgive my presumption. I have always acted on these principles myself. Whenever I know the parents of my pupils to differ from me, I studiously avoid, in conversation, allusion to the points of difference. If they come and ask me what they shall do to be saved, I tell them as well as I am able. Whenever I am liable to discuss points where there may be difference of opinion, their attendance is perfectly voluntary.

"I do not know how to refer to the very kind manner in which you have spoken of me. I can only say that I do not deserve it, but that I know of no man whose approval I should be more glad to receive. I will send you a pamphlet or two. Let me hear from you soon."

To these principles, so far as we know, he always adhered. It was not that he had a slight estimate of the importance of the points in which the several denominations differ from each other. But he felt that there were limits to his responsibility, and that he had no right to violate, on any plea, the rights of another.

Alike from the reminiscences quoted in Chapter IX. of the preceding volume, and from the tone of all his addresses and communications, it has, we presume, been evident that Dr. Wayland regarded education as a question open to argument, subject to inquiry and change. At a later day (perhaps in 1855 or 1856) he wrote to Rev. R. Anderson, D. D., —

"I consider that a great step is made in a reformation when it has been granted that the present system is open to examination, and not stereotyped for all ages. Wherever this is done, light will break in. All my labor about education 'hath this extent — no more.' It begins to be admitted that college systems may *be examined*. When this is done there is hope of amendment."

This feeling found expression in his little volume, published in 1842, entitled, "Thoughts on the Present Collegiate System in the United States." In this book he is rather occupied with defects than with their remedies. He was not satisfied with the kind or the degree of education imparted in the American colleges. He ever sought to elevate the standard of instruction, and to enlarge the number of those to whom the blessings of education should be extended. Though not pointing out in detail any line of policy, the volume now referred to, or at least the state of mind which gave rise to it, was the parent of important movements in the future.

In reference to this work he writes to Rev. Dr. Anderson, —

"I cannot tell you how much I am obliged and encouraged by your kind letter. I wrote with fear and trembling, apprehending that I might very likely stand alone and be considered a disturber of Israel, a sort of Dorr in the literary camp of New England. I, however, felt so strongly convinced that I was in the right that I concluded to venture; and your letter encourages me to hope that I may do some good. As it is, we are multiplying little men and forming no great ones; and the community, having no leaders, is tossed about with every wind of ultraism."

To John N. Wilder, Esq., of Albany, who had written in regard to the movement then on foot to establish a university in Western New York, he wrote: —

"What I want you to think of is, first of all, not to erect dormitory buildings for students. It leads to half, or more than half, of the trouble in colleges, and besides absorbs money that might be much better employed. If you start on this principle, it will save you from much expenditure.

"But pray observe another thing. Try to establish an institution that shall teach what people will pay for learning. As it is, colleges are merely making lawyers, ministers, and doctors; and these will not support one half of the colleges at the north. Try the application of science to the arts. I think that this will support itself, and aid the professional school."

It has already been remarked that President Wayland desired so to aid those who were in pursuit of an education as in the highest possible degree to elevate the standard of scholarship. With this view he proposed to the corporation to devote the income of certain funds, bequeathed by Hon. Nicholas Brown, to the establishment of premiums for excellence in various branches of study. And he himself founded the "President's Premiums," for the purpose of advancing the scholarship of those entering the university. The Rev. Henry Jackson, D. D., also established premiums for excellence in the studies pursued by the Senior class. Among those who competed successfully for the various classes of premiums named above, are many persons who have since attained the highest eminence in literary and professional life.

We have more than once alluded to the labors put forth by Dr. Wayland for the advancement of popular education. He, however, did not feel that it is by schools alone that this object can be promoted. He regarded popular libraries as indispensable to the cultivation of a fondness for reading and of general intelligence. The town of Wayland, in Middlesex County, Mass. (formed from portions of several adjoining townships), had received its name in honor of the president of Brown University.

"On commencement day at Brown University, in the year 1847, President Wayland, in an informal manner, expressed a desire to do something, according to his humble means, to help the inhabitants of the town of Wayland to a town library. He said that he wished not only that the inhabitants of the town might enjoy the advantages to be derived from such a library, but also that other towns in its vicinity might be induced by this example to establish for themselves similar libraries. He proposed to make a donation to the town, of five hundred dollars for this purpose. At the suggestion of Judge Mellen, the donation was tendered upon the condition that five hundred dollars should be obtained in the town by subscription or otherwise;—the whole amount of one thousand dollars to be devoted to the purchase of books for a town library.

"Five hundred and thirty-four dollars were quickly raised by subscription, and President Wayland immediately placed his donation in the hands of Mr. Mellen." *

The free library, thus originated in the town of Wayland, was opened for the delivery of books, August 7, 1850, and has ever since been in beneficent action.

"After the Wayland Library was in successful operation, the suggestion was made to have a 'Library Celebration,' in which every one could participate, the expense to be borne by the town. This suggestion at once re-

* For the facts relating to the Wayland Library we are indebted to a pamphlet by Rev. Jared M. Heard (a graduate of Brown University), entitled, "Origin of the Free Library System of Massachusetts."

ceived the approbation of the inhabitants. The wish was universal to invite Dr. Wayland to be present upon the occasion, as the guest of the town.

"All the necessary preparations for such a celebration were made with great cheerfulness and promptness.

"The 'Library Celebration' took place August 26, 1851, and will long be remembered by those who witnessed it. The writer hopes that an effort will be made at an early day to publish an account of these exercises. A most interesting occasion it was for several reasons. First, from the cause that originated it, which was most justly stated in the following words by Dr. Wayland to Judge Mellen, the president of the day, while seeing the people, old and young, crowding the church in which the celebration was held: 'This gives me a higher idea of New England character than anything I have before witnessed. Your inhabitants have assembled without distinction of age or sex, to celebrate, with joyful festivities, not any great victory, not any great political event, but *the founding of a library.*'

"Another reason for the interest of this occasion was the unanimity and heartiness with which it was entered into by the inhabitants of the place.

"The exercises at the church consisted of an address by Judge Mellen to Dr. Wayland, in which he thanked him in behalf of the people for his generous donation, and extended to him a cordial welcome. This address was followed by one from President Wayland, which it is hoped may one day be published.

"In his introductory remarks, this gentleman stated the whole idea from which sprang his wish to have free public libraries established. He said, 'Our fathers founded schools where we are taught to read; when we know how to read, we want something to read,—we want books.' And from this simple idea in his great mind originated the movement which has resulted in giving to our state the free public libraries so successfully established in various parts of it."

But the benefits of Dr. Wayland's act of true liberality were not confined to a single town. As the immediate result of the events above alluded to, an Act was passed by the legislature of Massachusetts, in 1851, which empowered all the towns of the state to raise money by taxation for the support of free town libraries.* From this law, and from the action of Dr. Wayland which gave rise to it, have sprung the magnificent free libraries which now enrich Boston, Worcester, New Bedford, and a great and constantly increasing number of towns, and which have already conferred a degree of intellectual benefit that we in vain attempt to estimate.

The following letter from Rev. E. H. Heard, of Concord, Mass. (the adjoining town to Wayland), affords illustration of the influence of the system thus inaugurated:

"CONCORD, MASS., November 24, 1851.

"F. WAYLAND, D. D.

"Rev. Sir: Since you were the prime mover in the free library movement which is now going on in this state, I thought I would write and inform you what progress has been made in the work. The people at Wayland were never more interested than now in their library. At their last town meeting they voted to put the books belonging to the school districts into the town library. And you can hardly find a house in town in which there are not some of these books. They also voted to raise sixty dollars for the library this year.

"And there is to be a town library in this village. The proprietors of the circulating library voted to give it to the town, provided they would raise the largest amount of money allowed by law, every year, with which to increase it. The town accepted it, and voted the required sum. There are six or seven hundred volumes, and the tax will amount to about one hundred and fifty dollars. Many of the adjoining towns are also taking measures to establish libraries. And the time is not far distant when there will be a library in every town in the commonwealth. And other states will not only adopt our common school but our town library system.

"Thus, by your foresight and benevolence, the town of

---

* This act was prepared by Rev. John B. Wight, a member of the legislature from the town of Wayland, who was also allowed, by the courtesy of the house, the honor of reporting it, without reference to a committee.

Wayland has been enabled to take the lead in a work which will affect the moral and intellectual condition of the people, not only of this state, but of the whole country. And many will yet regard the establishment of town libraries in this state as the crowning benefit which, through your instrumentality, has been conferred on the country. For this, like other acts of benevolence, will be inspiring and creative, and will excite others to rank themselves in the same fellowship by deeds of kindred benevolence. And thus, ages after you shall have passed from these transitory scenes, the offspring of your own benevolent action will be multiplying in numbers and shedding ever-increasing blessings on our happy country.

"Long may you continue to reap the reward of your labors, so vast and of such surpassing value, in the heartfelt gratitude of the people of the whole country.

I am, sir, with the highest respect,

Your obliged servant,

EDWIN H. HEARD."

The following letters of Dr. Wayland belong to the period embraced in this chapter, 1841–1849: —

"Rev. Dr. Anderson: I hear you are going to the Mediterranean; and being in town on business, I snatched a moment to see you, to tender to you again my best wishes, and to assure you of my warm personal attachment, and my love to the work in which you are engaged. May the blessed Savior be with you by sea and on land, among men barbarous and civilized, Christian or pagan. May he prosper your way in the manner best suited to his infinite wisdom, and give you the desire of your heart. May he grant you that wisdom which He who sees the end from the beginning alone can impart, and return you, in due time, to your family, your labors, your country, and the church of Christ. If in anything I can secure your pleasure, command me."

To Rev. Dr. Hoby, Birmingham, England: —

"The last packet from England brought the sad news of the death of John Foster, *clarum et venerabile nomen*. The last great Baptist light on earth is extinguished. The greatest man in our Israel is fallen. I do not think that you have lost so fine a mind in England since Canning.

Southey was learned, classical, a thorough master of English, a poet, and an historian; but he fell immeasurably short of the vigor of Foster. Robert Hall was, I suppose, surpassingly eloquent, a writer almost without fault, and a classic in the language, vying with almost any who have ever written it. But none of them approaches the massive cubic sense of Foster. No one appeals with such irresistible effect to the conscience and common sense of mankind, and neither of them ever has had a transforming effect on so many minds as Foster. He drives his weapon to the hilt at every blow. Were I to characterize his style by any terms I know of, it would be, '*Britons, strike home.*' He never fails to strike home like a true Briton. And then he was so simple in manner, so thorough and heart-felt in piety, so unaffected in his greatness, so apparently unconscious of his power, so humble, that I presume he really thought much less of himself than any one that knew him thought of him; in fine, he was in every respect so remarkable a man that we are filled with despair at the thought that we can never expect to see such another raised up among us."

To Baptist W. Noel, London: —

"Rev. and dear Sir: I know that you will not consider as an intrusion a letter from one who can claim no other personal acquaintance with you than that derived from a few moments' conversation at your chapel, Bedford Row, some nine years since.

"I have just completed the reading of your volume on the Union of Church and State, and I should do injustice to my feelings did I not embrace the earliest opportunity to express to you the sentiments with which it has inspired me. I do not remember ever to have read a work on any subject with such profound and delightful emotions. Every sentence which it contains seems to me pregnant with most important truth — truth that must tell on the interests of the church in all coming time. I bless God that he has put it into your heart to write and publish it; and that his Spirit has guarded you in so remarkable a manner from acrimony and unkindness, while it has led you to adopt a faithfulness which cannot be surpassed.

"But I well know the penalty which you must pay for all this. I cannot measure the storm which will be raised against you from those whose worldly interests are attacked. But, my brother, be of good cheer. God has pledged himself to sustain you, for you have held forth his simple truth. You have left everything worldly for the sake of that truth, and he cannot forsake you. A multitude of those who love Christ will bear you on their hearts before the mercy-seat. Whatever hosts of earth surround you, the mountain will be filled with chariots of fire and horses of fire, which will be your sure defence.

"Nor is this all. Free churches and ministers need your words of rebuke, caution, and encouragement. Their piety will be increased by the efforts to which you incite them. You will behold now, or in heaven, millions blessing you for every sacrifice; and, above all, the Savior will accept it as done for himself.

"One idea alone has occurred to me, which I do not see that you have noticed. It is the injustice done to the supporters of the Establishment by the union. They pay for religious instruction five, eight, ten, or twelve hundred pounds, and are frequently served by a curate at one hundred. They receive only a tenth of what they pay for, and the rest is often spent in dissipation or vice.

"Excuse me for thus extending to you the hand of fellowship across the water. I have taken the liberty to send you a copy of some sermons which I have lately published. I hope they may reach you. You will see that our thoughts have partly been directed in the same channel."

To Rev. Dr. Hoby: —

"I rejoice at the position assumed by your government in relation to protective duties. If Sir R. Peel carries out his plans, as I think he will, it will do more to advance the cause of civilization than any measure that has been accomplished for centuries. It will be followed, from choice or necessity, by all other nations, and being followed, will bind nations so thoroughly together, — it will render them so necessary to each other, — that wars will be almost impossible. This will be specially the case between your country and ours. We shall be but one in fact, one in language, in religion (saving Puseyism), and we shall be able together to keep the peace of the world. May God of his infinite mercy grant it. I hear of many of your world's conventions that are to be held this year in London. What they will effect I do not know. I, however, believe that the mild, dignified, and forbearing manner in which you have treated this country, will do more to bring about peace and take away the war spirit than anything else that has been or that can be done."

To his uncle, Rev. D. S. Wayland, Bassingham, England, May 22, 1848: —

". . . I see no objection to the course of the government, as I understand it. To be sure, I would not live under such a system; but this is another matter. If the Queen is the head of the church, and responsible for its management, as much as for the administration of justice, there is no reason why she should not appoint bishops as well as judges. I do not see any use of bishops, or the whole of your hierarchy. I think Christianity would be better without it. But, were I an English prime minister, with my present views, I would appoint such men as I believed to be for the good of religion and in favor of religious freedom, to the extent of the royal prerogative.

"But these perplexing questions belong to the nature of the union of church and state. The only wise course is to separate them forever. I am glad of the appointment of Dr. Sumner to the archbishopric, and of Bishop Lee to Manchester. I knew the latter in Birmingham, and took to him very much.

"We are receiving, with every steamer, most stirring news from Europe. The movement of the Chartists is very like that of the insurrectionists in Rhode Island a few years ago. I feel, therefore, as if I understood your position better than I should otherwise have done. I fancy that the revolutions on the Continent are more gratifying to me than to you. I am an untamed republican, but not a sectarian one — a lover of representative governments, in opposition to dynasties and every form of absolutism. I believe that freedom of opinion in matters civil and religious (our old Roger Williams doctrine) will come out of this trouble; that soul liberty will advance towards universal acknowledgment, and thus the race will have a chance, at least, for development. I know there will be a flood of error, but this must be met by a flood of truth. For Louis Philippe I have no regret, except as for an unfortunate man. He has been selfish, absolute, and treacherous. I hear that our Sovereign Lady Victoria says openly that he has lied to her, as I believe he has always done when he thought he could gain by it.

"The indications in France and Germany are good. I shall not live to see the results of all this, but my children may. I cannot but believe that a new era has dawned upon the race, that another seal has been opened, and another page in history commenced. You have no idea of the energy instilled into a human being by individual self-reliance, and the feeling, that, under God, every man depends upon himself. But I know this is heresy, and I will not add another word. Let us unite in prayer that God will overturn and overturn until he brings in the desire of all nations, or at least that amid this overturning, he will direct all events to his own glory."

CHAPTER III.

THE REORGANIZATION OF THE UNIVERSITY.

THE college Commencement of 1849 passed off successfully; the exercises of the graduating class were of the usual degree of interest; the dinner was held in Rhode Island Hall, whose ample and well-lighted apartment afforded a grateful contrast to the low, dim, dingy Commons Hall, where the dinner had usually been served. The after-dinner speeches expressed a warm attachment on the part of the graduates to the institution which had nourished their intellectual life. The next day, at the meeting of the corporation, the president read his annual report, which contained these words: —

"The undersigned deems this a suitable occasion to carry into effect a purpose which for some years he has had in contemplation, and to devote the remainder of his life to pursuits which require the uninterrupted command of his time. With this view he respectfully requests to be relieved from his present engagements, and hereby resigns the office of President of Brown University and Professor of Moral and Intellectual Philosophy. . . . He asks that this resignation may take effect at the earliest practicable period within the present collegiate year."

These words were a surprise to all who heard them, — a surprise as painful as it was profound. And the emotions experienced by the members of the corporation were but representative of the feeling of the entire community, academic, commercial, and industrial.

The corporation at once appointed a committee to express their desire that he would withdraw his resignation; and he consented to continue in the discharge of his office for the current year.

The step that he had taken, however unexpected to others, was the result of deliberation on his part. Four or five years previously, he had mentioned his purpose in his correspondence with Dr. Nott. It is not impossible that the act, long contemplated, had been deferred until he should have witnessed the graduation of his two older sons.

He desired to have leisure to prepare for the press several works not yet published, and to revise, with the aid of leisure and of a matured judgment, those hitherto issued.

This, however, was not the only reason. The college for fifteen years had shown a steady decline in the number of its students.* Its income from all sources fell short of its expenses, and the inevitable tendency was towards bankruptcy.

But it might be said, let an appeal be made to the public for an increase of funds, in order to afford the college the support that it cannot derive from pupils. To this course there were strong objections. The college evidently was not answering any public demand. It was doing only what a great number of colleges, all over New England, could do just as well. To appeal to the public for money was, in reality, only to ask them to contribute for the support of the officers. To do this, while he felt able to maintain himself, did not accord with the president's self-respect.

But there was no reason to suppose that the public

* The number enrolled on the catalogue for

1835-36,	is 195.	1842-43,	is 167.
1836-37,	" 196.	1843-44,	" 169.
1837-38,	" 187.	1844-45,	" 157.
1838-39,	" 188.	1845-46,	" 140.
1839-40,	" 177.	1846-47,	" 146.
1840-41,	" 172.	1847-48,	" 141.
1841-42,	" 175.	1848-49,	" 150.

would respond to such an appeal. Indeed, an effort which had recently been made to raise fifty thousand dollars for the college had been entirely futile.

To Rev. Dr. Bartol, October 5, 1849: —

"... I was much obliged by your letter, specially because it touched the precise nerve of the question, and presented the point on which, in my opinion, it all hinges. The question I have asked myself in this matter has been simply this: Have I that power of available labor that will enable me to be more useful with the full command of my time, than with the command of a portion of it only; or, in other words, have I strength enough to stand alone, or do I require official position to support me? I must admit that, after considerable doubt and serious hesitation, I have with diffidence come to decide in the way which perhaps indicates undue self-confidence. I know that this is an experiment; but I prefer to make it. I know that I am liable to overrate my own powers; but I am encouraged by this fact in my past history, that I have been supposed to do what I have done, better than, when I undertook it, I supposed myself capable of. This gave me confidence, perhaps unwarrantable, in my own decision. The event must decide.

"In this, I know I am considered, by many persons, unwise. There are those who speak of the importance of position and official influence, and the folly of abandoning it. My view of the matter is this: if a man is equal to a place such as this, the place confers on him no honor or power. If he is unequal to it, he may as well leave it to others. Besides, I do not think so highly of official station, and the fuss there is about it, as many men. It is in many respects a trammel, and a man's power is very much in the ratio of his freedom. With such views I have acted, and I more and more believe I acted wisely; and I think most men, who are competent to judge, agree with me.

"Still there is a remote possibility that my plans may be counteracted. Should men here wish to do something noble and of great use to the state, and should the carrying it out depend upon me, I may feel obliged, against my will, to remain for a time. This is the only contingency which I see which can alter my views."

The expression of the wish of the corporation that he should remain at the head of the university prepared the way for a full communication of his views; and on March 28, 1850, he presented his "Report to the Corporation of Brown University," a pamphlet of which it is not, probably, too much to say, that its eminent ability was recognized by those who approved and by those who opposed its conclusions, and that its appearance constituted an era in the history of collegiate education in America.

Without aiming at an exact analysis of this pamphlet, we shall seek to present concisely his later views of education, availing ourselves, for this purpose, of the Report, of his Address at Union College (1854) on "The Education demanded by the People of the United States," and of his Lecture before the American Institute of Instruction (1854), and of other published works, as well as of the manuscript reminiscences from which already the most interesting portions of this memoir have been derived. While, for the sake of brevity, we shall not throughout employ his exact language, every sentiment will be such as he has expressed.

We find the number of students in Brown University steadily diminishing. It is not urged by any one that this decrease results from a want of ability on the part of the officers, or from any inferiority in the instruction imparted, to that afforded in other colleges. It is the unsolicited testimony of the officers of the professional schools, that our graduates hold at least an equal rank with the alumni of other institutions. The diminishing number of our students, as compared with the attendance at other colleges, is due to the fact that we have no means of reducing the cost of tuition, and giving education away. If funds were provided by which education might be rendered nearly or quite gratuitous, and pecuniary assistance afforded to the pupils, young men might be attracted from other colleges or allured from the active into the learned professions, and thus the number of students be increased. But whether the real interests of education would be thereby promoted is scarcely a question.

"And it may be doubted whether this would be more than a temporary expedient. The reduction of tuition might avail so long as our terms were lower than those of other colleges; but so soon as theirs were reduced to the same level, we must provide the means for still further reduction. It seems undesirable that the colleges of our country should, by any contingency, be enlisted in a competition of this nature." — *Report.*

But we find that in all the colleges of New England the number of students is decreasing relatively to the population, and that each year the colleges are compelled anew to appeal to the public for the support which they confessedly cannot derive from the pupils whom they are able to attract; and this, too, amid a population constantly increasing in numbers, and increasing yet more rapidly in wealth and intelligence, and universally thirsting for education. These amazing facts seem susceptible of but one interpretation — that the colleges are not meeting the educational wants of the community. The facts justify, nay require, a reëxamination of our collegiate system.

"It would seem that our whole system of instruction needs an honest, thorough, and candid revision. It has been for centuries the child of authority and precedent. If those before us made it what it is, by applying to it the resources of earnest and fearless thought, I can see no reason why we, by pursuing the same course, might not improve it. God intended us for progress, and we counteract his design when we deify antiquity, and bow down and worship an opinion, not because it is either wise or true, but simply because it is ancient."—*Address.*

The earliest colleges of America were modelled as exactly as possible after Oxford and Cambridge. Designed, like those ancient universities, primarily for the education of the clergy, they established a four-years course of study, filled up almost entirely with Latin, Greek, and mathematics. As new colleges arose in America, they copied, with undeviating fidelity, the exact organization of their seniors. "There seems a fatal tendency, in the formation of systems of education, blindly to follow precedents, without examining the laws on which they are founded, or the results which they have attained." We have all "copied the universal model, without considering how entirely unsuited to our condition must be institutions founded for the education of the mediæval clergy, and modified by the pressure of an all-powerful aristocracy." Thus the college of the later half of the nineteenth century aims to imitate the college of the early half of the thirteenth; and the American college, whether founded amid the learned leisure of the oldest form of New England society, or among the farmers of Illinois, or the miners of California, offers to all but one unvarying type of education.* No regard is had to the infinite variety existing in human minds, nor to the progress of man during the centuries, nor to the demands growing out of the changing aspects of human society.

It is true that some changes have been grafted upon the original model. While a predominance is still given to the classics and mathematics, yet a great number of new branches have been introduced into the system, until the four-years course now includes twenty or more studies. Attempting to pursue all these in the limited time spared from the classics and mathematics, the student finds himself unable to do more than feebly grasp the rudiments of each; he makes himself master of nothing; he is not "taught in college anything with the thoroughness which will enable him to go safely and directly to distinction, in the department he has there entered, without returning to

* And it may be added, that where our American missionaries propose a college for the youth just rescued from barbarism and heathendom, they seem to aim at the precise reproduction of the old-fashioned New England college.

lay anew the foundations of his success." * However strongly marked are the indications that God has designed him for excellence in some one branch of knowledge, yet he is compelled by the requirements of the college course to spend so much time upon studies which are repugnant and comparatively useless to him, that he gains but a meagre knowledge of his chosen department, and purchases superficiality in the studies which he loves, at the expense of a toilsome but almost complete ignorance of those which he dislikes.

The effect on the instructor is scarcely less disastrous. "He has no motive to increase his knowledge. He already knows more than he has any opportunity to communicate. There is no stimulus to call forth exertion. There is no opportunity for progress."

"It has already been remarked that the first and most prominent place is held by mathematics and the classics. Of the former of these it need, perhaps, only be said, that we do not so teach them as to make mathematicians. I suppose that the acquisition of an abstract truth in mathematics is almost valueless, unless it is carried out into its applications, and the student, by such applications, is enabled to use it for himself. If this is done, there is a probability that the principle will be remembered. If it is not done, it will be speedily altogether forgotten."—*MS.*

As to the classics, "I observed that nearly half of the time occupied in the college course, as well as two or three years of preparatory study, was spent on the Latin and Greek languages. I observed that this knowledge was very soon forgotten, and that every year we graduated young men who could not construe their diploma, and that in a few years afterwards not one in twenty could read a sentence of Tacitus or a line of Homer. The sentiments of these authors could have no effect on the mind, for the sentiment evidently was not appreciated.†

* George Ticknor, Esq., as quoted in the Report.

† The writer was present when a lady said to President Wayland, with an appearance of considerable solicitude, "Dr. Wayland, I should think that the morals of our young men would be very much injured by reading the classic authors, in which drunk-

This was obvious from the bald and unintelligible translations which disfigured our examinations. I observed also that those who were the best linguists among us were by no means deeply imbued with the sentiments of the classic writers. This kind of learning did not seem to have imparted richness to their minds. They very rarely quoted their most admired authors, or uttered sentiments which indicated that by reading the classics they had imbibed the spirit of the objects of their idolatry. With no other language than English, Burns had approximated more nearly to Horace than men who had spent years in the study of the Roman bard.

"Again, when the present course of education was established, all the knowledge which the human mind had acquired was contained in these languages. The nations of modern Europe had, at best, but a language without a literature. But how great the change produced by the last four centuries, or even by the century which dates back from the present year! All the most important knowledge or thought of our race is found outside the classic languages. The world has awaked as from a long sleep, and invention and discovery from every part of the globe press upon us with a rapidity that amazes and confounds us. Yet not a word of all this is to be found in the classical languages. Surely such a change in the knowledge of our race would indicate the necessity of a change in our plans of education.

"If it be said that the study of grammar and of con-

---

enness and every form of vice are celebrated and made attractive." He replied, "Madam, it might, at first sight, appear so; but, in fact, the young men understand so little of the classics, and enter so little into their spirit, that I do not really think that such studies do them much harm."

It will, of course, be understood that Dr. Wayland had no disposition to ignore the benefits that may be derived from a wise and generous pursuit of the classics. What he designed to urge was, first, that the place assigned to these studies in the system of modern education, and the amount of time allotted them, should be determined by a view of their educational value as compared with other branches of learning; and further, that they should be so pursued as to secure, in the highest attainable degree, all the advantages which they are adapted to confer.

struction is a valuable discipline for the student, it may be replied, this is true, but it is by no means the only one. And if the construction of language be the only valuable form of youthful discipline, why should we not also study Sanscrit and Arabic, and most of all, the old Gothic languages, which are sufficiently difficult and have the additional advantage of being the fountain from which flowed the noble English tongue?

"But supposing that this form of study has advantages for confining the attention, strengthening the memory, and (if properly pursued) for sharpening the powers of discrimination, are there not other studies which seem capable of conferring equal advantages? The works of God, in nature, animal and vegetable, in history, in geology, are all formed upon a plan, and are the mere realization of the ideas of God. Their classifications, their relations to each other, and their relations to time, are indications of wisdom with which no classic can compare. Why should we suppose that the thoughts of man are more appropriate food for the human mind than that which we may know of the thoughts of God. In morals the mind enlarges by conceptions of God — his perfection, his love, mercy, kindness, and truth, and by training our minds into harmony with his character. Why should it not be so with the human intellect? Why should we not study the laws of God in creation, the relations of these laws to each other, and the magnificent generalizations which they suggest, that so we may learn the modes of operations of the divine Being; that so we may (I speak it with reverence) train ourselves to harmony with the divine mind?

"I submit whether the study of the ideas of God is not likely to elevate and expand the mind as much as the study of the ideas of Virgil, Horace, or Homer. I would add, of Plato; but not one in a hundred, perhaps in five hundred, of our students, ever enters into the ideas of Plato."— *MS.*

"The knowledge of facts leads at once, by the principles of the human mind, to generalization. Hence the mind at a more advanced stage would desire to understand the classifications of physical science. The more simple principles of animal and vegetable physiology might be comprehended at a much earlier age than is generally supposed. The structure of plants might be so far unfolded by living specimens, that every walk in the fields would be to a child a miniature voyage of discovery. The classifications of animals and insects, their habits and modes of life, would form another most interesting line of investigation. I apprehend that this kind of education would be an admirable preparation for more abstract study. . . . And besides this, we should thus spread before the youthful mind the volume of the works of God, and render the world we live in a source of ever-renewed wonder and delight. I know of no part of my early education that I would not thankfully exchange for the ability which, under good instruction, I might possibly have acquired, of understanding and interpreting the ideas of God in creation, and of thus being brought into daily and intimate relation with my Father, who is in heaven." — *Lecture before American Institute.*

"The power of forming conceptions which shall lead to discovery in science, or to the practicable in action, is clearly of vast importance. Can this power be cultivated? On this question there can be no doubt. It steadily increases with the progress of the human mind. We naturally inquire whether the cultivation of this element of intellectual character has been regarded with sufficient attention by those who form our courses of higher education. A large part of the studies which we pursue add very little to our power of forming conceptions of any kind whatever. A larger infusion of the study of physical science, not merely as a collection of facts, but as a system of laws, with their relations and dependences, would be of great value in this respect. We thus study the ideas and conceptions of the Creator. We become acquainted with his manner of accomplishing his purposes, and learn in some measure the style of the Author of all things. Surely this habit of mind must be of unspeakable value to a philosopher in the discovery of truth, or to a man of affairs in devising his plans, since these can only succeed as they are in harmony with the designs of infinite wisdom and benevolence." — *Intellectual Philosophy.*

It appears, then, that the existing system of collegiate education is open to serious objections. It gives to classical studies an amount of time utterly disproportionate to their real value; it has no adaptation to the diversities of mind and genius, to the age, to the country, or to the demands of the people to whom it is offered; it compels the student to study much that he does not want, and does not allow him to go beyond the rudiments of the pursuit on which his livelihood and his usefulness are to depend; and it tends to produce a superficial habit of mind in those who yield themselves to its influence. It is adapted mainly to candidates for the learned professions, especially for the ministry. It excludes the great body of our population — the productive classes — from its advantages; for if they come to our colleges, they do not find the knowledge that they want, or they find it held at so high a price in time as to be beyond their means. But most of all does it rob those who repair to the colleges, and who, when youth is gone, and manhood, with its demands, is upon them, find that though they have paid the price, in time, they have received only an education not thorough in itself, and not suited to their needs.

To remedy these defects, the Report proposes to abolish the four-years term of study, and to lay aside the effort to teach within the period of four years a round of studies requiring a much longer time; to teach thoroughly every study that is taught, and to afford the student the opportunity to prepare and perfect himself in the branches of knowledge which he pursues; to throw open the college to all who desire knowledge, and to allow each person to study what he wants, without compelling him, as a condition, to study what he does not want; and to establish such new departments as may be demanded by the present state of human knowledge, and by the wants of the productive classes.

It was further proposed, not as a necessary part of the reorganization, but as promotive of a high education, that the emolument of the instructor should be made in some degree dependent on his success in imparting knowledge, and should be, in part at least, graduated by the number of his pupils;* and further, that the academic degrees should not be given in course, but should represent a definite amount of attainment, rather than the mere lapse of time since the candidate entered college, or since he graduated.

The statutes of the university enacted in 1850, embodying the practical applications of the principles of the Report, state, "In order to become a candidate for the degree of A. B., the student, having been regularly examined for entrance, must have been proficient in nine courses of one year each. . . . It is the design of the corporation to require for the degrees of Bachelor of Arts and of Philosophy an amount of study which *may* be accomplished in three years, but which may, if he pleases, occupy the student profitably for four years; and to require for the degree of Master of Arts an amount of study which *may* be accomplished in four years, but which, if generously pursued, may occupy the student with advantage a considerably longer time. And the Faculty have the power to direct in all cases the discontinuance of a third study, or the addition of a third to two already pursued, if such diminution or addition of labor will, in their opinion, be for the advantage of the student."

The object of these provisions is obvious. The degree was conditioned upon the amount of attainment rather than upon the time consumed in securing the attainment. Many pupils, perhaps the majority, would be unable to pursue with proper thoroughness three studies at a time. For example, how many young men could carry on a course

* It is, perhaps, worthy of note, that President Wayland urged this feature of the plan from a conviction of its importance, although he of course knew, as the event proved, that as his own department of ethics and metaphysics was remote from the line of popular studies, he would be the first to suffer pecuniarily from the new provision. But his watchword was, "I go for the human race."

of history, metaphysics, and Greek tragedy, and perform the reading and independent investigation required by these studies? The Faculty, using the power wisely put in their hands, would restrict the pupil to two studies, and his faithful pursuit of these would insure more mental maturity than the superficial study, without original thought, of three branches. Thus it would seem that the provision elevates instead of lowering the standard of education. The same remark applies with yet greater force to the requirement for the degree of A. M. It need scarcely be said that the carrying out of these provisions would require a large amount of conscientious fidelity on the part of the Faculty of instruction.

In favor of the change of organization above proposed, the Report urges three arguments. First, it is just. All classes of the community are alike entitled to the benefits of high education. Second, it is expedient. The number of students now in attendance will not be reduced; the standard of education will not be lowered; large numbers of the classes now excluded from the college will seek its benefits, and the blessings of high education will be universal throughout the community. Third, it is necessary. The present system cannot maintain its place. If unable to find in the college the education they need, the productive classes, the mechanic and the manufacturer, will establish institutions for themselves, to which the body of the young will be attracted, and the colleges will "become very good foundations for the support of instructors, but few will be found to avail themselves of their instruction."

If it is objected to the proposed plan of organization, that it would diminish the attention paid to the classics,—

"The reply is easy: If, by placing Latin and Greek upon their own merits, they are unable to retain their present place in the education of civilized and Christianized man, then let them give place to something better. . . . But is there not rather reason to hope that by rendering this study less compulsory, and allowing those who have a taste for it to devote themselves more thoroughly to classical reading, we shall raise it from its present depression, and derive from it all the benefit which it is able to confer?"

If it is objected that such a change is opposed to the wisdom of all our ancestors, it may be replied, —

"This is a question which cannot be settled by authority. We are just as capable of deciding it as the men who have gone before us. They were once like ourselves, men of the present, and their wisdom certainly has not received any addition from the slumber of centuries. God gives to every age the faculty for perceiving its own wants, and discovering the best means of supplying them, and it is, therefore, desirable that every age should decide such questions for itself. We cannot certainly decide them by authority."—*Address.*

As the plan proposed would involve the establishment of several new professorships, and the extensive modification of the college buildings, it was deemed needful for the inauguration of the experiment, that the sum of one hundred and twenty-five thousand dollars should be added to the funds of the institution.

Such was the spirit of the Report presented to the corporation. The corporation ordered it to be printed, with a view to its being finally acted upon at their next meeting.

During this interval, the president, wishing to gain all possible aid from the light of experience, travelled with his friend Mr. Zachariah Allen, of Providence, to Charlottesville, Va,. for the purpose of observing the condition of the University of Virginia, in which a system had been adopted somewhat similar to that proposed in the Report. The result of his observation, so far as it related to the practicability and efficacy of the system, was highly favorable. He was particularly impressed with the earnestness and enthusiasm of the officers of instruction. It would be wrong to affirm that the impression made by the young men assembled at the university, and by the general aspect of society in Virginia, was in a high degree pleasing. A single circumstance affected him deeply. One evening a number of students came to the house of one of the Faculty, by whom Dr. Wayland was entertained, and desired to see the president of Brown University, and to hear a short speech from him. He accordingly addressed to them a few words, as they stood on the lawn before the house. They listened respectfully, and with a gratified curiosity, yet with a manner in which a close observer might see an air of hostility and suspicion towards the speaker. After they had retired, his host said to him, "Not long since, one of the professors, who was my dearest friend, had incurred the ill will of some of the students; and upon the spot where those young men stood this evening, I saw him lie in the agonies of death, murdered by the hands of his pupils."

The corporation met May 7, and adopted the Report and its recommendations, with the condition that the amount named above should be subscribed by or before the 5th of September, 1850. It is probable that there was not in the corporation a majority who fully approved of the plan; yet they were unwilling to take the responsibility of opposing a measure which, in the judgment of the president, promised the only means of saving the college from decline, and of opening to it a field of enlarged usefulness.

The author of the Report had no occasion to offer the complaint uttered by Dr. Johnson after the publication of one of his pamplets — "Sir, it has not met with opposition enough." Perhaps no pamphlet upon education ever published in America was more severely criticised. In New England, the North American and the New Englander reviewed it adversely; the North American conducting the criticism with an absence of personalities, and in the tone and manner in which educated gentlemen of liberal views are accustomed to discuss questions of high public concern. The tone of the Reviews generally was unfavorable. From a great many sources came elaborate defences of the old system, and particularly of the classical course of study.

The Bibliotheca Sacra for 1851 contains an article on College Education, by one of the most eminent and truly scholarly divines of America (Professor B. B. Edwards), which is almost entirely devoted to a defence of the classics, and which, though not mentioning the Report, has obvious reference to it.

The newspapers, truer exponents of popular thought and feeling, were almost unanimous in welcoming the movement, and in looking hopefully for its success.* And the people, the mechanics, for themselves and for their sons, hailed the approach of a brighter day. On the railroads, by the wayside, at the work-bench and the forge, men talked of the enlargement of education, and saw in him who had suggested the change a benefactor of humanity.

The author of the Report did not deem it necessary to reply to the animadversions of critics; and we shall not undertake to do imperfectly what he might have done conclusively had he thought it needful.

To Rev. Dr. Bartol: —

"I have no doubt that the doctrines set forth in the Report will meet with opposition. It is somewhat disagreeable to be held up personally before the public, but I suppose it is necessary to success. The other view cannot be taken without unfolding and really laying bare the ground on which it rests. When this is done, I think that its condemnation at the bar of public opinion is certain. A philosopher who believes the middle ages to be the glory of Christianity, must be opposed to my notions, as most surely I am to his. The real opposition, I almost fear, proceeds from a desire of maintaining the exclusive-

* It would be scarcely pardonable to omit mention of the valuable aid rendered by the Providence Journal.

ness and rank of what are called the learned professions, and a corresponding indisposition to render science and liberal culture universal. All I can say is, that I believe myself to be working for man in all his relations — for man universal, as created by God, entitled to the right of equal and liberal culture. I think that men will so understand it. . . ."

He felt, probably, that it was a matter not to be determined by theory nor by argument, but by experiment, fairly tried. The hearty subscription of a sum considerably beyond the required one hundred and twenty-five thousand dollars, almost entirely by the citizens of Providence, insured the inauguration of the experiment; and accordingly, in September, 1850, the college was opened substantially upon the principles of the Report. Of the system which was then adopted, the author, at a later day, writes, —

"It did not go so far as I would have chosen, and did not, with sufficient freedom, carry out the principles on which it was founded. It was partly a compromise between the old ideas and the new, and was, perhaps, the best arrangement that could be adopted." — *MS.*

But, at any rate, the "new system," as it was popularly called, was a great advance upon the ancient plan of collegiate education. It continued in operation during the remaining five years of his presidency; and with what result? Did it extend to an enlarged number the blessings of high education? Did it maintain, and even elevate, the standard of intellectual attainment? Under its auspices, was the general character, social and moral, of the college preserved?

The number of students enrolled on the catalogue of

1848–49, is 152
1849–50, " 150

Upon the adoption of the new organization, the number was, in

1850–51, first term,	174
" second term,	195
1851–52,	225
1852–53,	243
1853–54,	283
1854–55,	252

The little State of Rhode Island furnished ninety students — a number larger than proceeded from any other state, and amounting to two thirds the entire number that had been enrolled on the catalogue under the old organization.

But it had been darkly predicted that with the liberty of choice given, the severer studies would be neglected, and ease of attainment alone would influence the student in his selections. It appeared that, instead of thirty-nine who had studied geometry in 1848–9, the class, in 1851–2, numbered sixty-three, and in the following year seventy, and in the next year seventy-four. The class in trigonometry, which had numbered forty-two, rose to sixty-five. "But the classics, the type and summit of liberal and humanizing influences, would be utterly neglected: not a student would pursue these, unless forced into them by a kind, but rigid authority." For a year or two there was a falling away, but the catalogue soon showed that one hundred and seven were studying Latin; * and the number of candidates for the degrees of A. B. and A. M., for which classical study was required, was one hundred

* And of this number, it will be remembered, every one was pursuing the study because he deliberately chose it, and the instructor was not compelled to keep back the really forward and studious, that he might bring into something like an alignment those who, forced into the study, asserted their manhood by a faithful and conscientious indolence. He had only to guide the hearty enthusiasm of those who *wanted* to learn.

and sixty-one, while the candidates for a degree in 1848–9 had been but one hundred and forty-five. The class in rhetoric, which had numbered forty-two, rose to sixty-four. The class in chemistry from thirty-five rose to eighty-two.

From 1851 to 1858, inclusive, two hundred and forty-one graduated with the degree of A. B. or A. M. This afforded an average of thirty and a fraction annually, not counting, of course, those graduated with the degree of Bachelor of Philosophy. The number of graduates with the degree of A. B., from 1830 to 1850 inclusive, was five hundred and seventy, an average of twenty-seven and a fraction annually. Thus it would appear, that facts justified the language of the Report, "There is no reason why this class of pupils [those preparing for the learned professions] should be diminished."

As to general demeanor under the new organization, we may quote briefly from the annual report of the executive board to the corporation, for 1851: —

"During the year ending September, 1850 [the last year of the old system], the absences averaged thirty-three to each student; during the year 1850–51 [the first under the new system], seventeen to each student. And it is to be remarked, that, owing to the absences being reported daily to the president, a much greater degree of accuracy is attained than under the previous system.

"During the first term of the present year (1850–51), the total number of demerits incurred was two thousand and twenty-five; during the second term, with an increase of students, the number of demerits was one thousand and twenty-five. During the first term, eighty-nine incurred no demerit, during the second term, one hundred and twenty incurred none."

The last paragraph is quoted not as affording any ground of comparison between the old system and the new, but as exhibiting the improvement made by the new system upon itself.

During the first term of the following year, owing to temporary and incidental causes, the standard of demeanor was low, and much disorder prevailed. But during the second term, the executive board reported that the college was in as good a state of discipline as it had been at any previous period.

At the close of the year ending September, 1853, the board report to the corporation, —

"The conduct of the students has been in general commendable. Since the middle of the first term, no case has occurred requiring public censure."

The board also state, —

"From the account of the register, it will be seen that the collections have never been made so satisfactorily as within the last two years, and that the loss by bad debts for this period will be very small if there be any. The finances of the university are in a prosperous condition. Should the number of students continue to increase, or should the number of entrances maintain its present rate, the corporation will have the means of making important additions to the number of courses taught in the university. It is by thus using our prosperity as the means for attaining still greater prosperity, that we shall be able to accomplish the purposes which should ever be had in view by one of the oldest universities in our country."

For the year ending with September, 1854, the executive board report, —

"The whole number of students in attendance during the past year has been two hundred and ninety-six. The attendance and conduct of the students have been, on the whole, satisfactory. During the first term, the number of absences and of demerits was such as evidently to require special attention. Several young men were advised to return to their friends, and two were dismissed for cause. The second term manifested a decided improvement, and the conduct and attendance became perfectly satisfactory."

The report concludes as follows: —

" The present condition of the university is full of hope. The principles which we have adopted seem to receive the approbation of the community. Our income is sufficient to meet our expenses, and to leave a small surplus. When our lands become available, considerable additions may be made to our means. An opportunity will then be afforded of enlarging our courses of instruction, and carrying out more perfectly the principles which we have made the basis of our present system." *

To President Manly, of the University of Alabama: —

"August 9, 1851.

". . . The year before the experiment we entered forty-seven. The past year we entered ninety. . . . Every prophecy of evil has failed; and the college never before stood in the public estimation as it does at present. It can be carried through; if it fails, we are the persons in fault.

" We make no difference in our young men. All study alike in the same classes, and all could room in the college, if there were accommodations. We prefer to break up the distinction among classes and courses, and to consider every young man who comes to study, and who conducts himself correctly, as being as good as any other young man. Our young men studying for A. B., B. P., and select courses, are in every respect as deserving and as good scholars as any we have. There is every encouragement, so far as I can see, for trying the experiment."

To the same: —

"March 15, 1852.

" I think our prospect good. New cases are coming daily to my knowledge, where we shall be able to do good to men, who, otherwise, would have stopped at an academy."

It has already been seen that the number enrolled upon the catalogue was nearly doubled under the new system. But it was by no means designed to limit the advantages

* The Report of the Executive Board for 1855 we have been unable to find among the documents on file in the university.

of high education to those who had leisure to enter upon regular courses of study. Desiring to make the university a blessing, not alone to the candidates for a profession, and to the children of affluence and leisure; feeling that it had not yet discharged in full its mission in behalf of the creators of wealth, — the productive classes, — the president and those associated with him devised other and wider plans of usefulness. In 1852 a course of lectures was given by Mr. W. W. Pearce (instructor in Analytical Chemistry) upon the Principles and Processes employed in Calico Printing."

In 1853 Professor Chace (to whose able coöperation, it is but justice to say, the successful working of the new organization was largely due), having been appointed to the chair of Chemistry applied to the Arts, determined, in accordance with the original design of the department, to render it as available as possible to the mechanics, manufacturers, and artisans of Providence. The number of persons, and the amount of capital, employed in the manufacture of jewelry in the city, naturally suggested the class to be first addressed. Having, by patient and widely-extended observation and experiment, made himself acquainted with the subjects to be discussed, he announced a course of eight lectures upon "The Chemistry of the Precious Metals," addressed to the jewellers and other workers in those metals. The course embraced the following subjects: —

The relation of the metals to oxygen; the relation of the metals to the more important acids; the composition and properties of the acids and salts chiefly employed in acting upon metals; the formation, constitution, and properties of metallic alloys; the composition and action of solders and fluxes; the tempering of metals; the refining, parting, and coloring of metals; electro-silvering and electro-gilding.

An audience of about three hundred and thirty-five

assembled, filling Rhode Island Hall.* The lecturer explained to them the laws and principles governing the processes of their art, pointed out numberless ways of avoiding failure, waste, and loss, and showed the steps necessary to conduct each operation to a successful result. They listened with profit, and, it seems not too much to say, with delight. One said, "I see why it is that I have so often failed. I have been doing, or trying to do, these things all my life without ever knowing *why*." Another said, "if I had known these things years ago, it would have saved me thousands of dollars." At the conclusion of the course, the jewellers presented to Professor Chace a beautiful and significant token of gratitude for the benefit they had received from his instructions — a large silver pitcher, of elegant workmanship, made by the hands of those who presented it. Upon its sides were engraved scenes taken from the workshop and the lecture-room. The testimonial, designed to commemorate the alliance now inaugurated between science and industry, was itself an event, and afforded an illustration of the true mission of knowledge, and of one of the functions of a university.

These courses of lectures were intended as but the commencement of a series of similar movements, to diffuse among the laboring and productive classes the knowledge appropriate to their several callings. The new system included, among its features, courses of lectures on all the prominent applications of chemistry to the arts of life — on the working of the different metals, on the principles of combustion, the laws of heat, the most approved methods of warming and ventilating buildings, on the prin-

* Affording almost an exact realization of the anticipation expressed in the admirable address of Professor J. W. Draper (1853): "I heartily join in the sentiments recently expressed by an eminent clergyman, and trust that the time is not distant when we shall see the New York mechanic passing up the steps of the university, and depositing the tools he has been using behind the lecture-room door."

ciples and methods of dyeing and bleaching. It included also within its scope similar lectures on the applications of science to the mechanic arts, on the construction of machinery, the economy of power, the strength of materials, and on mining and engineering. It further proposed the establishment of an amply-furnished laboratory, open to mechanics of every class, who could there perform experiments and make analyses. Thus, with every year, the college was gaining in popular favor, and was conferring its blessings on every class. While no less useful than formerly to the candidates for the learned professions, it was also giving to the people of Rhode Island, and to their sons, an education which should fit them for whatever calling they might choose to pursue; which should lighten their toil, lessen their hours of labor, and render more safe their often perilous processes; which should make their daily life no longer a drudgery, but elevated, heroic, and promotive of their own and of the general wealth and happiness.

In 1854 Dr. Wayland delivered an address at Union College, upon "The Education demanded by the People of the United States." In no one of his many utterances did his powers do themselves ampler justice. His mind had worked itself clear on the subject of education, and the experience of the past four years had fully justified his convictions. In this address, while taking the same general direction as that followed in the report, he speaks with greater confidence and with a higher inspiration. Without attempting an analysis, we quote a few paragraphs.

On the assertion that useful, practical knowledge is destitute of disciplinary power: —

"Is it, then, to be supposed that God has made for our brief probation two kinds of knowledge: one necessary for the attainment of our means of happiness, but incapable of nourishing and strengthening the soul, and the other tending to self-culture, but leading to no single practical advantage? Shall we believe that the God and Father of all has made the many to labor by blind rules for the good of the few, without the possibility of spiritual elevation; and the few to learn nothing that shall promote the happiness of the whole, living on the labors of others, selfishly building themselves up in intellectual superiority? . . . We might surely suppose that that, which God had made most necessary to our existence, would be, in the highest degree, self-disciplinary. . . . We cultivate our powers of every kind by exercise, and that study will most effectually aid us in the work of self-development, which requires the original exercise of the greatest number of them.

"There are two methods by which we can determine the truth in this matter. First, we may examine any particular study, and observe the faculties of mind which it does and which it does not call into action. . . . Or we may ask, What are the results actually produced by devotion to those studies which are allowed to be merely disciplinary? We inquire, Are mathematicians better reasoners than other men in matters not mathematical? Are classical students more likely to become poets or artists than other men? or does their style, by this mode of discipline, approach more nearly to the classical models of their own, or of any other language?

"It is by such considerations as these that this question is to be answered. We have long since abjured all belief in magical influences. If we cannot discover any law of nature by which a cause produces its effect, and are unable to perceive that the effect is produced, we begin to doubt whether any causation exists in the matter."

Mental culture designed to be universal: —

"Skill in invention, united to the miraculous power of steam, is removing from human sinews the most laborious parts of every operation. . . . God is thus lifting off from us that oppressive severity of toil which paralyzes intellect and benumbs the power of emotion. The mind is thus rendered physically capable of thought and reflection. . . . We see here a tendency to realize the beneficent designs of the Creator. It is evident that God intended all men to think, and to enjoy all the advantages of intellectual culture, for he has given to all men all the powers adapted to thought and culture. It is equally evident that he intended all men to labor, for labor is essential to physical health and enjoyment. And, moreover, men think the better for working, and they work the better for thinking. He, however, never intended that labor should crush the power of thought. His design concerning us will not be accomplished until every man shall be able to secure a competence by an amount of labor which shall leave his spiritual nature free and unembarrassed, nay, the better prepared for its work, on account of the physical labor in which it has been engaged."

We may suppose the following words to have had their origin in the successful endeavor, lately mentioned, to carry the blessings of science into the workshop: —

"The practice of every art depends for success on a knowledge of some social or physical law. To such a community as ours, knowledge is, then, a matter of imperative necessity. Without it, unless by accident, man must labor in vain, and consume his capital without remuneration. But if it be said that, after all, the men who avail themselves of the laws of nature in their daily pursuits, do not resort to our colleges, the reply is easy: If they resorted thither, would they find what they want? Our teaching of nature's laws is designed not for men who expect to use their knowledge, but for those who expect immediately to forget it. Let, however, instruction be given, adapted to the wants of the community, on any scientific subject, and the instructor, wherever he can find men, will rarely want for hearers."

The discussion of the main subject of the address closes as follows: —

"Is it not imperative on us to set an example for ourselves? In a free country like our own, unembarrassed by precedents, and not yet entangled by the vested rights of by-gone ages, ought we not to originate a system of education which shall raise to high intellectual culture the whole mass of our people? When our systems of education shall look with as kindly an eye on the mechanic as the lawyer, on the manufacturer and merchant as the minister; when every artisan, performing his process with a knowledge of the laws by which it is governed, shall be transformed from an unthinking laborer into a practical philosopher; and when the benign principles of Christianity shall imbue the whole mass of our people with the spirit of universal love, — then, and not till then, shall we illustrate to the nations the blessings of republican and Christian institutions."

In 1856, at the dedication of the Norwich Free Academy, he said, —

"I regard with special interest the announcement that young men are here to be fitted for the practical employments of life. . . . I look upon the practical arts as a great triumph of human intellect. Our admiration for this sort of talent is legitimate. We do well to revere the genius of Milton, and Dante, and Goethe. But there is talent in a cotton mill as well as in an epic. And I have often been deeply impressed, as I have stood in the midst of its clattering machinery, with the thought, How great an expenditure of mind has been required to produce these spindles, and looms, and engines!

"Besides, we shall do well to remember that the agencies which have revolutionized society and advanced civilization have been inventions in the mechanical arts. I rejoice, therefore, that the studies in this school are to be, in part at least, of a practical cast. It will do a great and noble work if it shall foster and develop practical genius to be engaged upon practical things."

In 1861, after alluding to the principles which have been dwelt upon above, and the results aimed at, he wrote in his reminiscences, —

"The college commenced, accordingly, to act in conformity with these views, and, so far as I am able to discover, justified their truth. Difficulties were indeed experienced, but they arose not from any inaccuracy or want of wisdom in the plan. So long as I was connected with the college, it continued to be thus carried on, and satisfied my expectations."

Again, in 1864, at the centennial dinner of the university, he said, —

"It was upon such principles as I have thus briefly stated that the new arrangements of this college were commenced. Of their adaptation to the present state of civilization, and especially to that of our own country, it is, perhaps, premature to speak. Time will decide upon their truth or their fallacy. It is worthy of observation, however, that the changes in collegiate organization of late, so far as I know, have all been in this direction. Nor is this true of this country alone. The Universities of Oxford and Cambridge are adapting their courses of study in such a manner as to meet the demands of the different classes of the community, and are becoming accessible to classes who were formerly not allowed to enter their sacred enclosures. . . .

"I hope that you, gentlemen, may yet see these views 'familiar as household words' to the whole civilized world, so that every seminary of higher education shall scatter broadcast over the whole community, over every rank and every class, over every profession and every occupation of life, 'the benefits of knowledge and the blessings of religion.' Rhode Island gave to the world the first practical example of a commonwealth founded on the principles of 'perfect liberty in religious concernments;' and this principle is now making the circuit of the civilized world, and awaking the nations from the slumber of ages. It will be a pleasing matter of reflection for us, gentlemen, if we shall be permitted to see this little college taking the lead in another glorious reformation, and being the first to offer to our brethren, in every walk of life, all the blessings of broad, generous, universal intellectual cultivation."

Shall we, then, hesitate to say that the system of education pursued in the university from 1850 to 1855 was successful? And if so high a degree of success was attained notwithstanding many disadvantages, — was attained when to an organism not new was applied a new principle, when the impulse went forth from one man almost alone, without the coöperation, and with the opposition of many, upon whom absoluteness of success greatly depended, — shall we not say that the system has demonstrated its practical value, and has shown that under favorable or even under fair auspices, the result would have been as benign as the humane aspirations of its originator could desire?

Many facts show that he rightly estimated the demands and the tendencies of humanity. The University of Virginia (already alluded to), continuing upon its enlarged and liberal courses of instruction, became the leading institution in the south, containing in 1861 not far from seven hundred undergraduates. Very many of our colleges have made provision for a generous scientific culture. The United States, by act of Congress, has granted munificent endowments for the support in each state of "at least one college, where the leading object shall be, without excluding other scientific and classical studies, and including military tactics, to teach such branches of learning as are related to agriculture and the mechanic arts, in such manner as the legislatures of the states may respectively prescribe, in order to promote the liberal and practical education of the industrial classes in the several pursuits and professions in life." The Massachusetts Institute of Technology, endowed by the public and private munificence of the immortal Commonwealth to whose name it at once owes and imparts renown, has entered, without any period of immaturity, upon a career of broad and almost unlimited usefulness. It offers to the members of every class the privilege of a high education, at once liberal and productive, without exacting as a condition the study of the ancient languages. In addition to its regular and its special courses, it has established evening classes for the free instruction of persons of both sexes above the age of eighteen.* Among these evening classes were, last winter, the elementary class in French, numbering one hundred and sixty, and the class in grammar, rhetoric, and composition, numbering one hundred and twenty, besides smaller classes in mathematics, navigation, anat-

* These evening classes are established by a grant of money from the Lowell bequest.

omy, and physiology. The whole number of applications for tickets to these evening classes (exclusive of the students in the regular course, who are not admitted), was between five and six hundred. On Wednesday and Friday afternoons forty-eight tables in the laboratory are occupied by teachers in public and private schools, for instruction in chemical manipulation.

In these steps towards a universal and a truly liberal education, in the pamphlets of Professor Atkinson, Dr. Bigelow, and President Barnard, in the address of Dr. Hedge before the Alumni of Harvard University (1866), and in numberless other utterances of the advancing age, is to be found the true rejoinder to the adverse criticisms upon the "Report."

And the same tendencies, less marked, perhaps, but unmistakable, are visible in other lands.

Such was the position of the university in the summer of 1855, in the twenty-ninth year of the presidency of Dr. Wayland — the fifth of the new organization. He might, with humble gratitude to the Author of every noble work, review the changes since he entered on his office. He found the college with less than ninety students. He had seen its numbers rise to two hundred and ninety-six. Eight hundred and thirteen had graduated under his presidency. He found it with three professors; it now had eight. It then had no library, nor apparatus worthy of the name, no laboratory, nor cabinet, nor any means of securing any of these. It now had an admirable apparatus for philosophy and chemistry, a good laboratory, a valuable cabinet, a library of thirty thousand volumes, and a fund of twenty-five thousand dollars, by which the library was increasing at the rate of one thousand volumes annually. It then had two public buildings; it now had four. It then had about thirty thousand dollars of funds; it now had one hundred and fifty-six thousand dollars, in addition to the library fund. It then conferred its benefits on a few members of privileged classes and professions; it now was irradiating every workshop with its benign light, and was blessing mankind.

And its future seemed as bright as its recent history had been progressive.

CHAPTER IV.

LABORS GROWING OUT OF THE REORGANIZATION.—RELIGIOUS EFFORTS.—MECHANICS' ASSOCIATION.—AGRICULTURE IN RHODE ISLAND.—NATIONAL UNIVERSITY.—LIFE OF JUDSON.—APOSTOLIC MINISTRY.—CORRESPONDENCE.

IN June, 1850, Dr. Wayland wrote to Deacon Lincoln,—

"You must be patient with me about letters. I am pressed beyond measure in things which do not allow of haste. I am in the most laborious part of the year for me in college without any relief. I am working at my plan of organization, attending to what I can of the subscription, and harassed by a multitude of anxious cares and delicate arrangements."

And again, in July,—

"Last night, at about eleven o'clock, the committee had its last meeting on the Report [embracing the laws of the college]. . . . Then comes the meeting of the corporation; then the preparation for commencing the course; and then, if I live, a year of responsibility such as I have not yet seen."

After speaking of the point thus far reached in the subscription,—

"This is all that we know of. The time presses heavily, and I wonder sometimes that I can sleep o' nights; but it is all in better hands than mine."

Of the labors and cares of the years 1849–55, from the hour when the first suggestion of a reorganization was made, to the close of his connection with the university, it is impossible to convey any just idea. His ordinary duties as president and as instructor must be discharged. Then the plan for the reorganization must be created, objections anticipated, and the report written. Upon the adoption of the report, there arose the work of the subscription, to which he gave time, and labor, and correspondence. Then came the draughting of new laws. Upon the opening of the new year, each member of the college — those formerly members as well as the recent entrances — was personally examined by the president, that his studies and courses might be assigned. The president was the centre of everything. If any complaint was made, if any difficulty needed to be obviated, recourse was had to him. The executive board, between May, 1850, and July, 1851, held thirty-five meetings, at each of which he presided. Some of these were exceedingly laborious and of great length, extending far into the night. During the following year (1851–2) nineteen meetings of the board were held. Besides these, there were the meetings of the Faculty. And the public attention, which had been attracted to the new system, led to a vast amount of correspondence.

To his sister: —

"June 26, 1851.

". . . The fact is, I have, for a year, written nothing but business letters, so that I hardly know how to write anything else. I have inquiries of all kinds about college, and have had an amount of official duty thrice as much, at least, as ever before. I have lectured daily, and examined weekly essays for my class. This has taken a large part of my time, so that I do not know when I have made a visit. I sometimes feel disheartened with the life I lead, but it seems appointed to me, and the rule of our life should be, that man must not live by bread alone, but by every word that proceedeth out of the mouth of God; that is, by whatever God sends us. For two years I have not known what relaxation means. After Commencement I shall, probably, have a little more time. But all depends on business which I cannot control."

And throughout, if any work seemed so unusually difficult that others shrank from it, it either fell to him, or he, of his own accord, assumed it. It was apprehended that the preparation of the catalogue for the first year would involve extraordinary labor, as it must contain a great amount of new and explanatory matter, and as the old arrangement of classes was entirely abolished, and the names must be classified on new principles. The president said at once, "I will do it;" and he did it.

To Rev. Dr. Hoby: —

"July 22, 1851.

"I am obliged to confess that I am a bad correspondent. For two years I have not known rest or leisure until within a few days. We have commenced important changes in our college arrangements, adopting some new principles, and cutting loose from your old university plans. To do this it was requisite to raise one hundred and twenty-five thousand dollars. The work has begun, and it has now gone through one year of its course. We have thus far been successful, and the prospect is, that we shall be able to carry it through with great advantage to the cause of education. But the care and responsibility have been exceedingly oppressive. If it had failed, on me would have fallen all the reproach. Through the great mercy of God, however, it now looks prosperous — and to him be all the glory. But I would not, for any earthly consideration, go through the same work again.

"I have not seen any of your friends. I have been, and am generally, so confined at home, that I rarely see any one, unless some one, in passing this way, calls upon me. My lot is to turn grindstone and work steadily in one place."

He was so made that it was an impossibility to see anything with which he was connected go wrong; he must either relinquish it, or he must, at whatever cost, make it right. At this time he felt even an enhanced sense of responsibility. The eyes of the public were on him. The system was of his creation and proposal. On his recommendation it had been adopted; in confidence in his capacity, and often on his representations, the means for its establishment had been contributed. It *must* succeed. During the first term of the second year, under the new arrangement, his cares and anxieties were greatly increased by certain annoying circumstances, purely incidental in their origin, and in no manner connected with, or growing out of, the natural working of the system.* He preserved perpetually an undaunted front. Probably the absolute certainty of physical prostration and death would not have moved him till the system was fairly established. Indeed, such was his iron will, that neither to himself nor to others was the draught on his strength apparent. Yet how these things told upon him, is shown, in some degree, in the following letter, written during the vacation succeeding the term recently alluded to.

To his sister:—

"It is true I have been unwell for some time — not from disease, but from over labor and mental anxiety. My work and care have been for some time rather too much for me, and I have, almost for the first time, spent as much of the vacation as I could in doing nothing. I was so worn out that the writing of a letter was a burden to me, and I have hardly written one but from sheer necessity.

"Your fear of my suffering from homœopathic treatment was groundless. I did not need, and I did not take, medicine. I wanted nothing but mental rest. You are, perhaps, in danger of thinking too highly of medical treatment of every kind. The most accurate researches show that people get well as certainly without treatment as with, if well cared for in other respects. This holds true, at least in very many diseases. I observe that all the best physicians give but little medicine; and the older they grow,

* It was the opinion of his physician that he never ceased to experience the effects of the strain to which his brain was at this time subjected. Indeed, the varied, and, to a considerable extent, unshared responsibilities which rested on the president, might well have destroyed the health of a younger man.

the less do they give, and the less is their confidence in medicine. Such is my belief, or rather my want of belief, as to this matter."

Meanwhile his care for the moral and religious culture of the college was unwearied, nay, was deepened, as the numbers for whom he felt himself responsible were increased. During much of the time he preached on the Sabbath in the chapel. And never, certainly, did he with more eloquent earnestness pour forth his soul for the conversion of his pupils. One occasion — the Annual College Fast Day of 1852 — was memorable. On the evening preceding, he received, by telegraph, news of the sudden death of his early playmate and tenderly attached sister, Mrs. Stone. His heart yearned to look on her features once more, before they were concealed in the grave. But the divine voice seemed to say, "Let the dead bury their dead, but go thou and preach the gospel." He preached from the words, "But ye, beloved, building up yourselves on your most holy faith, and praying in the Holy Ghost, keep yourselves in the love of God." The sermon was mainly a warning expostulation addressed to those who, having professed religion, were in danger of failing to keep themselves in the love of God. It was an occasion of profound solemnity.* During the same year, also, he instituted among the officers a weekly meeting for prayer in behalf of the students. And he was frequently at the Wednesday evening prayer meeting. He desired to attend, as often as he could without detracting from the familiar character of the meetings.

In his own home, too, there were claims upon him of peculiar tenderness. His youngest son, for many years an invalid, was, during the years 1850–51, in a condition so critical, that at times his life was endangered. He required

* The late Rev. Bradley Miner, of Providence, a man of singular correctness of judgment, said to the writer, "It was one of the most awfully solemn sermons I ever heard."

ceaseless attention, and on his account the president slept on a lounge, ready to rise and minister to his wants. It is probable that he had not, during that winter, one night of unbroken sleep.

His public labors outside of the university were never more arduous. At the invitation of the legislature of Rhode Island, he addressed that body, explaining the features of the new system, and securing their approval.

In 1849-50, a course of lectures having been proposed before the Association of Mechanics and Manufacturers, he was asked to open the course, and consented, feeling a strong sympathy with the objects of the Association — the elevation and culture of the mechanics of Providence. His subject was, "The Elements of high Civilization existing in Rhode Island." The lecture was written expressly for the occasion, and was never used again. Indeed, it was so special in its character, that to employ it elsewhere would have been almost impossible. It bears the marks of haste in composition; but it contains thoughts worthy of fixing the attention, not alone for the hour, but for all time. The definition which he gives of civilization is profound and radical, and the address is imbued throughout with his characteristic public spirit and large humanity. How inspiring is the delineation of a community whose members should have realized the idea of a high Christian civilization! "Upon such a nation, God himself, according to his invariable law, would shed down his richest blessings. The land tilled by industry and skill would yield its largest increase. Its waterfalls would pour down wealth. Its mines would unveil their treasures. Its harbors would be loaded with the riches of every clime. Piety would gladden every fireside, and the consolations of the gospel would watch beside every death bed. Happy is the nation that is in such a case, yea, happy is that people whose God is the Lord." As was to be expected in addressing a Rhode Island audience, he did not forget a tribute to one of his favorite heroes, the eminent founder of the first commonwealth that established absolute spiritual freedom.

In September, 1851, he gave the annual address before the Rhode Island Society for the Encouragement of Domestic Industry. This, too, was prepared especially for the occasion, and aimed to direct the farmers and manufacturers of the state to the means by which they might render the industry of Rhode Island in the highest degree productive. The familiarity which he exhibited with the subjects discussed, illustrated the breadth of his intelligent sympathy. To the farmers especially he spoke from the heart. If he had a passion, it was the culture of the soil. The address breathes throughout his desire to see every man, whatever his class or trade, raised to a higher level of knowledge, goodness, and happiness.

In 1852 he received from Harvard University the degree of Doctor of Laws. While he set a very low value upon titles as such, yet the assurance thus afforded that his labors in behalf of education were held in favorable estimation by gentlemen of high character and enlarged public spirit, afforded him unaffected pleasure.

During the winter vacation of 1852–3, he acceded to the request of a number of eminent gentlemen who were interested in the movement for establishing a National University, and attended a meeting, for this purpose, at Albany. He made an address in the State Capitol, upon the principles of university education. Many members of the legislature, then in session, were present, to whom the address was a revelation. They had hitherto regarded high education as something remote from popular interest, calculated only to aggrandize an intellectual aristocracy. Now they saw its relation to the elevation and enfranchisement of universal humanity.

Upon the death of Dr. Judson, the feeling was universal that a life so peculiarly devoted to the glory of God and the welfare of man should not be left without a suitable record; and, after the return of Mrs. Judson to America, the executive committee of the Missionary Union, having consulted her wishes in the selection of a biographer, voted to request Dr. Wayland to prepare the Memoir. The request found him already overwhelmed with labor, and purposing to devote such hours as he could with difficulty snatch from the college, to a revision and re-writing of his Moral Science. But to exhibit for the imitation of mankind the life and character of this most noble of men, especially when thus he could repay to the widow and orphan a portion of the debt that humanity owed to Judson, was a duty to which all else must be postponed. If his brethren who had been associated with the missionary, and if she who knew him best, and to whom his fame was very dear, regarded Dr. Wayland as the most suitable person to discharge the duty, he would not gainsay the decision.

The work was attended by peculiar difficulties. He was to write the memoir and delineate the character of one whose life had been spent on a remote continent, whom he had scarcely known personally, having seen him but for a very few days, and having never, so far as we are aware, enjoyed any correspondence with him. For nearly forty years Dr. Judson had been prominently before the Christian world; the leading events of his history had become as household words; his published journals and those of Mrs. Judson had been widely read. On the other hand, by far the greater part of his private correspondence, with his family at home and with his missionary associates, had, from a variety of causes, perished. There was little material accessible to the biographer, except such as had for many years lain open to universal observation. Dr. Wayland writes to Rev. Dr. Peck, —

"The want of all material for the Life of Dr. Judson is

pressing and painful. I do not see what can be done about it. Fire and water have done their worst with regard to all his letters and manuscripts, and what is in print has been made public in every form. I hope you have something for me at the Rooms. Pray cause all your correspondence to be examined, and send me everything you can get. From all the circulars we have, as yet, received nothing; I believe not a line."

To present the subject in a light that should be fresh and impressive, and at the same time truthful, was not a work of easy accomplishment.

The presence and aid of Mrs. Judson were of inestimable service. He writes, —

"I saw her very frequently, and was in the habit of conversing with her with the utmost freedom respecting missions in general, and the missions to the East in particular; and, in fact, on almost every subject connected with the progress of religion in the world."

In the preface to the Memoir, Dr. Wayland ascribes to her aid a large share of whatever value the work may possess. During its preparation she spent several months in Providence, in his immediate vicinity, and was for some time a member of his family. The high estimate which he formed of her character (expressed in his letter to her biographer), and her sincere regard for him (which was touchingly exhibited in her request that he would preach the sermon at her funeral), remind one of his striking remark, found in an early chapter of this Memoir, that, in order to render the intercourse of social life perfect, each sex must have something in common with the other. To outward view, no two persons could be more unlike than the great, robust, practical man, capable of "toiling like an ox" (as his friend Dr. Pattison has sometimes said), braving almost unconsciously the buffetings of the world, and the woman, inexpressibly fragile, sensitive, imaginative, filled with genius. Yet, in reality, they had much of sympathy. Her frail nature was inspired by a heroism and a sense of duty as strong as his; and in him there were a vividness of sentiment, a tenderness of feeling, scarcely surpassed in woman. Since his death, a lady who knew him well, and to whose religious life his words had been blessed, said, —

"There was one remarkable trait in him that I never heard spoken of. I never knew any one who understood women as he did, or who could influence and control them like him. He sympathized perfectly with all their weaknesses and trials. It was easy for them to open their hearts. They had no difficulty in confiding absolutely in him; and this confidence was always safe. I have often told him things that I told to no other being, knowing that they would die with him and with me."

The assistance of Mrs. Judson aided greatly in removing the embarrassment growing out of the scantiness of material for the Memoir. But the needed time he could gain only by devoting his Saturdays and his scanty vacations to the labors of examination and composition.

Early in September, 1853, the Memoir was published. It is probable that rarely has a religious biography been issued which has secured the approving opinion of critics so diverse in character. The ordinary reader found himself carried on by the interest of the narrative; the pious experienced a quickening of devotion from its deep spirituality; and those who had no sympathy with evangelical views could not but admire the simplicity of the style and the lofty heroism of the life which was recorded.

Theodore Parker writes, —

"It contains less information about the Buddhists than one might look for, but the noble Memoir of Mr. and Mrs. Judson is beyond all praise. Yet they carried absurd dogmas to the Burmans, who had a plentiful supply of their own. Had the same pains been taken at home to remove poverty, ignorance of natural laws, to abolish slavery, drunkenness, and prostitution, and to teach piety and morality in general, what a good result would have come from it! Bigotry must be expected in a missionary.

He says to one he tried to convert, 'A true disciple inquires not whether a fact is agreeable to his own reason, but whether *it is in the Book.*' The 'Creed for his Burman Church' is a dreadful document. Judson's character is truly noble. If the only results of missions were to raise up such men, it were enough; for one such man is worth more to mankind than a temple like the Parthenon."

Of course it was not to be expected that the book would escape adverse criticism. By some persons it was objected that too much space was given to the journals and letters of Judson, and that the hand of the biographer was not sufficiently seen. By others it was urged that the views of Dr. Judson upon matters of missionary policy had taken a tinge in passing through the mind of the biographer, and that in some instances he presented his own opinions rather than those of Judson. This impression, perhaps, was not absolutely unnatural, for so coincident were the views of both, that the one might well seem to be presenting his own when he was most faithfully delineating the opinions of the other. It is within the recollection of the writer of these lines, that, while Dr. Judson was a guest at the house of Dr. Wayland, in November, 1845, the formation of the American and Foreign Bible Society having been alluded to, Dr. Judson said, "Dr. Wayland, that is the only subject on which I ever differed from you in opinion." Mrs. Judson, after reading the manuscript, writes, April 12, 1853, —

"Dear Dr. Wayland: . . . You have made me your debtor for evermore. It does not of course become me to speak, except to one point of your work, however much I may enjoy its eloquent simplicity and perspicuity; but from the mere beauty of truthfulness, it has given me such genuine satisfaction as I never expected to feel in the management of this one subject. I believe that language is incapable of a more faithful daguerreotype. I am more than pleased. I am deeply grateful to you, and to the great Power who, I believe, has guided your pen. I have no suggestions in regard to your conclusion, and but a very few trifling ones in matters merely verbal."

Mrs. Wade, who, with her husband, had been associated in missionary labors with Dr. Judson since 1823, writes to a friend, from Maulmain, —

"How do you like the Memoir of Dr. Judson? We think it remarkably truthful. It is thought by some that Dr. Wayland has made the book express his own views of missionary work, rather than those of Dr. Judson. But the truth is, two great minds, looking carefully into the work of evangelizing the heathen, would come to very nearly the same conclusions, though little acquainted with each other's views, and residing on different sides of the globe. We, who knew Dr. Judson so long and so intimately, well know that his views of missionary labors are remarkably well expressed."

We cannot avoid inserting, alike for its appositeness at this point, and for the great value of its general views, the following letter from, confessedly, the highest living authority on the whole subject of foreign missions (of whom Dr. Wayland once said, "Anderson is the wisest man in America").

"Missionary House,
Boston, November 7, 1853.

"My dear Brother: Your Memoir of Dr. Judson I have read with more interest and profit than any other missionary biography since Henry Martyn's. Indeed, it is unique in value for men of my cloth. The volumes are exceedingly suggestive, and all the more so and more valuable for your not concealing the eccentricities, peculiarities, defects, whatever they were, of the great subject. I have not had much time for general reading since our annual meeting, and I cannot read you as fast as I can most others, and I have marked certain points for recurring to them again. Our missions have been supplied with the Memoir, and I wish all our brethren may read it with the care and thought it deserves. Dr. Judson's firm rejection of all work preparatory to preaching the gospel, except learning the idiomatic language, is admirable, and so is your unequivocal sanction of his views. Blessed that heathen people whose first missionaries begin their work as he did. . . . Dr. Judson appears to me to have been made for just the position he occupied. He was great as a pioneer. He had, perhaps, all the strong qualities that were needed in his sphere. In some of these he resembled the apostle Paul. Whether those high qualities that fitted the apostle for the 'care of all the churches' could have been developed strongly in Dr. Judson, we may not know. He is an original. In some respects he is a fine model. But it is in connection with the development and illustration of some fundamental principles in missions, that he especially interests me. I think that he was right in the main, and that the Christian world will at length come substantially to his way of thinking, and that you have done a great service to the cause of missions by your impartial development of his proceedings and character. Few would, or perhaps safely could, have been as bold as you have been in some points of importance. You have purchased the 'good degree' which gives you boldness to speak with authority.

Yours truly,

R. Anderson."

It need scarcely be stated that Dr. Wayland presented the copyright of the Memoir to Mrs. Judson. He also paid all of the personal expenses incident upon his connection with the work, and paid for the greater number of the copies of the book which he presented to his personal friends. He counted it, he once said, a high honor to have the opportunity of doing this act, and he would not, in however slight a degree, mar the satisfaction it afforded him.

Fidelity to history perhaps demands mention of the fact that, under these circumstances, in October, 1853, a publisher in New York, acting (as he alleged) under the "written approval of some of the wisest and best of Christians," advertised as in press a "cheaper and more popular" Life of Dr. Judson; designed, of course, to take the place of Dr. Wayland's work. For a sufficiently full narrative of the events connected with this publication, and for Mrs. Judson's correspondence on the subject, we refer the reader to Dr. Kendrick's deeply interesting

Memoir of Mrs. Emily C. Judson. It is sufficient to add here, that although the volume alluded to never emerged from the obscurity into which it was born, yet the promise of its appearance had the effect to check considerably the circulation of Dr. Wayland's work, and of course to impoverish in the same degree the widow and orphans of the man who had poured his little patrimony, and all his scanty earnings, into the mission treasury, who "bore in his body the marks of the Lord Jesus," and who, after a life spent in the service of Christ, had left to his family only his name and his prayers. It would be false to deny that these events were a source of profound painfulness to Dr. Wayland. That such purposes should find a lodgment in the hearts of men called by the Christian name, distressed him more deeply than words could express.

The Memoir was republished and copyrighted in England simultaneously with its appearance in America. Although its circulation was naturally less considerable abroad, it took a place at once in the first class of biography. Several years afterwards, a member of Dr. Wayland's family, while visiting England, found himself the recipient of many acts of courtesy and kindness from those who knew him as a relative of the author of the Memoir of Judson.

To a personal friend, in reply to an invitation to lecture: —

"November 18, 1852.

"I am really very much obliged to the people of —— for thinking so well of me; but it grieves me to think how sadly they would be disappointed if they were to hear me. They would say with Solomon, 'As a fining pot to silver, so is a man to his praise.' But, in fact, I could not go without a dereliction of duty. I am engaged in Dr. Judson's Memoir, which takes all my time. I am doing it for the widow and the orphan, and they need it. And, besides, I do not think my talent, whatever it is, lies in this direction. People go to these occasions to be amused and astonished. I can neither amuse nor astonish. I have never been very successful in this line."

To Mrs. O'Brien:—

"June 2, 1853.

"The Memoir is done, so far as I am concerned. It has taken all my time since September; and this morning I feel relieved of a pressure that has not left me since I commenced it. I think it will be useful and interesting. Indeed, I feel a more than usual confidence in it. Mrs. Judson thinks it truthful. If it should prove otherwise than useful, I shall regret it, for it has taken a year of my time when years begin to grow few. Still, I have done it for the Master. My time is his; and I trust that I have given this to him, and have done it as well as I could. If he is willing, in his great compassion, to receive it, I shall have reason to rejoice, and I will rejoice. I presume it will be liked and disliked, as is the fate of most that I have written. I have made several efforts to see you, but 'have been let hitherto.' The fact has been, that when I got hold of this work, and the work got hold of me, I could not leave it without feeling that I was wasting time. This is the only way of doing anything, exposed as I am to interruptions."

To his son:—

"October 21, 1853.

"As to Guyonism and the 'threefold cord,' I have indicated my general views. I do not believe in any one's taking the modes of moral improvement indicated by others. This runs into the rites and austerities of the Romish church. I do believe in a man's taking the New Testament and applying it to his own practice in such way as he finds to edification. The rout made about Judson, on this account, was absurd and very weak. It indicated a sick and puling appetite in the moral character of the churches. Christians may be covetous, fashionable, attend balls and waltzes, and it is looked at kindly; but if a man takes unusual means to make himself better, the saints are in commotion."

In June, 1853, he was suddenly summoned to preach at the funeral of Rev. Dr. Sharp. It would be gratifying to quote from this tribute to his early friend and the friend of his father. But this pleasure will not lie within the reach of the present generation, as the manuscript of the sermon was deposited beneath the corner-stone of the First Baptist Church in Boston.

He had accepted an invitation to preach the annual sermon in July before the New York Baptist Union for Ministerial Education, and he prepared for this occasion the discourse afterwards known as "The Apostolic Ministry." This sermon received in its preparation more than usual labor, and was twice written. It was preached at Rochester, on the day preceding the Commencement of the university. The discourse was two hours in length, and was relieved by a brief intermission and the singing of a hymn. By its singular clearness of style, vigor of thought, and earnestness of feeling, it commanded the attention of the audience throughout. A Unitarian clergyman, who was present, said, "Some might call it a long yarn, but I call it rather a long cable." It was shortly afterwards issued in two editions of four thousand each. Subsequently, it was included in the "Sermons to the Churches." It has also been republished in England.

He remained for some days in Rochester, and attended the Commencement of the university, the anniverary of the Theological Seminary, and the inauguration of his former pupil, Rev. E. G. Robinson, D. D., as professor of theology. After spending a day or two in the wheat-growing country south of Rochester, he went to Niagara, and returned to his home by way of Saratoga, where he passed a few days. The journey afforded him a little much-needed rest, and was almost the only relaxation he had enjoyed for several years.

To a candidate for the ministry, then engaged in teaching: —

"September 26, 1852.

"I am glad that you are interested in your work. Do it well, and do it on system. But never let it be absent from your mind that you are preparing for the ministry. Make that always your end and aim. You should, therefore, always have a portion of your time set apart for this work. Have some ministerial study ever going forward, that you may be making progress in this direction. You had better preach, — once a fortnight, for instance, — to improve yourself and others. Do not, however, preach until you are prepared. Study your sermon and the delivery of it. Make plans; keep making them; write sermons as you can; make a most prayerful effort to deliver them well. Learn to do this, and leave the rest to God."

To the same: —

"I would commit some Scripture every day, and have always some book of devotional character in reading. I am greatly delighted with Neander on John. I have almost completed the second reading, and shall read it again. This is more than I can say of any book that I have read for years. I would advise you to read and study it carefully. It treats of the great and essential relations between man, the Messiah, and the Father. They are relations frequently taken for granted by the writers of the New Testament, and underlie and determine the most solemn and important ideas. Hence to have them clearly developed in our own thoughts, will give us great aid in understanding the Word. I cannot tell you how much I thank Mrs. Conant for translating it so well. It is worth a cart-load — I hope I may be pardoned — of German philology."

To a son, who had written to congratulate him on his fifty-seventh birthday: —

"March 13, 1853.

"I thank you for your expressions of gratitude and filial love. With countless imperfections I have endeavored to do my duty to my children, without any conscious desire of anything but their good. I have endeavored to encourage you in the pursuit of whatever was independent, virtuous, self-reliant, and disinterested, and have labored and prayed for your salvation and usefulness in the cause of Christ. I bless God that my labors, through his boundless grace accompanying them, have not been wholly in vain. Every birthday reminds me of the lessening portion of life, of which a year is annually a larger part. I feel more and more that what I do I must do quickly; and yet my opportunities for doing good are but imperfect. But above all things I would always bear in mind how much inward work there is to be done, how much sin to subdue, how much heavenly affection to acquire, before I can be meet for that world towards which I am so rapidly tending. Pray for me, that I may be permitted to finish my course with joy."

An article had gone the rounds of the papers stating that Dr. Wayland was engaged in investigating the phenomena of the so-called spiritual rappings, and anticipated very important results from these developments. A friend wrote to him, suggesting the propriety of denying, through the public journals, this absurd statement. The circumstance is utterly without interest, except as his reply illustrates his manner of dealing with similar unfounded statements and personal attacks.

"'Fudge!' as Mr. Burchell said. I had nothing to do with their putting the article in the paper, and am in no way responsible for it. I presume it was put in to have me answer it, and make capital out of it. The best way is to let it alone, and to let it die out of itself. I have no opinion on the subject, except that I believe the fact of the motion; what makes it, I have as yet no means of knowing."

To a former pupil, an instructor who had experienced some annoyance and ingratitude from his scholars: —

"I regret that you are thus troubled; but things of this kind are good for us, if they work the fruits of righteousness. The case before you is painful, but not remarkably so. One of the commonest forms of trial to which we are subjected is the ingratitude and unkindness of those whom we disinterestedly intend to benefit. This is a source of pain which has followed me all my life. But who ever suffered so much from this source as the Captain of our salvation? It was his meat and drink daily. In our own case, the reason of it is evident. In attempting to do good, we are looking at the good to man, and are pleased with it, and so forget that we are the servants of God, and must do it for him. He removes the supports on which we were unconsciously relying, to teach us that we must look for our reward to him alone.

"But things being as they are, what is to be done? I reply, Gain piety and wisdom. In the first place, thank God for this very trouble. He saw that you needed it, and therefore sent it. Thank him for his faithfulness. But, then, how to use it? Gain victory over it. Leave no means untried to conquer every feeling of resentment towards everybody. Pray for them, love them, and look upon the thing without a single natural emotion; let all your feelings be Christ-like.

"When you have attained this elevation, you can look down upon the whole matter, and it will shrink in dimensions, so that 'the crows will look scarce so gross as beetles.' You will then be able to make up your mind on every point, as it comes up, with perfect equanimity and correct judgment. When we get into this atmosphere, everything stands in its true light, and we are not likely to err in judgment. Such are the principles I should suggest. The application of them to the particular case I cannot well make. If your manner needs correction, correct it. The order proper for a recitation I would maintain, or I would have no recitation."

To a son, then at Rochester: —

"June 22, 1853.

"I fear that you are calculating too much on our visit, and I feel troubled about it. When we set our hearts on anything, we are likely to be disappointed. Consider the uncertainty of life and health. I fear that your friends have exaggerated expectations of me. I am not eloquent, and it is very likely that my ideas will by no means be well received. I must tell them what I think, and that is not likely to be always acceptable. Bear these things in mind. Leave it all with God, and ask him to bless my coming, without allowing yourself to have any high-raised expectations about it. I know it results from your affection; but this may lead us astray."

To a candidate for the ministry: —

"October 2, 1853.

"In your last letter you speak of meditation on the Scriptures as the best means of understanding the Word. I hope you will keep this in mind. In every science there are central points, from which you can with ease behold the whole. In morals, moreover, it is necessary, in order to understand a doctrine or a law, that you be in the proper moral condition. Now, this is the case in theology especially. You do not get at the meaning of the Word by learning what men have dogmatically written about it. I would give more for a book of earnest devotion than a dogmatic treatise, in order to the understanding of the Scriptures. But this all leads to one point. The mystery of the cross is evidently the grand moral centre from which every other doctrine takes its departure. If a man were fully imbued with this, if he could look upon it as angels look, every doctrine would open to him as clearly as daylight. This, however, requires moral preparation—a heart in harmony with the cross. Let it then be your great effort to read the Bible with this view; to pray earnestly to understand this; and this key will unlock everything. Neander on John illustrates this. It is all about the work of Christ, and his relations to the Father; and it is remarkable to see what light it throws on everything else. Have this always in mind, and from time to time write down your thoughts; they will be the seeds of sermons."

To the same:—

"November 24, 1853.

"The sermon [Apostolic Ministry] will, I hope, be received as a true exposition of Baptist and New Testament sentiments. But only the power of the Holy Ghost can make it effectual in the hearts of men. I grieve to see the decline of our churches and numbers from the plan of Jesus Christ; but all is in the hands of God. Cultivate expository preaching. Nothing enriches the mind of the hearer and preacher like it. We thus come nearer to the thoughts of God."

To the same:—

"January 28, 1854.

"As to making sermons, the rule is, that any man of ordinary sense and advantages can do what other men do.

When you get into the work, and your mind is turned to it, it will aid you greatly. You will have at once truths which you see need to be enforced; and the necessity of doing a thing adds greatly to our power of doing it. I rejoice to hear of the appearance of good around you. Let me know more about it. Give yourself wholly to the work. You will learn more of the dealings of the Holy Spirit with man in this way than in any other. Observe the truths which affect men, the way in which they must be presented in order to affect them, and the various excuses and subterfuges of the human heart. A minister learns more from a real revival of religion, with prayer and reading of the Scriptures, than in any other way. But he must be thoroughly in it, and labor, not with the left hand, but *manibus*, *pedibus*, *unguibus et rostro.* As to your enterprise in carrying the gospel to a neglected part of the city, I hope you will urge it on to the end. If my sermon does no other good than to lead to this result, it will abundantly repay me for all the trouble of preparing it. You say that you feel inwardly moved to this. Always attend to these inward monitions. They are apt to proceed from on high, if they come to us when we are calm and unheated, and especially when they are at variance with our love of ease and self-indulgence. You will rarely find them deceive you, if duly mixed with prayer, and humility, and self-distrust, and faith in the power of the Holy Ghost. Try to follow the thing out as nearly as possible in the manner of the Acts of the Apostles."

To a candidate for the ministry: —

"I have let your questions as to study 'simmer' (as Sir Walter has it) in my mind for a day or two. I am of opinion that I would read through the New Testament carefully, at least as far as the Revelation. You get thus the bearing and spirit of the whole, and form an opinion on each book. After that you may read theologians. But after you have read the New Testament through, you will be the better able to compare their proof-texts, and to judge for yourself. I am still of opinion that the New Testament, as it has been given to us, is the best book; and I would get hold of this first, before I went into the results of men's doctrines and theories in regard to it. This will strengthen your confidence in your own views of the truth as it was declared by Christ and his apostles. The New Testament is unlike any other book; the study of it, faithfully and humbly carried out, cultivates originality. The study of other books leads to authority. The great centre is Christ crucified. From this every other doctrine takes its bearing. If we have true views of this, everything else will take its place, and assume its true proportion."

To the same:—

"... You can do nothing better than commence with Christ and his apostles. Why should you drink the truth diluted and adulterated by man, when you can go to the fountain?

"The preaching is weak, because at present men preach theology instead of the Scriptures. Nothing gives vigor to the mind, like deep contemplation of pure truth. Peter was an illiterate man, Paul a learned man, and yet 1st Peter will compare with any of Paul's Epistles for power of thought and rich, varied, and compressed exhibitions of truth. Keep to your idea of blending general culture with professional study, to enlarge and diversify your mental energies."

To his sister:—

"February 16, 1854.

"I regret I was not more conversable, as it is called, and more interesting when I saw you. But it is my misfortune. There is upon me a sort of habitual sadness, a want of interest, a kind of despair of ever effecting anything, and a feeling of inability to labor, which I think is unusual to me, at least unusual as a habit. I do not know whence it arises. My general health is good. I am inclined to attribute it to overwork, for two or three years, some time since. I see nobody except on business. I have no taste for society, as it is where I must see it, if I see it at all. I have no intimate companions. I incline to be alone, and when I am in company, am silent for the simple reason that I have nothing to say. I am never silent by design, but always by necessity. You must, therefore, excuse me for being so uninteresting, for I am not half so uninteresting to others as I am to myself. This looks like a Jeremiad; it is not. When I can get out more in the spring it will, I presume, pass off. The cares of college press me, and I have long wished to get rid of them. I am waiting for an opening of Providence."

To a former pupil, a lawyer: —

"You must, I think, be convinced of the effect which business is producing on your mind. You know, as well as I can tell you, that we are created with a moral as well as an intellectual nature, and that the former is by far the more important. You know also that every part of our nature develops by cultivation and exercise, and withers and grows inactive by neglect. Now, your present business occupies almost entirely the intellectual part of your nature. You are engaged in devising what, for yourself or others, is best for this world, and specially for one of the least important matters of this world — earthly possessions. There is nothing about it that lays hold of the moral elements of character. These are cultivated by prayer, adoration, repentance, striving after holiness, self-denial for the good of others, and devoting ourselves to the promotion of some good cause, some cause by which men will be made better for time and for eternity. You see how your present avocations tend (unless counteracted) to influence the development of character, and you see how the tendency must grow stronger by every day's exercise, until eternity, and all that relates to the moral character of man, will suffer a disastrous eclipse. You have referred this subject, time after time, to a later period. What later period can you conceive of, which will not be more unfavorable than the present?"

CHAPTER V.

THE NEBRASKA BILL. — THE BURNS CASE. — ADDRESS AT UNION COLLEGE. — INTELLECTUAL PHILOSOPHY. — CORRESPONDENCE. — NEED OF REST. — THE PRESIDENT'S RESIGNATION. — THE LAST COMMENCEMENT.

DURING the winter and spring of 1854, Dr. Wayland, was, in common with all good men, profoundly moved by the proposed passage of the Nebraska Bill. To his son he wrote, —

"I am glad to hear of your interest in the Nebraska question. It is the most important that has occurred in my time. We need to have the religious feeling aroused on the subject. It is now intolerably torpid. Keep within a sound discretion, and go forward in the business."

At the meeting of the citizens of Providence, March 7, 1854, he was present and spoke. Waiving all incidental and side issues, he opposed the bill on the broad ground that it was designed to establish slavery throughout all the territories concerned. He said, —

"I protest against this bill, in the first place, because it proposes to violate the great elementary law, on which not only government, but society itself, is founded — the principle that every man has a right to himself. Second, as an American citizen, I protest against this bill. Third, as a citizen of a free state, I protest against this bill. Fourth, I protest against it as a Christian."

His speech was published in full in nearly all the leading papers of the Northern States, both secular and religious, and was regarded as unanswerable. The National

Era declared that no such specimen of compact logic had been addressed to the American people since the death of Daniel Webster; and the south attested the power of his words by angry denunciation, and by the exclusion of his books from such of the southern institutions as had hitherto used them. He had never given up the hope that the iniquitous measure referred to would be disavowed and discountenanced by the good men and Christians of the Southern States, many of whom had by letter, and in conversation, expressed to him their sense of the evil of slavery, and their desire for its removal. It was with pain that he was forced reluctantly to abandon this hope. With great justice, an eminent Baptist minister in one of the border states, observed that the southern people would hear Dr. Wayland after they had ceased to hear any other northern man.

To his son, on the occasion of the Burns case in Boston: —

"June 2, 1854.

"Keep down your passions; pray for the country; try to look as patiently as possible upon wrong-doers. In the mean time, proclaim the principles of right, their obligation and supremacy, and nerve men to be willing to suffer loss in consequence of them. What is wanted is to extend and deepen the feeling of resistance to oppression, and of determination at all hazards to be free from participation in it. When this is universal, united, and moral, nothing can withstand it, and the agents to carry it on will soon appear. Do not allow yourself in strong excitement, but rather lift up the case with both hands, and all your heart, to the Judge of all the earth; plead his promises and his perfections, and wait for the indications of his providence. This seems present duty. Write, publish, inform the people, direct the present feeling in proper channels. This is all I see at present."

To a former pupil, a lawyer: —

"July 29, 1854.

"The times look grave. I hope that the spirit of the north is at last aroused. It seems to me that the thing to be done is not to be committed to any rash or sudden measure, but to deepen, extend, and unite the anti-slavery feeling. I never before have been deeply moved by any political question. May God direct it all to the advancement of truth and righteousness. Do not be anxious to take extreme, but rather solid ground, and thus carry all sober men with you.

". . . I want the spirit of freedom and sense of right extended in every direction, not by violence that cannot be defended, but by showing the right, and keeping people out of the wrong. I never knew anything so intensely and cumulatively abominable. It is a matter of deep and anxious thought. You should study it carefully, and make up your mind on all the points, so that, if a time comes for action, you may be prepared with good reasons for yourself and others."

To the same: —

"Keep out of passionate excitement. Study the constitutional principles, and the slave laws, and think out for yourself every case liable to occur, with all its terminations. You may be called on in such a case. If so, it will be of vast importance to be fully prepared in advance. You may be invited to address an assembly. Any one can advise them to resist, but a jurist should be able to show them their constitutional position in all its bearings, and the true ground for their conduct. From all I can learn of the whole country, the feeling is such as I never knew before. What we want is, to deepen it, place it on fixed principles, extend it, and give unity to it. If this is done at the north, we shall see some change. The southern men are doing all we could desire in ripening this state of public opinion. May God prosper the cause of justice and humanity."

In reply to an inquiry about the Kansas and Nebraska emigration scheme: —

"I do not see clearly enough through the business to form any opinion. I do not think I have time at present to think it through, and therefore should not dare to give an opinion that would influence others to take so important a step. It is very painful to advise to a step which turns out badly."

In reply to an invitation to preach at a distance from home: —

"I cannot make any promise. I am pressed very closely, and have (besides work at the Intellectual Philosophy, which must be done in time) to deliver an address at Union College, and one at the Institute of Instruction, which meets here in August. I am now doing rather beyond my strength, and cannot afford to lose a day or an hour."

To a minister: —

"What you say of free institutions is true and important; but then I am opposed to uniting this, or anything else, with the preaching of the gospel. These other and more externally impressive ideas undermine and subvert the preacher as such. The Christian view is to look up to God, and to arouse the Christian feeling in men. To abolish slavery is a good thing, but it is not religion. Let the dead bury their dead, but go thou and preach the kingdom of God. Read the corresponding passages, and you observe that Christ places preaching the gospel above every other thing. I have no faith in any other means for curing the evils of this present. Northern men, if it were profitable, would themselves hold slaves in the present state of religion amongst us. What is needed is a general revival of religion in this country. Nothing else will save us. Since the bill has passed, I can only look to God to overrule it for the cause of righteousness. It will be a new event in the government of the universe, if such villany does not plague the inventors. God is infinitely wise and long-minded."

In reply to a letter from his son on his fifty-eighth birthday: —

"My days are fast gliding away. I feel the change produced by advancing years. My spirits are not so good as they once were. I am less able to meet difficulties. I cannot labor as much as formerly, and for the winter have barely been able to drag through my work. Age will claim its due. I am admonished that the night cometh."

Upon the 25th of July, 1854, he delivered an address

at Union College, upon the fiftieth anniversary of the presidency of Dr. Nott. Of the subject and spirit of the address we have already spoken. The scene was affecting when he reached the closing passage, and the aged instructor, weighed down with fourscore and two years, arose, surrounded by his graduates, many of them far advanced in years, and holding high civil stations, while one who had been his pupil forty-one years before, now on the verge of threescore, thus addressed him: —

"Venerable man! We rejoice to see that thine eye is not dim, though thy natural force is somewhat abated. We thank you for your care over our youth; we thank you for those counsels which have so often guided our manhood; we thank you for that example which has ever so clearly pointed out to us the path of earnest duty and self-forgetful charity. Long may you yet live to witness the happiness which you have created, and to cherish the genius which your inspirations first awakened to conscious existence. And when the Savior, in whose footsteps you have trodden, shall call thee home to receive thy reward, may death lay his hand gently on that venerated form, and gently quiet the pulsations of that noble heart. May thy fainting head recline upon the bosom of the Redeemer whom thou hast loved; may thine eye open upon visions of glory which man may not utter; and so may an entrance be abundantly administered to thee into the joy of thy Lord. Heaven will account itself richer, as it opens its pearly gates to welcome thy approach; but where shall those who survive find anything left on earth that resembles thee?"

Returning home, he prepared the introductory lecture for the twenty-fifth annual meeting of the American Institute of Instruction, which assembled in Providence August 8th. In this address he reviewed the changes which had taken place in popular education in America since he last addressed the same body on the 19th of August, 1830. The progress already made seemed to suggest the possibility of yet further advances; and he concluded with urging the consideration that we should aim to render our system of education in the highest degree useful, by basing it upon a study of the powers of the human mind, and of the order in which these powers are matured. In the portions of the discourse which looked to the future, as in all his later utterances, it was evident that in his view the method of education was an open question, and that to use past experiences and successes, not as a final resting-place, but as a means to new discoveries and nobler conquests in the future, is one of the first duties of the American teacher.

To Rev. Dr. Cutting, in reply to a request that Dr. Wayland would write out, in detail, his views of a professional education for the ministry: —

"September 2, 1854.

"I really am unable to do anything in the premises at present. Some time I may make a book about it. I am now carrying through the press an Intellectual Philosophy. I have a new Moral Philosophy, in my head in part, and in part on paper, and a work on Evidences, two thirds done. This is my line of present duty. The shadows in my path begin to lengthen. The sun has long since passed the meridian, and inclines to the west. I work as hard as I can. I think I am able to do these things now; in a few years, even if I live, it may be impossible. It has required some self-denial, and very steady work, to do my duty in college and to discharge other important duties. I have been constantly at my work all vacation, having had only one holiday. . . ."

During the autumn of the same year, he published The Elements of Intellectual Philosophy. This work grew out of the lectures which he had for many years delivered to his classes in the university. Its character and purposes cannot be better explained than in a few words from the preface.

"I have not entered upon the discussion of many of the topics which have called into exercise the acumen of the ablest metaphysicians. Intended to serve the purposes of a text-book, it was necessary that the volume should be compressed within a compass adapted to the time usually allotted to the study of this science in the colleges of our country. I have, therefore, attempted to present and illustrate the important truths in intellectual philosophy, rather than the inferences which may be drawn from them, or the doctrines which they may presuppose. These may be pursued at any length, at the option of the teacher. If I have not entered upon these discussions, I hope that I have prepared the way for their more ample and truthful development."

While the volume has not attained the preëminence and circulation reached by the kindred treatise upon moral science, yet it may be doubted whether any work is to be found, better fitted by the absolute clearness of its statements, and by the training imparted to the mind of the reader, to prepare a pupil for an extended course of metaphysical study. Without deeming it within the demands of a biography like the present, to consider his character as a metaphysician, or the relation that he holds to the leaders in philosophy, we beg leave to direct the attention of the reader to a most interesting and discriminating discussion of these points, found in the North American Review for July, 1855.

On the 1st of November he preached, at the ordination of his son in Worcester, the discourse upon "The Church a Society for the Conversion of the World," which afterwards appeared among the "Sermons to the Churches." And, during the period embraced in this and the previous chapter, he prepared the greater part of the sermons in that volume, as well as a large number of others, intended for the regular service in the chapel, or for special occasions.

To a minister recently settled: —

"October 8, 1854.

"I am greatly pleased at the indications mentioned in your letter. Have the prayer meeting, and feel your way for another. The singing is greatly important. We generally have two or three singers to do this portion of the worship of God. It is totally destitute both of æsthetic and of devotional effect — a mere impertinence. Try for something else. Get the people to see that it must be accomplished, and then it will be. The effect of such music, with good tunes, in preparing the people to hear, is very great. I have seen a congregation solemnized by singing, so that preaching was like sowing on well prepared soil.

"I am working hard at my little book (Intellectual Philosophy), and then I trust that I shall write nothing more that does not bear directly on the kingdom of Christ."

To the same: —

"November 7, 1854.

"As to the day of fasting, I would take the greatest pains to have it a real thing, and to escape formality. The first meeting is better spent in trying to awaken confession and penitence; the second, in the exercise of faith and trust, and reliance on Christ. I would have an object, and strive to carry it out, not leaving it to mere random conversation and general prayers."

To the same, writing on the day devoted to fasting and prayer: —

"You and your people have been much on my mind to-day, and will be till I sleep. I pray that you and they may receive a Pentecostal baptism, and that from to-day a new era may commence, which may from you overspread our churches."

To the same: —

"I have just read Jay's Life. There is a good deal in it that is senile, but there is valuable instruction. His views were very much like mine. He determined to be a *preacher*. Commencing at sixteen, he maintained a high reputation until eighty-four. He was not only a highly esteemed, but a most useful preacher. It would be well for you to determine whether you mean to be a preacher or a reader of theology. The aims are different, and to be sought by different ways. There is nothing that I so much regret as that I did not make myself a preacher. I have too late come to the impression that I might possibly have suceeeded, if I had labored for it."

To a young minister: —

"February 16, 1855.

"It seems that you are about building. This is a great temptation. Men under such circumstances are strongly urged to preach so as to build up a society, and not to convert men. Be careful of this, and let it be your aim not to get men to take pews, but to enter the kingdom. If they do the last, they will certainly do the first. Do not build an expensive church. It will burden your friends, and render the establishment costly, and thus drive off the poor, to whom the gospel is to be preached. Have it neat, commodious, well ventilated, and plain. This best becomes Christians."

To his sister: —

"I am glad you like my book [the Intellectual Philosophy]. It has cost me many hours and years of thought, in one way and another. I have tried to make it plain. Whether I have succeeded or not, time must determine. At all events, it has all gone through my own mind, and is not made by the scissors. This is more than can be said of many books that have been published on that subject."

To the same: —

"You are very kind in inviting us to come to you. The fact is, I am just preparing to build a house, and until this is under way I cannot say anything, or I should have written to you before. I will come if I can, and shall make every effort to do so.

"I rejoice to hear you are all well and happy. It does not fall to my lot to enjoy much in this way. I wish it did. I am in the perpetual treadmill."

To a former pupil, a member of one of the earliest classes which President Wayland instructed in Brown University, recently elected to the United States Senate, who had first used his franking privilege to write, expressing his sense of obligation to his former instructor: —

"March 6, 1855.

"Your very kind letter arrived this evening; and though it is late, and I have some work to do, I should not sleep soundly if I allowed it to be for a moment unanswered.

"As I read it, my eyes became moist, and my tongue grew thick, and I could easily have wept, though not much given to tears. Amid my many failures, and what I cannot but consider great want of success, it is more cheering than you can imagine, to know that my labors have not been in vain, or at least that one of my pupils, who has arrived at deserved distinction, is kind enough to take this view of them. I well remember the old chapel, and can see you rising to recite there, as though it were yesterday. If I then did you any good, I rejoice at it, for thus I did good to virtue and humanity.

"I have followed you year by year, ever since you left us. Few have marked every step of your upward progress with more sincere pleasure — I had almost said pride — than myself. More than all, I have been delighted to learn that as your influence increased, it was everywhere exerted in favor of virtue and religion. I always knew that when any question arose involving the interests of piety or humanity, you would be found on the side of Christ and his cause.

"And now a wider field opens before you. When I look at the position of this country, and the talent committed to it by God, and the power of the Senate over the destinies of humanity, I can hardly conceive of a more responsible position. Every important act of that chamber tells upon the civilized world — it may be for generations to come. My dear ——, may God baptize you with a spirit of power, and wisdom, and singleness of mind, and eloquence, and fortitude, and humility, and gentleness, and unfailing faith, and habitual prayer."

To a minister: —

"I am glad to hear of any seriousness among your people. Let me advise you to give yourself wholly to the work. Preach on the sinfulness, the helplessness, the accountability of man, his totally lost state, and the way of salvation by Christ. Do not, however, discourse upon these topics, as if you were preaching to the inhabitants of another planet, about what was going on here; but bring the truths down to the consciences and hearts of your people. Urge the evidences of piety, and arouse those that are asleep. Always, when you write, leave some three or four pages for the most pungent, personal, affectionate address and persuasion you can offer. Take high ground, as a messenger from God to sinners under his displeasure. This discoursing about things in general is ruining our churches and destroying the power of religion. Always remember that you make a blank failure, if your people do not go away obliged to make a personal application of all you say."

To a minister: —

"You wish that the work of God could be carried on without revivals. I wish so too. I wish that there were no special revivals; that there was no need of them, because the churches were always revived, that is, always in earnest. But if this is not the case, if they slumber for years, what but occasional revivals can prevent their sleep from becoming the sleep of death? I think you should labor not for a revival of six weeks, but for one of six years. Revivals show what God is willing to do always, if we are ready to receive his blessing."

To the same: —

"... We want to preach the truth, but we want to preach it so as to raise us in the estimation of men, attract the intelligent and wealthy, and make the gospel of the Son of God *respectable*. It is difficult to emerge from these influences, and to rely on the naked word, wielded by the right arm of the Spirit of God. Yet here is our strength. I would labor and pray to get all these things under my feet. I do not mean that a man is to speak carelessly, or foolishly, or awkwardly. These are not the teachings of the Spirit of God. It takes more pains and effort to get one's heart imbued with the Spirit than to write an intellectual sermon, as it is called. It is much more difficult to renounce self than to do the hardest work to please and glorify it.

"Get out of yourself so far as you can, and lie low at the feet of the Savior, perfectly willing to be everything, anything, if he will only give you souls for your hire. Humble yourself under the hand of God, and he will build you up. When *he* builds you up, you will probably stand."

To the same: —

"If you sincerely desire the salvation of the souls of

your people, and are laboring for this, you have all the promises of God to rely on. Jesus says, 'Lo, I am with you always, even unto the end.' God never causes such labor to be thrown away. You may plead all his promises, and freely claim all that he has said. But we must allow him to choose his own time and manner; and he is pleased when we, with child-like confidence, rely on his veracity; and if the vision tarry, wait for it. The promise of God cannot fail. Go on, then, cheerfully, not anxiously, knowing that it is yours to blow the trumpet, but that it belongs to Omnipotence to overthrow the wall. You may compass the city six times, and the walls remain solid as the hills; but on the seventh time they will fall down flat. God means to have all the glory himself, and he ought to have it; and surely we should rejoice in his carrying on his work in such a way that he shall secure it. Be, then, earnest, steadfast, enduring; but do all in faith, and trust in God."

In 1854 an eminent and learned college president in New England, in writing to acknowledge the receipt of the Intellectual Philosophy, had expressed what was the unavoidable sentiment of every one who remarked the results of Dr. Wayland's life.

"I wonder, my dear sir, how you find time to accomplish so much. It is but a few months since I read (and with great pleasure) your life of Dr. Judson; and now you have published another volume, which must be the embodiment of no small amount of laborious thought. I have considered myself a hard-working man. But I find it almost impossible to finish anything; and the *disjecta membra* of my toils as a scholar lie around me like the materials of a building which the carpenter can find no time to put together."

Alas! the explanation became in time painfully obvious. Like a steamer whose fuel is exhausted, he was supplying the motive power from the fabric of his own being. There has already been apparent, in many of his letters, a growing sense of weariness, which was indeed dispelled whenever a new call of duty was heard, yet which settled again upon him whenever the temporary demand had been answered. Ever accustomed to watch closely the phenomena of his own mind, he detected the imperious claim which nature, in various ways, was making for repose. His physician unhesitatingly told him that he must not longer remain pressed with the duties of his present office. His own convictions accorded with this opinion.

"I was convinced that I could not have discharged my duties for another year. . . . I was treated with the greatest kindness by the corporation and by the Faculty. They desired me to continue with less labor. But I thought that no arrangement of this kind would be for the good of the university. So long as I was responsible, I could not help doing all that responsibility involved. If I did not act thus, the institution would suffer."

At a special meeting of the corporation, held August 21, 1855, President Wayland read the following letter: —

"BROWN UNIVERSITY, August 20, 1855.

"TO THE CORPORATION OF BROWN UNIVERSITY.

"Gentlemen: After more than twenty-eight years' service, the conviction is pressed upon me that relaxation and change of labor have become to me a matter of indispensable necessity. These, I am persuaded, cannot be secured while I hold the office with which you have so long honored me. I therefore believe it to be my duty to resign the offices of president of Brown University and professor of moral and intellectual philosophy. If it be agreeable to you, I desire that this resignation may take place at the close of the present collegiate year.

"In sundering the ties which have so long bound us officially together, I shall not attempt to express the sentiment of gratitude and respect which I entertained towards the gentlemen of the corporation of Brown University. For more than a quarter of a century we have labored together in promoting the cause of good learning, and specially in advancing the interests of this institution. Those who, like myself, were young men when I entered upon office, are with me beginning to feel the approaches of age. Yet during this long period, no spirit of dissension has either divided our councils or enfeebled our exertions. We have beheld this university, year after year, advancing in reputation and usefulness, and diffusing more and more widely the blessings of education. Let us thank God for giving us this opportunity of conferring benefits on mankind, and for crowning our labors with so large a measure of success.

"Permit me, gentlemen, to tender to each one of you the assurances of my grateful regard, and believe me to be,

With the highest respect,

Your obedient servant,

F. WAYLAND."

He writes to Rev. Dr. Bartol:—

"... I am glad to see that you look upon my resignation as I have done, and, what is somewhat remarkable, for precisely the same reasons. Had you and I conversed together fully, and had you given my reasons in brief to another, you would not have altered a word from what you have written. The work was wearing upon me, and would in a few years have worn me out. It has become burdensome. It is almost entirely secular. A president is held responsible for what he cannot do, and this is sadly grinding to a man's conscience. I am happy to see that, now the thing is done, almost every one says that I have acted wisely. This, as you suggest, is a matter of substantial comfort, and adds to the great pleasure which I feel every moment when I reflect upon the fact that my work as president of a college has ceased—a comfort and peace which I have not felt for many years. I trust, therefore, that I have not acted unwisely. May God grant his blessing upon my doings, and render the remainder of my life useful to my fellow-men, and acceptable to him."

The corporation, convinced that his decision was fixed, accepted the resignation, and adopted a series of appropriate resolutions.

We quote from the Independent the following graphic delineation of the events of Commencement Day, 1855. The account appeared under the head of "Editorial Correspondence," and was, as we suppose, from the graceful pen of Rev. J. P. Thompson, D. D., who, on the evening preceding, had addressed the Missionary Society of the University.

"PROVIDENCE, September 5, 1855.

"... To-day there is but *one* Providence, and that is the city on the hill, the light of whose university cannot be hid; and there is but one name spoken in Providence, and that is the name of the retiring president, which has given to college and to city a world-wide fame. The only use of railroads just now is to bring hither from every quarter the sons of Brown and members of the great fraternity of letters, to join in a parting testimonial to Francis Wayland. ...

"This day (Wednesday) is appropriated to the proper Commencement exercises. After the degrees were conferred, the chancellor of the university, Dr. Tobey, presented to Dr. Wayland the resolutions which had been adopted by the Board of Fellows and Trustees in accepting his resignation. Dr. Tobey is a member of the Society of Friends, and, though not himself a graduate of any college, has manifested a lively interest in the cause of education. He is a man of generous culture and of handsome address. He adheres to the strictness of Quaker phraseology, and expresses himself with that peculiar neatness and taste which characterize the Friends, especially in matters of compliment. In presenting the action of the trustees, he said, 'President Wayland, I herewith present thee a certified copy of the resolutions now read in thy hearing. Wilt thou be pleased also to accept from me personally the assurance of my high regard for thee as a citizen and an instructor of youth, with the desire that Heaven may smile with prosperity upon the evening of thy days?'

"The valuable document presented by Dr. Tobey, enumerating the various services of Dr. Wayland to the college, was drawn up with excellent judgment and taste, and was the more interesting from the quaintness of its style. The Quaker chancellor did not scruple to give the retiring president all his titles of vain and worldly pomp — D. D., LL. D., &c., while yet he accosted him with the familiar *thou*.

"Dr. Wayland had the good taste not to attempt a speech. With evident emotion he said, —

"'Mr. Chancellor, I beg you to accept, for yourself and for the gentlemen with whom you are associated, my grateful acknowledgments for the kindness with which you have been pleased to estimate my imperfect services.

"'If the corporation of Brown University believe that I have faithfully endeavored to do my duty, I desire no higher earthly reward.'

"The whole scene — the 'unbaptized Quaker,' the representative of the extremest spiritualism, in his prim habit and with his precise and well-ordered phrase, contrasted with the sturdy Baptist, the representative of the intensest form of an outward ordinance, yet overflowing with spiritual emotion; these two sects, whose forerunners were outlawed from the old Puritan colony of Massachusetts, now met in that shelter which Roger Williams founded for 'persons distressed for conscience,' and fraternizing in behalf of a sound and liberal Christian education — this was a scene which some painter's pencil or some poet's pen should have caught upon the instant to transmit to other generations. Will not Longfellow raise for us the spirit of Roger Williams to look upon the Providence of today?

"After these exercises came that indispensable conclusion of a Commencement, the public dinner. Tables were spread under a large tent in the college grounds, and several hundred sat down to the feast. At the close of the dinner, Judge Thomas, of Worcester, presented a series of resolutions adopted by the Alumni, highly complimentary to President Wayland. These he introduced by a happy and feeling speech.* . . .

"Dr. Wayland rose to reply, but said, 'his heart was liquid, and he could pour it out like water.' As, however, everybody demanded something from his lips, he proceeded to give the secret of that success which all agreed had been attained by Brown University in the last thirty years. I can only give an outline of the great thoughts and principles which Dr. Wayland uttered with a simplicity and candor which showed *the* secret of his power. I beg every one, — especially every young man, —

* The greater part of Judge Thomas' remarks has been quoted in a previous chapter.

whose eye may run over this letter, to ponder these weighty words of one of the wisest of teachers.

"Dr. Wayland referred to the fact, that when he entered on the presidency there were but three professors and two college buildings; the library was small and seldom used, and there was no apparatus. There were no recitation-rooms, but recitations were held in the rooms of students, week by week, in rotation. Now, in its grounds and buildings, its library and lecture-rooms, its apparatus and professorships, Brown University is as well furnished as any college in New England. The secret of this success, so far as he was concerned, was as follows: —

"1. *A resolute and honest consecration to the work to be done.* He had cut loose from whatever interfered with that work. He kept himself from amusement, — for which he had no taste, — and even from favorite studies, and gave himself to the work of building up the university.

"2. *A dogged instinct to do his duty.* He had a fixed determination to go through with what he had begun, and to take up every duty as it came. No doubt, in the matter of discipline, some had thought him a 'regular old despot.' But God only knew the *agony* he had endured when called to inflict pain on any student or his friends. The pain *they* had suffered was nothing when compared with *his*. He had tried to avoid discipline, but could not. And now, as the rejected suitor appealed from Philip drunk to Philip sober, so he appealed from impetuous and excited young men to the men he saw before him, matured and subdued by experience. *They* must decide on his acts as an instructor; and there was no pupil of his whom he would not be glad to meet anywhere, for he knew that towards all he had done his simple duty.

"'3. *Never to act for to-morrow, or next month, instead of to-day.* It has been my rule to do to-day what I have to do, as well as I know how. The way to prepare for to-morrow is, to do with a whole heart the duty of to-day. Sometimes young men take up teaching as a temporary employment, while preparing for a profession; but their *heart* is not in it, and consequently they break down as teachers, and carry with them into their profession the reputation of men who have already failed. Do your present duty, and never be mousing around for something else.

"'4. *Adherence to general principles.* Have confidence in general principles. Our wisest men — for I take it for granted that our politicians are our wisest men — often mistake from want of confidence in principles. Things follow their tendencies. Take a law of right and carry it through, and accept the good and bad together. You can't have the good of a principle without the evil. But follow the principle. It will bring you into narrow places, and up steep defiles; but keep on, and you will see a glory beyond, that will repay the labor and toil of the ascent. For myself, I am built railroad fashion. I can go forwards, and, if necessary, I can back; but *I can't go sideways.*

"'5. *Whatever of knowledge I have of men or mind, I have gained from the New Testament of the Lord Jesus Christ.* Study the Bible if you would be wise. Count it your highest honor to be useful to your fellow-men.'

"These remarks were received by all with deep emotion."

On Friday afternoon, when the bell rang for the opening exercises of the new term, Dr. Wayland was walking through George Street, not far from the residence of the late Professor Goddard. He stopped and listened. To one of his former pupils, who was just passing, he said, —

"No one can conceive the unspeakable relief and freedom which I feel at this moment to hear that bell ring, and to know, for the first time in nearly twenty-nine years, that it calls me to no duty."

CHAPTER VI.

HIS NEW HOME. — THE OUTRAGE IN THE SENATE. — "CHRISTIAN WORSHIP." — ELECTION OF 1856. — CORRESPONDENCE. — AN INTERESTING REMINISCENCE.

SEVERAL months previous to his resignation, Dr. Wayland had commenced building a house at the corner of Governor and Angell Streets. The lot was beautifully situated, sloping eastward towards the Blackstone River, with (at that time) nothing, save the trees, to interrupt the view of the water.

His first care was to prepare the ground which was to form the garden; and in doing this he put in practice the principle which he had more than once urged on the farmers of Rhode Island — thorough tillage. The land was subsoiled to the utmost possible depth, and all the stones of any magnitude were removed. The effect of this labor in relieving the ground alike from excessive drought and excessive dampness, was marked and permanent. As soon as the state of the ground admitted, he began to set out fruit trees of all kinds. Probably there was not a tree upon the place which his own hand did not plant.

In January, 1856, at the dedication of the Third Baptist Church in Worcester, he preached the sermon upon "Christian Worship," afterwards included in "Sermons to the Churches."

In this discourse he considers the radical idea of worship as existing under the heathen, the Jewish, and the Christian systems. He then traces in each case the legitimate influence of the idea upon the outward form, and particularly shows what should be the effect of the Christian theory of worship upon the construction of Christian edifices, and the conduct of Christian services.

His view of the several religious systems is searching and profound, and the sermon, while by no means wanting in directness and fidelity of personal appeal, is characterized, in a degree not usual in his later writings, by the graces of diction.

We quote a paragraph, not as by any means the finest passage, but as bearing perhaps, better than any other, to be severed from its connections.

"In the early ages of humanity, men, like children, think more readily through the medium of visible objects. Hence the idea of God is soon transferred to some representation of the Deity which can be seen and felt. Thus arose all the multiplied forms of heathen idolatry. Each nation, forming its own conception of the Supreme Being, embodied that conception in some material image. Then, again, the notion of the Deity became divided and subdivided, as some distinct supernatural being was supposed to govern some peculiar department of the visible creation. Thus every nation, and tribe, and city had its appropriate gods, to whom it specially looked for succor in calamity, and whom it adored as the author of every deliverance. Not only every trade and occupation, but every individual, had his supernatural friend, god, demigod, or deified hero, to whom his special service was due, and who was to him, in a peculiar sense, the giver of all good.

"It thus followed that a mutual intercourse was supposed to be established between the gods and men. The gods bestowed favors, and men made to them offerings of the things in which they specially delighted. The gods were present, either by representation or in person, and they received the sacrifices which the worshipper presented. But the common people were not worthy themselves to present their offerings to the gods. Hence a caste selected from the people, or holding their office by hereditary descent, was chosen by the god to mediate between him and men. And, again, since the gods were personally present, they must have a place of abode. At first the most beautiful and picturesque spots on earth were consecrated to their service. Thus, in Greece, the lofty hill-top, as it first received the rays of Apollo, the smiling valley, bearing on its bosom the rich gifts of Ceres, the solemn forest, as it whispered the praises of Jove, nay, every sparkling fountain, every mysterious cavern, every loud-resounding beach, had its presiding divinity. As wealth increased, men began to adorn and beautify their private residences. The deity must also have his appropriate dwelling-place. His house was the temple. This was his chosen abode, where, by his own appointment, he could be most acceptably worshipped. Hence he scattered blessings upon his friends, and hence he launched his thunderbolts upon his enemies. The splendor of the temple of the deity was the measure of the devotion of his worshippers. Hence the wealth of provinces was not unfrequently exhausted in providing a suitable edifice for the abode of the god. All that genius could conceive, or art elaborate, was poured out in profusion in honor of the patron deity. Hence arose those stupendous structures in India and Egypt, and those magnificent temples in Greece and Italy, the ruins of which cannot now be viewed without the profoundest emotions of grandeur and astonishment. The civilized world was dotted thickly with edifices and shrines, in comparison with which all that the Christian religion has done in the erection of forms of beauty and sublimity dwindles into insignificance.

"Of the moral results of the heathen temple worship, it is not my purpose here to speak. These may be best understood from the character of paganism delineated in the first chapter of the Epistle to the Romans."

In March, 1856, his residence being completed, he moved into it; we may suppose, not without many serious thoughts, as he looked forward to the events which, in the order of nature, the house would, in no very long series of years, witness.* Yet it was with many pleasant and cheerful anticipations that he became, for the first time

* It was worthy of note as an illustration of his conscientiousness, that, until he was a householder, he would not vote on any municipal question involving the expenditure of public money.

in his life, possessed of a home on which he might look as permanent, and found himself free from harassing avocations, and enabled to spend his time in the culture of his own soil, and in labors for the promotion of the happiness and holiness of mankind.

On the 7th of June, 1856, he took part in the meeting of the citizens of Providence, called out by the assault upon Senator Sumner. His appearance upon the platform was greeted by his fellow-citizens with a degree of enthusiasm, which was alike unexpected and grateful to him. In his remarks, as in his speech upon the Nebraska Bill, he put aside the incidental features of the matter under consideration, and sought to reach the grand principle involved. He alluded to the fact that there are but two forms of government — the government of law and the government of force. The recent assault he regarded as one of the steps in an effort to dethrone the government by law among us, and to inaugurate the government by force. He concluded thus: —

"The question before us is simply whether you, here and now, consent to this change in our form of government, and accept the position which it assigns to you, and whether you agree to transmit to your children this inheritance. For myself I must decline the arrangement. I was born free, and I cannot be made a slave. I bow before the universal intelligence and conscience of my country, and when I think this defective, I claim the privilege of using my poor endeavors to enlighten it. But submit my reason to the bludgeon of a bully, or the pistol of an assassin, I cannot; nor can I tamely behold a step taken which leads directly to such a consummation."

He was profoundly interested in the issue of the national election in 1856, and, it need scarcely be said, voted for the candidate of the Republican party. He was not, however, surprised at the result of the election, and had no doubt of the divine wisdom which permitted the event.

To Hon. C. G. Loring, Boston: —

"June 7, 1856.

"... Since I saw you, I have thought of but one subject — the condition of the Northern States. We have neglected the sighing of the captive, and said that slavery was, after all, a small matter; and God is giving us a taste of it, that we may see how we like it ourselves. The iron already enters my soul. I feel that we are governed, not by law, and the expression of the universal conscience of the nation, but by bowie-knives, bludgeons, and the lash. I hope that the conscience and love of liberty in this people will be aroused.

"You mentioned a thought to me to which I attach great importance; it is the formation of some plan of concert among the free states. We must have concert, and *act upon a plan.* It may require some time, and labor, and sacrifice, but it is worth them all.

"But amidst all this confusion God reigns, and the wrath of man shall praise him, and the remainder of wrath he will restrain. I try to uphold my hopes for my country by falling back on the character of God. There only is our trust."

To a minister, during the Fremont campaign: —

"September 20, 1856.

"The business of a teacher of religion, I think, is to press upon men the principles on which they should act. When he applies these principles to particular cases, so as to show men, as the minister of Christ, how they should act, he mistakes his office; certainly, as a general thing. You may on the authority of God urge his law. To tell men that they must vote for Buchanan, Fillmore, or Fremont, on the same authority, is to claim his sanction for your opinions. What is this but Romanism?"

To Dr. Bartol: —

"November 17, 1856.

"... Well, the election is over, and I am satisfied. We have at last a North. It is an expression of decidedly changed public opinion. We have now a basis of operations, and have only to be united, to keep alive the moral sentiment of the people, to diffuse light, and to gain the next tier of states, and the result is sure. If Fremont had gone in with new and undisciplined men, and a Senate and House against him, we should have been broken up. Now I think the chances of freedom are good — God prosper the right."

To a minister: —

". . . Let us try to do the work that seems set before us, looking to God for his blessing. He will take better care of the future than we can. I begin to distrust thoroughly all long-tailed human plans. God has not the least respect for them. The great power in morals is example, and no one can tell how far God will make this useful."

To his sister: —

". . . The more I see, the more I am in love with the true Baptist principles. They are in accordance with the teachings of the Savior. This Abrahamic covenant, and hereditary membership, are the curse of the church. I think much more gravely of their effects than ever I did before.

". . . You see the insidious nature of infant baptism. Manage it as you will, it leads to mingling the church and the world. It is the worm at the root of the spirituality of the church. . . ."

To a sister: —

". . . The past year has been one of mercy to our family in general; sickness has visited us, but death has not been permitted to invade us. We are all a year nearer to a change of worlds and to the judgment-seat. As I grow older, I am more and more impressed with those views of scriptural truth that were so dear to our beloved parents. I rejoice the more to hear them in the pulpit and to read them in the printed page. I deeply regret that they are no more dwelt upon by the ministers of the gospel. The present state of the churches shows the need of them, and until that need be supplied I have but little hope of any improvement in their condition. It has seemed to me that preaching is now directed to building up a society, as it is called, and not to making or improving Christians. May God send us a renewing, for all the influences of the Spirit are, as it seems, bestowed upon the heathen."

To the same:—

"... Your suggestion about society in your last bears upon a difficult point. That we are social beings is true and important. Columbus' idea of guiding a power which he could not resist, does not, that I see, find an example in the life of Christ. I do not see how we could guide card-playing, polking, and waltzing to any good result, any more than drinking champagne and whiskey, and intoxication. These seem to be numbered among the unfruitful works, with which we have no fellowship. If we had the moral power to go among those engaged in them, and reprove them, and mingle a prayer-meeting with them, it would be another thing; but this would be ill-bred, for we were not invited for such a purpose. I take a different view of it. Why should not reasonable and intelligent people have their own parties, and unite in innocent and profitable intercourse. This is not ill-bred. Let worldly people have their parties, and let us have ours. It may be said this would not succeed. Well, it may be tried. If it fails, then we can stay at home. It is very useless to preach to other people to abandon the world which we ourselves visibly cherish and pursue. So it seems to me, but I am open to conviction. I know, however, that I could not preach to people to die unto the world, if I frequented such entertainments as are common."

On his sixtieth birthday he writes to his son:—

"I thank you for your kind and filial expressions of affection. As I grow older, I feel more and more the need of kindness. I am not quite an old man, but am approaching to it. Soon, if I am spared, feebleness will come upon me. I hope to gather strength from my new avocations and labors, yet this will be as God pleases. But a small remainder of my life is left; and I desire to spend it for the good of man and the glory of God. I trust I have your prayers that this may be my course of life until the end. I find myself getting more and more unlike the men around me, and more solitary as I grow older. I cannot be a partisan; and he who is not, will have but few companions. I turn more and more to my children and relations, and am glad to have their sympathy and succor."

During the summer of 1856 he attended Commencement at Yale College. The following incident, communicated by a gentleman of deserved eminence in literature and education,* is appropriate at this point:—

"I never spoke with Dr. Wayland, nor did I ever see him but once; and I never heard him, except in a ten minutes' speech, off-hand; and yet, in that speech he did more towards shaping my ideas and plans in life than any other person has ever done.

"I had just returned from a three years' tour in Europe, whither I went immediately after graduating at Yale. I was so situated, that I might reasonably be supposed to be beyond the need of much exertion. I had done and written some things which my friends thought warranted me in adopting a pleasant literary life. I was reading, and trying to enjoy myself in New Haven, yet not satisfied, and anxious to *do* something.

"Lounging about the edge of the crowd at the Alumni meeting at Yale, in 1856, I was attracted by hearing his name, as he was called on to speak. He rose, and his appearance made an impression upon me, such that I doubt whether those who saw him constantly, now carry in their minds a more vivid portrait of him than I do at this moment.

"He spoke of the possible rise or decline of this nation, of the duties of educated men, and said that he believed this country was fast approaching a 'switching-off place' towards good or towards evil, and added that, in determining which way the nation should be 'switched off,' the west held the balance of power, and that the west was the place for earnest men to work in, to influence the nation. That was all; but it changed my whole life. I gave up law, literature, and politics, and thenceforward my strongest desire was to work anywhere and anyhow at the west in education."

---

* Hon. A. D. White, LL. D., president of Cornell University, New York.

CHAPTER VII.

VIEWS OF THE MINISTRY. — "APOSTOLIC MINISTRY." — "NOTES ON THE PRINCIPLES AND PRACTICES OF THE BAPTIST CHURCHES." — LETTERS FROM J. M. PECK, D. D., PRESIDENT ANDERSON, HON. W. LUMPKIN, R. ANDERSON, D. D., H. G. WESTON, D. D., DR. NOTT, J. W. ALEXANDER, D. D. — EXTRACT FROM ARTICLE BY DR. WILLIAMS.

WE will now retrace our steps in order to allude to a topic, the full consideration of which has, for the sake of unity, been deferred to this point.

In his sermon at Rochester, on "The Apostolic Ministry," Dr. Wayland, taking as his text the words of the great Commission, asks, "What is the gospel? What is it to preach the gospel? and, Who are to preach the gospel?" To the latter question he replies, "Every one who has heard and believed it." "Every disciple of Christ must be a discipler." To the promotion of this object, every endowment of every Christian should be devoted; and those persons who are specially called by the Holy Ghost, and fitted by peculiar qualifications, are to consecrate themselves singly to this labor. "The minister does the same work that is to be done by every other member of the body of Christ; but, since it is his exclusive business, he may be expected to do it more to edification." It was by acting on these principles that the early disciples secured such triumphs for the gospel. Thus was it that the nation of the Karens was evangelized. Thus, too, have the German Baptists multiplied beyond precedent; and such was the practice of our own denomination in America in its earlier days. He next considered the bearing of these doctrines upon Christian and ministerial education. The sermon closed with an appeal to the disciples of Christ, to exhibit a zeal proportioned to the demands of the nation, and the portents of the age.

In 1855 Dr. Wayland commenced, in the Examiner, (N. Y.), a series of letters, with the signature "Roger Williams," entitled "Notes upon the Principles and Practices of the Baptist Churches." Of their purpose he says, —

"The general design of these papers is twofold. In the first place, I have endeavored to present a popular view of our distinctive principles and practices, indicating, at the same time, their harmony with the precepts of the New Testament; and, in the second place, I have labored to impress upon my brethren the importance of a firm adherence in practice, to what they believe to be the truth." — *Author's Preface to the English Edition.*

He originally intended to prepare only eight or ten letters; but the subject opened before him; new topics suggested themselves to his mind, or were suggested by the letters of inquiry which reached him; and at last the series contained fifty-two numbers. The letters were commenced during the last year of his presidency, and were continued during a considerable portion of the following year. In 1856 they were collected and published in a volume. The "Notes," both as they appeared from week to week, and after their publication in a more permanent form, were favorably received. They do not bear the marks of elaboration, but resemble rather the familiar conversation of a man of large mind, extended experience, and elevated piety. Had the author consulted authorities more fully, he would have escaped some errors of detail; but it is doubtful if he would have preserved the singularly natural and transparent style which is one of the chief attractions of the book. He writes, —

"There was nothing in it which I supposed to be new.

It merely presents the views which have generally been held by Baptists, as things taken for granted, and which had never before been reduced to regular form. Men were pleased to read in print what they had always believed, but had never before seen collected together." —*MS.*

The volume was republished in England as Vol. I. of the Bunyan Library. In the Introduction to the English edition, the editor, Rev. J. H. Hinton, offers some just remarks upon the excellences and defects of the work, closing with these words: —

"It is but simple justice to say, that the reader will find the volume everywhere interesting, instructive, full of sound judgment and wisdom, written in charming English, and never violating a Christian spirit."

Dr. Wayland's purpose in these letters, as indicated in his words quoted above, unavoidably led him to consider some of the particulars in which the practice of the Baptist churches had varied from their principles, and to urge his brethren to "stand in the old ways." He was of opinion that, adhering to their principles, they would not fail to achieve great results for God, and especially to gather large numbers of those holding neither the highest station nor the lowest in society, the "middling interest;" among whom, in his judgment, was always to be found the most promising field for labors, looking to the moral and intellectual elevation of man. But he thought that he perceived a disposition to forget these principles, and to seek, by conformity to other sects, to gain the more aristocratic classes. This he regarded as a grave error. He was convinced that the practice of the denomination in regard to the qualifications and duties of the ministry differed from the principles which the Fathers, adhering to the divine standard, had held. An unwearied advocate of true progress, a radical in his views of education, he yet could not regard anything as progress which varied from the teachings and the spirit of the Bible; and he believed that the highest advancement of which man is capable is secured by obedience to the inspired wisdom. "The gospel is radical enough for me," he once said. And in proportion to this variation the ministry had lost in numbers and in power. He had already, in the "Apostolic Ministry," indicated some of the steps which would tend towards an increase in the numbers of the ministry. In the "Letters on the Ministry of the Gospel," published some years later, the increase of its efficiency is the leading theme. He devotes nearly a third of the volume now spoken of to considering both these points. The three productions really form one series.

He was deeply impressed with the fact that the number of Baptist ministers fell, by several thousand, short of the number of Baptist churches. He was of opinion that this want should be supplied, in part, by encouraging every Christian, whether ordained or not, to use all his powers for the service of Christ and the salvation of souls. Further, the number of laborers in the ministry would be enlarged, by encouraging persons engaged in secular business, yet possessing gifts of persuasive speech, to devote a portion of their time to evangelical labors. And the number of persons consecrating their whole time to the single work of preaching the gospel would be increased by removing any restrictions which had insensibly grown up (not warranted by Scripture, nor by the primitive usage of the denomination), and by allowing every one called of God to the ministry, to enter on the work of preaching, with such a degree of theological learning as the providence of God places within his reach. If he were able to devote a long series of years to preparation and study, let provision be made for him to do so. But if from age, or want of aptitude for study, or from poverty, or domestic circumstances, or from any other cause, such a course be out of his power, then let him diligently and conscientiously use such means of improvement and culture as God has made possible for him, and proceed in the work to which he has been divinely called, trusting in the promised aid of the Holy Ghost. That he was not mistaken in the opinion that the numbers of the ministry might thus be increased, would seem evident from a statement in his reminiscences.

"I have had several letters from ministers who had not had the advantage of a professional education, saying how greatly they had been consoled by this public declaration, that a man might be a called and accepted minister of Jesus Christ, without going through college or knowing a word of Latin or Greek. Others, who had given up all thought of the ministry in despair, had been encouraged to turn their attention to it."

An opinion has, we believe, gained some currency, that Dr. Wayland was opposed to the education of the ministry. That he regarded moral qualifications for this work as taking the precedence of all else, is, indeed, undeniable. But that he did not ignore or undervalue education, we will not undertake to establish by argument. If the record of his life and labors leave any room for doubt on this point, it would seem that it would be dispelled by the views advanced in the sermon on the Apostolic Ministry (pp. 46–57, as found in Sermons to the Churches). It would be difficult to find a more clear, terse, and unanswerable argument for Christian and ministerial education.

"I was said to be opposed to ministerial education, because I held that a man with the proper moral qualifications might be called to the ministry by any church, and be a useful minister of Christ, and that we had no right to exclude such a man because he had not gone through a nine or ten years' course of study. God calls men to the ministry, by bestowing upon them suitable endowments, and an earnest desire to use them for his service. Of those thus called, some may not be by nature adapted to the prosecution of a regular course of study. Many others are too old. Some are men with families. Only a portion are of an age and under conditions which will allow them to undertake what is called a regular training for the ministry, that is, two or three years in an academy, four years in college, and three years in a seminary. But does not every man require the improvement of his mind, in order to preach the gospel? I think he does. His faculties, all of them, are given him to be used in the service of God, and the more he can do to render them efficient, the more he will have to consecrate to that service. But this is to be conditioned by the circumstances under which he has been placed. A theological seminary should be so constructed as to give the greatest assistance to each of these various classes of candidates. Some may be able to take a smaller, others a greater amount of study. Let each be at liberty to take what he can, and then the seminary is at rest. It has done what it could. The rest is left to Providence." — *MS.*

Again, in the "Notes on the Principles," &c., he says, —

"If it be said that these views are opposed to an educated ministry, we reply, Is it opposition to an educated ministry to affirm that every man whom God calls to the ministry, should cultivate himself just so far as God has given him the opportunity? Is it opposition to an educated ministry to urge every minister to improve to the utmost his younger brethren, in whom he perceives gifts for usefulness? Is it opposition to an educated ministry to labor to improve the hundred instead of the ten? All that we propose is, that every one be encouraged to enter upon this work who possesses the qualifications which the Holy Ghost has established, and that every one who engages in it, be urged and aided to give himself all the means of improvement which the providence of God places in his power."

The writer of these pages once said to Dr. Wayland, "Is it your opinion that every candidate for the ministry should conscientiously secure just as high and complete an education as the providence of God renders possible?" Dr. Wayland replied, "That is exactly my opinion." A clergyman who, for a number of months, studied for the ministry under his instruction, says, —

"There cannot be a greater error than to suppose that Dr. Wayland had an inadequate or superficial notion of the preparation needed for the ministry. No one was ever more difficult to satisfy. An exegetical exercise, a sermon, or a plan offered for correction, that would pass muster almost anywhere else, he would criticise, exhibiting its short-comings, until the writer was glad to carry off the remains, and set himself to the task of re-writing it."

He was of opinion that the efficiency of the ministry might be increased, first, by admitting no one to ordination who had not given ample proof of a divine inward call, and of a personal adaptation and aptness to teach. Persons who entered the ministry under anything but the strongest and most unmistakable divine impulse, however complete their education, lowered its standard and reduced its power. Second, he would have the education for the ministry, whether in a seminary or under the advice of a settled pastor, so conducted as to be a moral rather than a mental preparation, and so as to lead the candidate as much as possible into a practical acquaintance with the duties before him. Third, he would have the entire ministry pervaded by a profounder spirituality, a larger acquaintance with the Word of God, and a more absolute forgetfulness of self, and consecration of every power to Christ; or, to employ his own words, —

"We need more prayer, more reading of the Scriptures, for our own spiritual improvement, as well as for public preparation; we need a more exclusive and entire consecration to our work; we need a victory over the world, which should trample under foot its applause, its wealth, its honors and distinctions, and be willing to become great by becoming little in the sight of men. The first thing for a minister of the gospel to attain, is conquest over himself; to be perfectly willing for men to say of him what they please; to bear the contradiction of saints and of sinners, if only he can, by preaching the simple truths of the gospel, be the means of converting men to Christ, and saving souls from eternal despair. When he has broken these fetters, and thus become a freeman in Christ

Jesus, he can enter upon his work, with a power of faith, with might in the inner man, which those who consent to bow down to the world, and do merely what those around them are doing, can neither attain nor understand." *

He was of opinion that the efficiency of the ministry would be greatly increased by faithful pastoral visitation.

"In such visiting, the pastor should make it his business to enter into the religious condition of every individual. With the Christian, he should converse on the evidences of personal piety, the motives to a holy life, the value of souls, and the importance of a life of entire consecration of ourselves to Christ. . . .

"He will pay particular attention to the children of every family, calling them to early repentance, and pressing home upon each one the gracious offers of mercy through the blood of the cross. . . . To the worldly and unrenewed in heart he will kindly, yet faithfully, speak of the vanity of the world, the hollowness of its pleasures, and the treachery of its promises, and will urge them without delay to seek for an interest in Christ."

He also believed that, by the relinquishment of manuscript sermons in the pulpit, and by the practice of expository preaching, the ministry would gain in power over the hearts and consciences of men.

The following corespondence is introduced as apposite in this connection: —

Dr. Wayland to Rev. Dr. Jeter, Richmond, Va.: —

"April 19, 1854.

"Your letter was really as cold water to a thirsty soul. It is now so long since I have heard from you, that I did not know but you had forgotten me. It was a great pleasure to converse in this way with you again. I am glad the Memoir pleased you. It was a very interesting labor. Dr. Judson rose in my estimation from the first to the last. He will take his place among the first missionaries of this or any age. . . . As to the sermon [Apostolic Ministry], I can say, with you, that the opposition of brethren to its doctrines has alarmed me. I did not know before, how

* Ministry of the Gospel, pp. 137, 138.

far Baptists in cities had swung from their ancient moorings. I do not think that there is a word in it that would not have been acknowledged by all Baptists when I was a boy. And yet, it is here considered as radically opposed not only to an educated ministry, but to all education. My brother, if the views which are held by many of our brethren be carried out, our denomination is done for. Let it be received as true, that a Baptist is not to preach the gospel without years of heathen learning, or, if he does, that he is nothing but a backwoodsman, of whom every one ought to be ashamed, and we are dead, plucked up by the roots. We leave the Acts of the Apostles, for the teachings of Presbyterians and Episcopalians. Look where you will, no denomination ever increased with this ministerial heresy. We began from nothing; how God has blessed us! But just as soon as we desert our principles, we cease to enlarge, and the Spirit of God is not with us. I hope that the brethren in Virginia will hold fast to the doctrine of the New Testament, and in this respect the distinguishing doctrine of the Baptists. It is most absurd for us to aim at the aristocracy; they do not want our kind of religion. We are a *middling-interest* people, and there is no better interest. The Bible does not encourage us to aim for the rich. Jesus Christ did not, and we had better follow his example. . . .

"Well, my brother, I rejoice to unite with you, in love to all who love the Savior. There are, and will be, divisions of opinion; but there is one Redeemer, one hope through grace, and one heaven, to which all who love Jesus Christ are tending. I am sorely grieved at this Nebraska business; but I love all my brethren in Christ, north or south, east or west; and I can rejoice with them in all that advances the kingdom of Christ. I shall always remember you with pleasure, and your visit here."

From the late Rev. J. M. Peck, D. D., of Illinois: —

"I regard your views pertaining to the Christian ministry, and especially the propagation of the gospel, not only as truthful, but as exceedingly important at this crisis in our denomination. Recently I have seen, in the Christian Chronicle, a report of your sermon, which confirms me the more in the correctness of your principles, and their adaptation to the exigencies of our churches. I am much gratified to learn that the sermon will go to press."

From President M. B. Anderson, LL. D., Rochester, N. Y.: —

"I have just finished reading your Memoir of Dr. Judson, and I cannot refrain from expressing the extreme gratification, which I have derived from the clear, comprehensive, and just delineation which you have given of the character of that great and good man. . . .

"By the remarks which you have interspersed with his letters, you have brought out the exact significance of his life, and the great moral lesson which it is divinely designed to teach. I have never felt more powerfully, than during the hours that I was reading these volumes, the glory of the simple gospel of Christ, when apprehended by faith, and honestly carried out into practice. I remember, when a boy, reading through the night the Memoir of Mrs. Ann H. Judson. I did not expect ever again to be so moved by the details of a life, with almost every part of which I had become familiar. I have, however, been more strongly moved than I was in my boyhood, but by a different class of emotions. I have felt crushed, under a sense of the inadequacy of my conception of the true ends of a moral being, under the government of God; of my failure to seize, as I ought, upon the great elemental principles of our Savior's system of mercy.

"I see in your sermon on the 'Apostolic Ministry,' merely a transcript of the great lesson you have drawn from the facts in the life of Judson. There are some points in that sermon which I could wish otherwise; but to the great fundamental idea developed in it *I adhere with all my soul.* I have tried, while an editor, to inculcate, with far feebler powers, a similar view of the gospel ministry. I have steadily refused to be ordained, while I had not the pastoral care of a church, so that I might be the better fitted to speak and act as a lay preacher. I have deliberately sunk the desire to attain distinction as a preacher (as the world at large understands the matter) in the desire to introduce among my brethren, and exemplify as far as my other duties would permit, the idea of talking about Christ to poor condemned sinners, not as a matter of professional skill, but as the spontaneous outpouring of a heart warm with the love of Christ. Though my 'talks' have been necessarily ill digested, prepared often amid the noise and distraction of the streets of New York, while attending to business which exercised my body alone, they have given me great enjoyment.

"I know that it is only needful for pastors to lead off in work of this kind, and to enforce the necessity and obligation of it upon intelligent laymen, to accomplish in our larger cities a work for Christ which shall bring about a new era in the history of our Zion. I have not a doubt, that, in and around the city of New York, a dozen large and vigorous churches might thus be gathered in two years' time. When irreligious men see persons enter upon such labor, with no hope of reward, either in money or fame, it has a moral power over them which can hardly be exerted by the paid missionary. Let laymen thus go forward and collect Sunday schools and churches, and God would provide pastors, as fast as the churches grew.

"I remarked incidentally that there were some things in your discourse that I could wish otherwise. I ought to say that they are trifles, such as do not hinder me from doing all I can to circulate it, and inculcate its main principles. . . . I hope you will excuse me for obtruding these remarks on your time and attention. I have written from the heart, because I have thought I should feel better for saying what I have. I hope you will not feel under obligation to spend time in replying. My main end will be accomplished, if I shall have said anything which may induce you to follow up the impulse which you have begun. Can you not write a work on the propagation of the gospel in large cities, which shall point out in detail the practical working of the general principles which you have laid down?"

From Hon. Wilson Lumpkin, of Georgia: —

"I have read and re-read your discourse on the 'Apostolic Ministry,' with all the thought and consideration which I could bring to bear on the important subject. I am so entirely satisfied with the value of the inestimable truths presented, that I dare not trust my limited range of thought to suggest a single modification of any paragraph contained in it. I have been a member of the Baptist church for fifty-two years, and most of that time an acting deacon. I have been deeply impressed, for many years past, with the conviction that the church of Christ was doing but a small share of what was necessary to be done, in order to hasten and secure the universal triumph of the Redeemer's kingdom on earth. Moreover, I have, for some time past, believed that the plans and efforts of our great and good men to regenerate and convert the world were deplorably deficient, and too much based on worldly wisdom and philosophy, without sufficient regard to the plain words of divine inspiration. I have felt that some great reform was needed in all denominations of our American church. But I have still worn the collar and worked in the harness prepared for me by others. I have looked in hope to our institutions of learning, including our rising theological seminaries, to furnish our destitute churches and people with a higher order of qualified men, to carry forward the work of the Lord. I have fully appreciated all the advances we have made in literary and religious culture; and yet I have been forced to see and feel that a greatly increased destitution in religious instruction pervaded many portions of our country. In direct proportion as the idea prevails that none are to preach a crucified Savior to a perishing race of precious immortals, unless they have come from the schools of the prophets, destitution spreads far and wide.

"But the question that has perplexed me most has been, What is the reform needed, and how shall it be brought about? For myself, although an old man, I felt that I was but a child in such great matters. In the first place, I had no well-defined plan of reform in my own mind; and, secondly, I had neither qualifications nor position for so great a work. But your discourse has revealed to me the great object which I have been in search of. It appears to me that it is imbued with the wisdom which comes from above, and is at the foundation of the reformation which can alone save the church from a downward tendency. Let the doctrines which you have advanced be inculcated and put in practice, and the Zion of our God will arise from the dust, and become the glory of the whole earth."

From Rev. R. Anderson, D. D: —

"MISSIONARY HOUSE,
BOSTON, February 13, 1854.

"... You state, very clearly, under your first head, what the minister of Christ is to preach; but you lay yourself out mainly upon the preachers. The views you take are of the highest practical importance, and we shall never get the amount of gospel preaching we need at home, nor feel like sparing a sufficient number of our educated and able preachers for foreign missions, until your views are those of the public mind. I believe I agree with you to the full extent of your reasoning, provided the question be, how nominally Christian nations are to be evangelized. I sometimes feel no small apprehension as to whereunto it will grow, when I observe the immense power exerted by our theological seminaries, on all questions relating to the creating and employment of the gospel ministry. I fear that the prevalence of a feeling that an uneducated ministry is worse than none (or what comes near to that), is a good deal owing to them. They have almost all the great batteries of thought in their hands. I am no enemy, but the firm friend, of these institutions, and would have them exist, and do all the good they can; only I would by no means have the community shut up to them. Let your idea of the simplicity of gospel preaching be repeated in ten thousand forms, until it is understood; and let all the preaching gifts that exist in the church be drawn into exercise, by men occupying high places of trust and influence, by churches and associated bodies of ministers, and, employed under their watchful and directing care. I no longer object to colporteurs, nor to lay missionaries in cities, nor to short courses into the home ministry when there is reason for it; believing that an uneducated ministry (with an experimental knowledge of the gospel) is infinitely better than none. Your reasoning is conclusive, as it seems to me, in respect to home ministries for evangelizing the people.

"But I am not prepared to send many laymen, nor yet to send many uneducated ministers, on foreign missions. Nor do I think it well to attempt sending a very great number of foreign missionaries into any one heathen country not territorially large. It does not work well. Your theory comes in here. It is the simple gospel we wish to proclaim, — what every true convert understands, and can make known to others; and I would rely chiefly on native force for evangelizing heathen nations; and only a small part of this would I require to be in any sense learnedly educated. Our theological ideas, the result of our home system of ministerial education, have gone too much into our foreign missions, and we have found it difficult to get a native convert ordained who had not been liberally educated. I have sometimes been almost reconciled to the scarcity of missionaries for a time, if it only have the effect to break down (as perhaps it is providentially designed to do) this unapostolic notion. I go for your discourse as regards home ministries; but I am rather increasingly disposed to send out a select body of foreign missionaries to be emphatically leaders and commanders of the people. And I see nothing in your discourse to induce me to think that your views are not accordant with my own. Go on, my dear brother, without fear or shrinking, and believe me as ever, respectfully and most truly yours."

Dr. Wayland to Rev. Dr. Anderson: —

"February 17, 1854.

"I am most happy to find that we agree in all that is essential as to the gospel commission. The point to which you except, I confess I have not fully considered, and will, therefore, hold my opinion in abeyance. The Moravians say that they do not desire for missionaries highly educated men; they have not found them to do so well. One thing is, however, certain; heathen countries must be evangelized by natives; no other plan is even conceivable. It is strange to observe, in our missionaries, the most deplorable calls for aid from home, and the comparison of the relative proportion of laborers in heathen and in Christian countries, and, at the same time, a settled plan to keep out of the field of gospel labor all the natives, or to reduce the number of them as much as possible. Some other views must prevail, and the churches, wherever they are, must be looked upon, not as wheat laid up in a garner, but as seed sown in a soil where it must spring up and bear fruit, if it be planted and watered by the Spirit of God. We are all looking too much to our own wisdom, and forgetting that there is any Holy Ghost. We are making a difference between the times of Christ and his apostles, and our own times, which I suspect does not exist. May God give us grace to understand his Word. I would give infinitely more for a spirit to receive the gospel as a little child, than for all the commentators, divines, and decrees of councils that have existed from the beginning.

"But I am prosy. Can anything be done to put these things in a new light before the churches? I find good men everywhere are alarmed at our present tendencies."

From Rev. H. G. Weston, D. D.: —

"PEORIA, ILLINOIS, December 4, 1855.

"I can no longer deny myself the pleasure of thanking you for the views which you are presenting of our duty and danger as a denomination. Your sermon on Ministerial Education, and your articles in the Examiner, I have read with tears of gratitude, thankful beyond expression that such truth is set forth in such a manner, and from such a source. A short time since, a leading Presbyterian minister in this state remarked that your sermon at Rochester was *the* sermon of the age. I thought, if this is apparent to a Presbyterian, how can it fail of approving itself to Baptists?

"Views more needed and timely could not be offered to our churches. We have so long and with so much complacency congratulated ourselves upon the good work which we are doing in moulding the views and practices of other denominations (a work unacknowledged by them), that we have forgotten the (to us) more important fact, that they are wonderfully transforming us. For years I have desired to see a thorough exposition of the theme, 'The unconscious influence of other denominations upon the Baptists;' but the few to whom I have dared to make the suggestion have considered the very idea a slander. Nothing at the present time is so crippling our energies as our wholesale attempts to copy Pedobaptists. The work to which God has called us we are leaving undone, and we waste our energies in vain endeavors to accomplish something which is not within our power. If, by any means, we can be induced to give up this vain attempt to combine things that are irreconcilable by nature, — this all-consuming endeavor to put new wine into old bottles, — if, by God's grace, we can be brought to understand our duty, and be content with it, our work will be already half done. We generally see clearly enough that the *theory* of the Baptists is radically different from that of the Pedobaptists; but alas! we lose sight of the inevitable consequence, that there should result an equally different *practice*. O that we could rid ourselves of this unwillingness to be singular in carrying out the grand principle of the New Testament! Would that we were content to be conformed to the principles, as we are to the ordinances, of the gospel, and that, in the one case as well as in the other, we esteemed it a very small thing to be judged by man or man's judgment!

"I will not weary you with expressions of gratitude for your exposition of the true nature of gospel preaching; but I could not resist the temptation of assuring you that thousands of hearts beat in warm response to yours, and that many prayers are offered that your efforts may be crowned with wonderful success.

"And now will you pardon the liberty I have taken, and believe me, &c."

From Dr. Nott: —

"I have read, with great interest, your book on the good old Baptist usages; and I sympathize more with its teachings than many of your own brethren seem to do. We, by our machinery, make ministers for cities and villages — I mean for what is called the 'upper crust' in them. But as to the great world, and the 'lower crust' of cities and villages, I know not what would become of these, but for the Methodists and Baptists. And of late, the Methodists and Baptists are following us, and we are following the Episcopalians, and they are following Rome, — at least in the outward aspect of our places of worship, and it will be well if not in the worship within. The Baptists, I am aware, are pretty far from Rome yet, and I pray that they may remain so."

From Dr. Wayland to Rev. J. W. Alexander, D. D.: —

"I have just completed your admirable Memoir of your father — now with God. A more charming biography I have never read. While you write as a son, it is as a son of Archibald Alexander. There is nothing filial that is not admirable, and not a word that could not be attested even more strongly by a host of witnesses. A more beautiful or noble specimen of Christian character can hardly be conceived. His gifts were great and abundant beyond the common lot of humanity; and God placed them where they shone with a radiance that illumined the whole church of Christ. The moment I looked upon the portrait, I remarked its likeness to Wilberforce. The latter, of course, I never saw; but I have seen his portrait by Lawrence, and the resemblance is remarkable. I saw your father only on two occasions. Once, about thirty years ago, I spent a few hours in Princeton, and called upon him. He received me with a cordiality and kindness which I should have expected only from an old friend, and showed me the place of repose of the mighty dead. He invited me to stay with him; but I was unwell, and was obliged to hurry home, fearing an attack of fever, which I barely escaped. I have seen hundreds of remarkable men since, whose impression on me has entirely passed away; but this interview with him is fresh and green in my memory. Many years afterwards I heard him twice one Sunday, in Dr. Spring's church. He preached a sermon to Christians, admirable throughout, but not, that I recollect, marked by any of those bursts of eloquence of which he was so capable. A high pulpit and a city audience is not the place for those things. An old Virginia church, or court-house, crowded around the windows, is the place for such eloquence. Those magic bursts of feeling must be rare among the conventionalities and respectabilities of a city congregation. The sound of a bell depends as much on the quality of the metal as on the vigor of the blow.

"I now see why Princeton has made good preachers. I agree with your Presbyterian doctrine very well on most points, especially on the marked prominence you give to the work of Christ. I differ from you in some respects. You make the gospel system more rectangular and closely articulated than I. You see clearly, where I only have an opinion. But you make preachers. The tendency of seminaries is to become schools for theological and philological learning, and elegant literature, rather than schools to make preachers of the gospel. With every year their general tendency is in this direction, as I think I have observed. I have thought this of Princeton. As I would have asked your father, so may I ask you, whether he ever observed it, and feared for this tendency. You will, I trust, excuse this long letter. I could not have satisfied myself without writing, and I have written more than I intended."

From Rev. J. W. Alexander, D. D.: —

"NEW YORK, November 15, 1854.

"I should at any time have esteemed it a pleasure and honor to find myself in a correspondence with you; but this becomes peculiarly pleasant when I have to acknowledge such a letter as yours of the 10th. All your warm recollections of my honored father give me high gratification. Nothing can be more just than your remarks about his preaching. In the pulpit he was two different men, and least of all was he himself when he came into the cities to preach. When he got on his high horse, in conversation, he was indescribably delightful; this happened only once or twice in a month or two, and never 'upon compulsion.' Most heartily do I assent to your remarks about the literary tendencies of our theological seminaries. I feel it in my heart. Having left the desk for the pulpit, I feel it more. Alas, alas, that in an age and land demanding life, soul, activity, eloquence, fiery zeal, martyrdom, so many noble young men 'quite mistake the scaffold for the pile,' and come out *scholars.* Hall and Chalmers show us that great attainments need not spoil the preacher; but few learn it in America. In the somewhat senile gossip of dear good Mr. Jay (just out) there is some good talk on this. *He*, good man, was the *beau ideal* of the unlearned preacher. But give me this rather than the other. . . . In a great many discourses, tear off the text, and I wager no man living can tell whether he is reading a Commencement address, a sermon, or an article in the Bibliotheca Sacra. Indeed, I have known the same manuscript go through all three phases, literally. In many admirable, even masterly sermons (so called), in New England and New York, the idea of sermon, *qua talis*, seems to me to be wanting. This strikes our English friends most painfully. Such are not the sermons of the late Professor Scholefield, whom I heard at Cambridge, of McNeil, Stowell, Leifchild, Brock, or Binney. Yet this school of preaching, i. e., the true, always pleases, even in New England. Pardon my undue freedom of talk. I have been severely ill for a month, and am taking reprisals on my friends."

Dr. Wayland to Dr. J. W. Alexander: —

"Do not be alarmed. I am not apt to be so mercantile a correspondent. I do not always reply by return of mail. But your views so thoroughly accord with mine that I must add a few words to my last note. What you say of the pulpit is true to the letter; and when to this style of preaching are added the indirect effect of Unitarianism, and the tendency to treat lightly and seldom the doctrine of depravity, and to generalize the atonement by Christ, until it fades away into an undefined and inoperative idea, what is to be expected? The pulpit is becoming of very small practical value, and the church of Christ is sinking into insignificance. Men do not preach to convert sinners, and subdue the world to Christ, but to 'build up a society,' to erect temples, and draw together the rich, practically excluding the poor. You feel this; but what must be my feeling to see this overspreading my denomination, which by every principle of its nature is opposed to it, and to which it is certain death? It is good to find any one who reads the signs of the times as I am compelled to do. . . . How far is the evil owing to our seminaries? If it is not radical and necessary, can they be improved, or shall we return to some other mode of preparation for the ministry? I doubt if Princeton ever again makes as good ministers as when your father and Dr. Miller were the sole teachers. . . . I write in haste, but the subject weighs upon my spirit. It is overwhelming to see the glorious gospel of the ever-blessed God turned to such use, and something held out in its name from which all that is essential and awakening is excluded. Are there any men among you who feel this? Can anything be done in a better direction? It is sad to think of at home, and it is spreading to our *foreign missions*. I have asked all sorts of questions. Answer them or not, as you please or have time. It is at least a comfort to me to pour out my sorrows in the ear of a brother who mourns over the desolations of Zion."

From Dr. Alexander: —

"November 17, 1854.

"I will in the first place take my head from the series of remarks in your truly welcome letter. My belief is, that the pulpit is sinking all over the country. It is worst in towns and cities, and at literary seats. The sermon becomes an oratorical, æsthetic, or intellectual refection. On this subject I cannot speak freely. *Peccavi!* I look for the 'physican, heal thyself.' If you were to drop into my church, you would find me sinning like others. The proximate cause of the evil is this: a *selfish disposition to gain character* for individual power, polish, 'mind,' and all that. I have often preached worse than I could, because I wanted to preach (secularly) better. Though the former of the two following reasons condemns myself, I believe the main reasons of our failure are, 1. *Manuscript sermons;* and, 2. The *absence of exposition*, as the great matter of preaching. Pardon my resorting to an egotistic way of expressing my thought. With a broken constitution I preach three sermons a week. The first I write and read — it is my main achievement for the week; the second I preach from a page of hints — say a skeleton; the third, which for many years has been an exposition in course, I deliver with no written helps at all. Now, my impression is, that most of the good wrought by my means is by 3 and 2, and very little by 1. But the grand cause lies farther back; it is want of fire, of faith, of feeling, of love, of grace. If I had religion enough, all my sermons would be like my expository lectures. I lament from the bottom of my soul that I ever took 'the papers,' as the Scotch say, into the pulpit. But even Scotland is going into it. I sometimes go into a Wesleyan church to warm up a little. Why! — they are as genteel and formal as so many Presbyterians.

"If I were not a poor feeble creature, whose work seems nearly done, and who cannot exemplify what he teaches, I would blow a trumpet of alarm. I think a revival of ministerial piety is the desiderandum; an outbreak as abrupt as that under Spener and Francke in Prussia, or the Wesleys and Whitefield in England. . . . This I say, being preacher, in a Gothic pile, to one of the wealthiest assemblies in America; I would, however, rather preach to negroes — as I did for a long time.

"Remembering the entire history of Princeton seminary, I can speak confidently as a witness, though I wish to be modest as a judge. On the whole, the difference between the style of preaching of the first and last students is less marked than I thought, till I came coolly to consider it; and yet the tendency is decided towards learned, elegant, rhetorical sermons. *Present impression on hearers' souls* is not thought of enough. My father saw this; he labored against it; his own practice was against it. But I do not know that he ever ascribed the evil to seminaries. In my poor opinion, the evil cannot be laid at the door of seminaries, as such, any more than of colleges. It is a startling fact that, generally speaking, the type of the preacher is his *college type;* the gristle becomes bone, alarmingly early; seminaries and colleges both show the widespread atrophy and *anœmia* of the churches. Professors, specially, are tempted to be learned, rather than warm. The idea of returning to mere pastoral preparation, frightens all.

"Much might be done if men in high stations could more fully testify their conviction that the great end of preaching is to save souls, and if the curse of occasional sermons and great sermons could be wiped away. Invite a man a few months beforehand, and you never expect him to preach Christ. Our former revival excitements had some good results as to this point. People saw that ministers were agreed, and were in earnest.

"My own particular mode of address is so cool and equable, that I am unfitted to stir up in this affair. Rich congregations like easy hearing. *Promiscuous* assemblies are what the gospel was made for. I deprecate all *chapel* preaching in colleges and seminaries. That *Baptists* should forsake their very strength, and come down to the poor level of ourselves, is amazing to me.

"If some author, preacher, and educator, like yourself, would adventure a small volume on this subject, it would have great weight. You and I, dear sir, must soon be gone. In what hands are we to leave the blessed gospel? It is a momentous question. You have brought this prolixity on yourself."

As these pages are preparing for the press, an honored Baptist minister, a theological instructor, has said to us, —

"When the Rochester sermon was published, I did not like it. But within the past five years I have read the New Testament carefully, with a view to seeing its bearing on the points touched upon in that sermon; and I have become a convert. I am convinced that the reason of our difference of opinion was, that he had read the New Testament more correctly than I."

Does not the recent liberal provision in the Andover Seminary, by which a theological course is opened for those persons who cannot command the time or means for a longer course of study, — does not the blessing of God resting on the labors of lay preachers, alike in the army, and at home — upon the labors of Stuart, and Durant, and Wilson, — do not these and kindred facts show that Dr. Wayland rightly read the demands of the times?

We may add, at this point, a paragraph from an obituary notice of Dr. Wayland, written by Rev. Abel Stevens, D. D., the historian of Methodism: —

"The *moral character* of this truly great man was the crown of his greatness. The practicality of his intellect characterized his moral life. Though evangelically orthodox, his extremely practical view of Christianity rendered him almost extremely liberal. A working religion was his ideal of Christianity. Dogmatics must give precedence to ethics; this *doctrinaire* must stand behind the 'doer of the word,' the evangelist, the missionary, the Christian educator, the Christian philanthropist, the Christian statesman. Many of us remember the bold, practical, evangelical liberalism of his famous Rochester sermon. It was a resounding tocsin summoning American Christianity from its fields of speculation, polemics, and formalism, to its more legitimate fields of evangelical work — work on the highways, on the frontiers, in the suburban abysses of vice and poverty."

We do not know how we can better conclude this chapter than by quoting, from the columns of the Examiner, a portion of a notice of the "Principles," &c., in which there appear unmistakable traces of the affluent and polished diction of Rev. Dr. Williams.

"We rejoice to find a scholar and thinker, so justly eminent, far beyond the bounds of his own denomination, and of his own country, as President Wayland, setting himself in the earnest, child-like simplicity which is one of the surest marks of true greatness, to the task of putting before this generation, in our churches, the ways of their fathers, and of endeavoring to revive in the hearts of the children the principles and practices of their spiritual ancestry. He is, in the good providence of God, rarely endowed for the work. His earlier volumes have taken their rank; and, as a thinker and writer, he cannot seem to any, whom his suggestions may most displease, to have criticised a culture that he did not himself possess, or to have disparaged the use of powers which he could neither understand nor emulate. Received in his visit to the shores of Great Britain by men like Dr. Arnold, of Rugby, Dr. Whewell, and the late Sir William Hamilton, as their friend and compeer in the walks of philosophy and of the highest education; when in the maturity of his powers, attainments, and honors, he sits down to say that in the Christian ministry a regular and classic education is not the first requisite, — nay, is often not a requisite at all, — it seems to us that there is a glorious abnegation of all undue honors for that professional education, by himself so long and successfully dispensed, which should make his testimony doubly impressive, and which clothes that testimony, in all its simplicity and directness, with a noble magnanimity.

"He was abundantly competent to have produced a work of more form and pretension; but he wrote for the body of the ministry, and for the membership of the churches. To attain his object in winning them as readers, these unstudied outpourings, as of a revered friend holding us in a rich, free, and hearty conversation, were, we think, the best form that he could adopt. He has called his volume but 'Notes.' It is not elaborate, though its views are often profound — the result, evidently, of long and devout pondering. It is, in style of utterance, — to use an image of Bacon's, — 'but the first crushing of the clusters in the press, not the protracted twisting that leaves the harsh taste of grape-skins and stems in the wine.'

"Our own denomination have, like our Methodist brethren, been honored of God, in the times of our fathers, to preach the gospel to the poor. Their converts and the children of their converts have become very generally advanced in worldly resources above the former level and average position of their first membership; but both Methodist and Baptist — and the last, perhaps, more than the first — are not in our times displaying all the power to win and hold the poor, which is the great need of modern civilization, and which, largely displayed, is the crowning earthly glory of the gospel. In endeavoring to recall our churches to the simple tastes and more enterprising and aggressive piety of their forefathers, Dr. Wayland has made many suggestions as to sanctuaries, modes of public worship, and forms of preaching, and views of a divine call to the ministry, that deserve, not only from the character of the writer, but from the present circumstances of our people, very serious regard. . . .

"He would retain the due influence of the pulpit, but would call to a more general recollection of the most scriptural positions taken by our fathers, as to the need of a call from the Holy Ghost for entrance on the ministry. He would dissuade from the undue reliance which some have had upon a regular course of education as indispensable for the modern preacher. If the friends of theological seminaries construe these remarks of his as denying the advantages of scholastic training, it seems to us that it would be an unhappy misapprehension. He would, as we understand him, but dissuade the exaggeration of the claims of such education, an undue and unspiritual reliance upon its power, and above all, such departure from the ways in which God led and blessed our fathers, as would make it an indispensable prerequisite to the ministry, that the man had received certain secular instruction.

"Homage to the due and paramount sovereignty of the Holy Ghost in taking his own workmen where he may choose, provided the church see in them the experience, holiness, and aptness to teach, that are among the evidences *externally* of his *internally* calling and qualifying the men, — homage cheerfully and evermore rendered to the perpetual presidency of the Redeemer in his own modern churches, — is but simple loyalty to the Master. This we suppose, although there may be divergencies in the mode of expression employed, to be the great aim of Dr. Wayland. If such be his meaning, it is, we think, but a law of Christ that cannot, in our judgment, be abrogated, or even infringed, with impunity. Shall men, then, it may be asked, no longer enter, and no more sustain, theological seminaries? By no means. Let a man who has leisure, and youth, and helping friends, get, there or elsewhere, all the useful knowledge that he can. But let the door into the pulpit be kept open, not only for such younger brethren, but for the man of mature age and more slender training. And, above all, let the Paraclete choose his own tools."

CHAPTER VIII.

DEATH OF REV. DR. GRANGER. — ACTION OF THE CHURCH. — THE WORK UNDERTAKEN. — THE PASTOR'S SPIRIT AND AIM. — PREPARATION OF HEART. — VISITING. — PERSONAL LABOR. — CHARACTER OF HIS PREACHING. — THE VESTRY. — CORRESPONDENCE. — PROGRESS. — DEATH OF MR. MOSES B. IVES. — CRISIS OF 1857. — CORRESPONDENCE.

ON the part of any who might take exception to these views of the ministry, the reply would not be altogether unnatural, "It is not difficult for one on whom the labors of the ministry do not fall, to urge ministers to a high self-forgetfulness, an earnest devotion, a renunciation of fame, of ease, and emolument." Example, therefore, though possibly more difficult, would be, after all, more powerful.

On the 5th of January, 1857, Rev. Dr. Granger, pastor of the First Baptist Church in Providence (a man of eminent ability, piety, and zeal), was removed by death.

At the request of the church and of the afflicted family, Dr. Wayland preached, on the 18th of January, a discourse suggested by this event, in which he expressed his high estimate of the Christian character, and the religious earnestness of the deceased pastor, and especially his sense of his labors and counsels as a minister of the Deputation to the American Baptist Missions in the East Indies.

Suddenly bereaved, the church acted in accordance with the instinct of the community in any hour of perplexity.

On the 20th of February the joint committee of the church and of the society for the supply of the pulpit, —

" *Resolved*, that Rev. Francis Wayland, D. D., be earnestly requested to undertake the performance of ministerial and pastoral labors for the time being, and until it may be thought best to make some other arrangement; and that he be requested to devote his time and energies to these ministrations in such ways as may be best adapted to promote the highest religious interests of the church and society.

" *Resolved*, that the compensation for these services be twenty-five dollars per week." *

It may be remarked that the committee had previously asked him to undertake the supply of the pulpit only. He says, —

" This I was unwilling to do, for I thought that some time would elapse before a suitable candidate could be provided, and I believed that the church needed, not merely preaching on the Sabbath, but great and faithful labor from house to house."

The committee agreed with him, and thence resulted the invitation first alluded to.

He had now nearly completed his sixty-first year; he had not yet regained the strength which had been expended during his laborious years in college. He was preparing one or two volumes for publication, — one of which had been announced, — and he was proposing to complete the long-deferred work of revising and re-writing his Moral Science. He might, without difficulty, have pleaded excuses enough for declining to undertake a labor of the arduousness of which he had not a light conception; nor could he for such a decision have been " judged of man,

---

* The second of the above resolutions is inserted as an evidence (if any were needed) that a regard to compensation did not supply his motive or measure his exertions. He believed that "the minister is an agent, whose principal is, not the congregation, but Almighty God." — *Ministry of the Gospel.*

or of man's judgment." But it was to a higher authority that he held himself amenable. "With him, *ought* and *ought not* were the words most powerful of all that could be uttered." He wrote to his son, —

"I shall probably do it, and commence in a few days. This will confine me a good deal, but it seems an opening for usefulness, and I could not with a good conscience refuse. Should I do it, I pray God to grant us a revival of religion, and to build up his cause here."

In his reminiscences he writes, —

"The moment I assumed the duties of pastor, I relinquished every other engagement and occupation. I laid away my manuscripts, put aside all labor for myself, and devoted myself to the service of the gospel. . . . I had published my views of the ministry, of the kind of preaching needed, of the other labors (besides preaching) devolving on the minister, and of the necessity of making every other pursuit secondary to this, if we expected the blessing of God. From consistency, as well as from conscience, I felt under obligation to follow my own directions, or rather what I supposed to be the commands of our Lord and Savior. If I can speak of my own motives, I do not know that I ever commenced any undertaking from a more simple desire to do the will of the Master."

These words but inadequately express the completeness of his concentration of thought and effort. Not only did he give up all authorship, he relinquished all reading. He did not, we believe, even read a review during the period of his pastoral labors. He employed in studying the Bible, and in prayer, all the time not consumed in needful exercise, in preparation for the Sabbath, or in visiting the congregation.

"My first and most important effort was to gain victory over myself. I presume almost any preacher would understand my meaning. I had held some important offices of a literary character. I had published some things which were more than usually successful. I had had some reputation as a good writer. Now, all these antecedents would seem to point to a mode of preaching in harmony with them; elaborate, and calculated to commend religion to the taste and imagination; in fine, to a kind of preaching addressed to the ten, rather than to the hundred. I could not but feel that to preach otherwise would appear to many as a falling off, a sinking away; that it would, in a word, induce many persons to think less of me.

"On the other hand, I knew that such preaching as perhaps might be expected from these antecedents, though it may gratify the taste of the few, is without moral effect on the many; that hearers do not understand or follow it; and that it is, in fact, nothing more nor less than to use the awful truth of the coming of the Son of God upon earth, as a stepping-stone to the preacher's reputation. It it using the solemn realities of eternity, of redemption, and the atoning sacrifice of the Messiah, for the purpose of feeding the vanity of preacher and hearers, and making the preaching of no value to the mass of those who listen. How could a minister of the gospel render up his account at the day of judgment, in the presence of the Searcher of hearts, and in sight of those to whom he had accepted the office of religious teacher?

"There seemed, therefore, but one course to be taken. I strove to yield myself without reserve to the Savior, to preach whatever he bade me, and in the simplest manner possible, so that no one could fail to understand me. I was sent to labor for the conversion of men, and that not at some future time, but now, by means of every sermon. I saw that the preaching which has in view the exhibition of truth in such a manner as to convert men eight or ten years hence, is fatal to souls. It teaches men to put off attention to religion to a future period, and that period continues always a thing of the future, until death comes and ushers the soul into eternity, with the time for repentance as distant as ever.

"The minds of many members were pervaded by an idea of the greatness of the church, and a desire that it should occupy a high social position. I had myself an earnest longing for the conversion of my personal friends and their children; but this notion of the greatness of the church in the eyes of Christ seemed to me quite unfounded and offensive to the Savior. I asked of God with importunity for souls, *souls*, SOULS, let them be young or old, friends or strangers, wise or unwise; I cared not who or in what position; publicans and harlots were as good as any. And I endeavored to inculcate this idea on the minds of the members of the church."

It may be remarked, at this point, that the Rev. Dr. Granger, the former pastor, had for many years been in failing health; for two years he had been absent in the East Indies; and during the entire period of his pastorate his singular executive ability had led his brethren to lay upon him many engrossing labors connected with the benevolent and missionary organizations (both state and national) of the denomination. The church numbered about four hundred members. The strong attachment felt by the members to the church led them in many cases to retain their relation to it, though living in very remote parts of the city. The result was to give to the body an appearance of strength quite factitious, and to render a faithful visiting of all the members peculiarly laborious.

Dr. Wayland writes, —

"I was well aware that the families of the church and congregation were in need of real, pastoral visitation. This had greatly gone out of use. Several of the families told me that no minister had called on them for many years. By the visiting needed among them, I do not mean a mere call of civility to inquire into the health of parents and children, and to manifest a neighborly regard for their welfare. This is scarcely the business of men charged with matters of grave importance. Such service is required of men in no other occupation of life.

"The visiting to which I refer is that which has for its end exclusively the spiritual good of those to whom it is made. This I attempted to carry on. I resolved that I would visit no house without introducing the subject of religion as a personal matter, and that in every case, unless it was manifestly best to omit it, I would pray with the family. I commenced this work immediately, and it was nearly a year before I could complete it. Several circumstances prevented my doing it in as short a time as I expected. My house was so far from the centre of the city, from which the residences of the members extended in all directions, that I was obliged to spend a large portion of my time on the road. I found also that I had not the physical ability to walk as I could some years before. It will be asked, Why did you not ride? I answer, To do so would frequently have required the time of another person; but most of all, I could not ride to see poor persons who never ride. It would have an appearance of social superiority, which is hostile to the spirit of the gospel. Besides, it was very difficult to find many of the persons whom I visited. It was on this account much easier to go on foot.

"I discovered that I could visit fewer persons in a day than I at first supposed possible. One cannot begin this work very early in the day, for no one cares to see you until the household labor is completed. Then comes the interruption of dinner, and for half the year the time between this and dark is very short. And, moreover, it takes more time to make such a visit as I have spoken of than an ordinary call. The condition of the parishioner's mind must be ascertained, that you may know what kind of truth is to be administered. If there are several persons in a family to be seen, a considerable portion of time is thus, of necessity (though most profitably), consumed.

"This kind of visiting, however, reached but a portion of the parish — the mothers and daughters. The male members of families were generally absent. It was necessary to follow them to shops, counting-rooms, or wherever they were accustomed to spend the day. I talked to men wherever I could find them alone, or could draw them away for private conversation. Sometimes I would meet them in the street, and accompany them far enough to give the necessary warning. In this manner I believe I held personal conversation on religion with by far the greater part of the adults of the parish. I say this, of course, in general terms, for accidents will prevent one from seeing persons; and when they live at a great distance, the opportunity may not present itself for going so far to see them again. And I will add that in all this labor, which became more and more pleasant and easy to me, I never once was treated rudely, or as if I was not doing the business most appropriate to a minister. Some cases I found of persons steeped in worldliness, who evidently did not wish to be disturbed; but by far the greater part were thankful, and were by this means personally attached to me and to the services of the sanctuary, and their hearts were opened to the instructions and warnings of the gospel. I record with sadness that in many cases, even of those who had been associated all their lives with professors of religion, I was told that I was the first one who had ever personally conversed with them on the condition of their souls.

"It will, perhaps, be thought that I had some natural aptitude for this kind of labor. Not at all. In the commencement of my ministry, it was as difficult for me as for any one. I gained upon it a little during my pastorate in Boston. I was in the habit, while in college, of seizing upon such opportunities as offered to converse solemnly with my pupils, though I confess with sorrow that I did not make these occasions as frequent as I might have done. When, however, I undertook this pastorate, I resolved, in the strength of God, that I would carry religion with me into every house I visited, and, so far as was in my power, edify saints and call sinners to repentance. Having resolved to do it, and having once commenced, the rest was easy. I found that it was of no use to begin afar off, and gradually come to it, through a long reach of indirect approach. If I tried this, I was in great danger of failing. My custom was, after the first incidental conversation, to address the persons directly, and inquire into the prospects which they had for eternity. It soon became known that this was my habit, so that sometimes, upon my saying to a family, 'I suppose you know what I have called for,' the ready answer would be, 'I suppose we do.'"

He carried this portion of his labor to the utmost limit of physical endurance; indeed, he trespassed against the laws of health, in a manner that in another he would have reproved, and that can scarcely be commended in him. Setting out from his home as early in the forenoon as would allow time for the houses to be in order, he would continue visiting till noon. Sometimes he would accept an invitation to dine wherever the noon found him, sometimes he would eat something in a restaurant, and not seldom he would continue his labors without any refreshment, sustained by meat which the world knew not of; for his meat and his drink were to do the will of Him that sent him, and to finish his work. And when the afternoon was ended, if there was to be a meeting at the church in the evening, he would go into the vestry, and would wait there till the hour of service. A friend has said, —

"A number of times, on Wednesday evening, I went into the vestry before the congregation had gathered; and at first, thought there was no one there. But presently I would see Dr. Wayland lying down on one of the seats; he was worn out with the incessant visiting and talking of the day, and was resting for a few minutes."

In his visiting he steered clear of the platitudes of religion, and while kind, sympathizing, full of charity, he probed the conscience by his searching inquiries. "What does your hope rest upon? How are you living?" And he rarely failed to ask, to the confounding of many a complacent professor, "What are you *doing* for Jesus Christ?" A visit from him was an event in the spiritual history of a household, and the impression was deepened as it became the topic of conversation with other families who had received a similar impulse.

He endeavored to proceed systematically, but was also greatly guided by the intimations of the divine Spirit. Sometimes he would say, "I must go and visit this or that particular family;" and on being asked, "Why do you go there, when you have been at work all day, and are already tired?" he would reply, "I must go, for I feel called there." Once he felt a peculiar call to visit a certain family, though he was ignorant of anything in their circumstances calling for especial notice. He went, and found the mother of the family sick of fatal disease. He enjoyed a very solemn and profitable interview with her, and it was the last occasion on which such a conversation could have taken place.

He referred any instance of successful labor to the same divine guidance. It was at one time strongly impressed on his mind that he must call and converse with Mr. S. He went to his counting-room, but failed to see him. On his return from this unsuccessful visit, he met Mr. M., and conversed with him. This conversation led to his conversion. "And then I knew," said Dr. Wayland, "that it was to Mr. M. that I had been sent, though I had supposed that it was to Mr. S."

He has said that he had no aptitude for introducing religious appeals in his conversation. Whether he had such facility naturally, we do not know; but no one could fail to remark, at this period of his life, that he was eminently wise in winning souls, and that the word spoken in season was like apples of gold in baskets of silver. This skill proceeded from a profound sense of religious realities, conjoined with a warm affection for those whom he addressed, and was perfected by many years of fidelity in the discharge of this duty. One can hardly say whether his earnestness in preaching the word out of season as well as in season, or his singular felicity in avoiding offence and in winning attention, was the more remarkable. Once he was spending the evening in a social party at the house of his neighbor, Professor ——. We imagine that this was before his pastorate began, as he rarely or never allowed himself even so slight a relaxation during that period. A young lady, whom he had often met, was present, who, though most amiable in character, was destitute of personal religion, and was in fact averse to evangelical views. He chanced during the evening to be alone with her, in a part of the room somewhat retired, and he said to her, "Emma, I am very glad to see you so happy; but you know that the birds want a cover to fly under when it storms." These kind words opened the way for a conversation. The next time he saw her, he sought to deepen the impression. Meanwhile he prayed for her without ceasing. She strove long against the influences of the Spirit, but at last yielded her heart to God, and became a very lovely and happy Christian. After a few years she was seized with sudden illness attended by delirium, and soon died. In writing to his son, and mentioning her death, Dr. Wayland said, "When all power of influence is lost and gone forever, it is a comfort to remember that you have tried to do good to one who has passed away." Very few circumstances in his life gave him more pleasure than the blessing which followed his word spoken out of season; and what shall we say of the hour when he, in his turn, was led to the enthroned Lamb, by those whom on earth he had guided to the Savior?

He was remarkable for perseverance in spiritual labor. One person says, "He was the only friend who ever talked with me. But he seemed determined that I should be converted, and that he would be the means. He took every opportunity to win me to Christ. When my children were very sick, and my heart was softened, he talked to me, and so he continued, until I was a new creature in Christ; all that there is in me of good, is due, under God, to him."

Meanwhile he had commenced preaching on the Sabbath, and in the vestry on Wednesday evening. He had, as he has said, gained a victory over himself, and renounced the desire of reputation and of literary distinction. "What things were gain to him, them he counted loss for Christ." But this renunciation was far from being synonymous with indifference to the character and adaptation of his discourses. He had drawers full of sermons; but to preach the gospel of Christ, in his estimation, was much more than to "supply the desk," or to "occupy the time." He felt that his sermons, prepared for another audience, expressing a state of mind far less earnest than he now experienced, and appealing with too little directness to the consciences of men, would not accomplish the end for which, with all his soul, he was striving. So he wrote always one, and often two, new sermons for the Sabbath, and prepared, without writing, entirely new discourses for the Wednesday evening service.

He made little use of adornment; if figurative language was employed, it was for the purpose of enlightening the conscience rather than gratifying the taste. He not unfrequently introduced illustrative anecdote, and with all the power of his great soul laid hold on the moral sense of his hearers. His sermons were not characterized peculiarly by logic, but by something — we know not how to name it — that bears the same relation to the conscience that logic does to the mind. He had, as he once said, little confidence in a moral truth that is reached by a long process of reasoning. He believed that the moral sense of men and the Bible were, by the Power that originated both, adapted to each other. Hence he believed, that if the truths of the Word of God were brought nearer to the soul, the effect must be felt. He would take a passage of Scripture, and would first very plainly show its meaning; then he would explain its bearing on the persons before him, considering them, perhaps, according to their station or calling in life, or according to their prominent traits of character. Much of his life had been devoted to the study of human character and motives. And now, using his power of moral analysis, — though it was always kept out of sight, — he read the hearts of men, revealed their motives to themselves, uncovered their subterfuges, and brought them face to face with their duty to God and man, so that a hearer must either say, "I will not do what I plainly see to be my duty," or else he must yield and obey. "His preaching was moral philosophy animated by the spirit of the gospel," a hearer has said of him. "There was one peculiarity in his preaching," said

Rev. Dr. Caswell, "in which he seemed to me to surpass all men to whom I have ever listened. It was in exposing the devices of the heart, and in hunting a guilty sinner from every subterfuge, from every refuge of lies, until he stood before himself in all the deformity of sin. He had deeply studied the laws and modes of action of the human conscience; and few, if any, of the world's great teachers have ever handled it more skilfully." Rev. Dr. Warren (of the class of 1835) once remarked, "No man ever ploughed through my conscience as Dr. Wayland did." "I never," said an experienced Christian, "knew any one make sin appear so hateful and so guilty." His ceaseless, prayerful reading of the Bible gave him topics; and his profound meditation took him out of the region of commonplace. As he dwelt on a text, new depths would open before him, until he almost lost himself in the greatness of his own conceptions. The writer was walking with him during the winter of which we speak, and Dr. Wayland alluded to a subject that had come into his mind for the next Sunday — "God our example." The sermon was afterwards published in "Salvation by Christ," with the text, "Be ye followers of God, as dear children." He spoke of the train of thought: "Example is the most powerful force in morals; this law God has established; and in his dealings with us he acts in accordance with it, setting us an example of the dispositions which he bids us cultivate. He bids us be benevolent, and he is ever conferring benefits on all his creation. He bids us show kindness to our enemies, and he is ever showering blessings on those who have done him all the injury in their power. He bids us sacrifice our all — ourselves — for the good of others." Here his voice fell, and he seemed overpowered; presently he said, "It is almost too much to say — one can hardly express it. He surrenders himself, sacrifices himself for us." When this sermon, which was among the earliest, was preached, a few hearers, of more than usual discernment, recognized in it what was to be the spirit of his ministry, and knew, with prophetic inspiration, that his was to be a ministry of sacrifice.

Certainly, never in his life did his sermons contain more of the divine ideas; and his constant intercourse with his people, his daily, almost hourly, sympathy with their anxieties, with their temptations, their dangers, gave to his words a present power, a life that carried them home to the bosoms of men. It was often remarked, that one could tell by the preaching on the Sabbath what features of character, what objections, what excuses, he had encountered during the week. The sins of common life he brought into the pulpit, and held them up that he might warn men against them — the frauds common in business, the ruinous example often set by professing Christians, the indulgence of disciples in worldly and sinful pleasures. He often said, in public and in private, that many a professor, blameless in his exterior and attendant on all the ordinances, was, by reason of covetousness, in as great a danger of losing his soul as is the drunkard, the swearer, the gambler. He was lifted by the divine Spirit above all fear or favor. After reproving, as he only could do, some prevalent sin, "Pardon me," he said. Then recovering himself, "But no, I don't want your pardon for telling you the truth." He once said, "I find, as I visit among you, professors of religion, members of this church, who rarely or never come to meeting, who do not pray, or read the Bible, and all say that they have no enjoyment in religion; and yet they would not give up their hope for a thousand worlds. They are trusting that they will yet be brought back to the enjoyment of the favor of God." Then, with startling earnestness, "And who are you, that God should work a miracle, and reclaim you while you are living in the neglect of every means of grace and every help to piety which he has revealed in his word?"

He sought to undeceive those who entertained the impression that God had regard for any particular church or organization, otherwise than as it is peculiar for its good works, its piety, its faith, its humility, and its holy activity. His whole soul sympathized with the indignant exclamation of Chalmers (often quoted by him) in reply to those who suggested that his zeal was inflamed by a desire to build up the Free Church of Scotland. "Who cares for the Free Church, compared with the Christian good of the people of Scotland? Who cares about any church, but as an instrument of Christian good?"

We presume it need not be said that he was profoundly impressed with the truth of the distinctive principles of the Baptist denomination. On suitable occasions he exhibited these principles in his preaching; yet never as barren theories; always as principles vitally connected with practice. Thus, in a sermon from Acts viii. 36, 37, — "See, here is water; what doth hinder me to be baptized? And Philip said, If thou believest with all thine heart, thou mayest," — after exhibiting clearly the teachings of this and of kindred passages in regard to the mode and the subject of baptism, he thus closes: —

"Such, my brethren, is an outline of our belief on this subject. We think that we are in this matter following in the footsteps of our Lord and Savior. But let us, in closing, observe the course of conduct to which this belief of necessity pledges us.

"We believe that no one is a subject for baptism unless he is a truly regenerate person. We reject the opinion that every citizen has a right to this ordinance, or that uniting with a church is a means of grace which unconverted men may employ for their spiritual improvement. Our doctrine is all expressed in the words of the text, "If thou believest with all thine heart, thou mayest." Hence it becomes us to take all the pains in our power to discover whether those who present themselves as candidates for this ordinance give competent evidence that they are regenerate persons, the sincere disciples of Christ. If we fail in this respect, of what use is our belief? What is the value of correct principles if they do not govern our practice?

"But this is not all. Our belief in this matter involves our belief in the spirituality of the church. We hold that no one has any right to continue a member of a church, save so long as he exhibits in his life the evidence of discipleship to Christ. We often err in the reception of members. We have not the gift of discerning spirits. Hence we are liable to admit to the visible church those in whom the seed has sprung up, but in whom it has subsequently been choked by the cares of the world, the deceitfulness of riches, and the lusts of other things. Such persons may continue through life guilty of no breach of human law, and yet give not the slightest evidence of being governed by the law of God. They may neglect the worship and ordinances of the house of God; they may choose their associates from among the worldly and profane; they may neglect prayer in the family and in secret; they may be worldly, covetous, extortioners, unjust, lovers of pleasure more than lovers of God. Men frequently, by a gradual decline, fall as far as this from the character of discipleship, and yet the decline has been so gradual that at no particular time did there seem any opportunity for discipline. But, if such is the case, of what use is our belief in the spirituality of a church? If we allow Christ to be thus dishonored among us, our belief in the spirituality of the church will not save us. Let us, then, exercise a godly jealousy over each other. Let us watch over each other in the Lord. If a brother is wandering from the path, let us labor to reclaim him. If we cannot reclaim him, we must separate him from our company. If our principles be true, we must carry them out; for thus alone shall we make manifest their excellence. If, while we hold the truth, we do not put it in practice, what do we more than others? Nay, we hold up the truth to reprobation, by showing, in our practice, that it is utterly valueless."

His preaching might perhaps have been called severe, coming from any one whose tenderness of heart, wide benevolence, and profound sincerity, were less apparent.

It was often remarked, that from no one else would such absolute plainness have been endured.

Thus, by manifestation of the truth, he commended himself to every man's conscience in the sight of God; and men, as they listened, and as their hearts were revealed to themselves, felt as though they were standing face to face with the day of judgment.

Simple and scriptural as he was in the pulpit, he was even more so in the desk of the vestry. He writes, —

"The weekly lecture on Wednesday evening was, I think, a useful service. I spoke without notes, after reflection, on a subject which, at the time, seemed appropriate to the wants of the hearers. I endeavored to set aside all formality, and to bring myself in direct contact with the consciences of the people. The audience immediately began to increase in numbers and in solemnity. The attendance was large through the summer, and, indeed, continued so until the close of my temporary pastorate. I seemed to speak from my heart directly to the hearts of my hearers; and, sometimes (to use the words of the apostle), 'I think that I had the Spirit of the Lord.' Why could I not preach so in the pulpit on the Sabbath? The audience was mostly the same. I do not think that I was afraid. I generally wrote my sermons. The writing was a sort of screen between me and my hearers. I deeply regret that I did not overcome this foolish habit. I should have saved much time for other labors, and I believe that I should soon have learned to preach more effectually.

"Does the difficulty of which I speak grow out of anything in the construction of our houses of worship? or is it owing to the time of holding the service? Persons are always more susceptible to impressions in the evening. Can anything be done to afford a remedy in this matter? I have heard many persons relate the same experience, particularly that excellent preacher, Dr. J. W. Alexander. I do not know a better thing for the ministry than would be done, if we could only remove the vestry to the church. I, perhaps, did something in this direction. At any rate, I believe that I so preached that my hearers understood me, and knew that I was anxious for their salvation.

But (I know not why) I could not, or did not, attain to the freedom, the nearness to the hearts and consciences of the people, in the audience-room above, that I attained in the vestry. Whether I am to recover my former health I know not. If, however, I should be permitted to preach again, I will certainly do what is in my power to learn to preach directly to men, looking them in the face, and not looking at the paper on the desk. Should I live to make the attempt, may the Spirit of God enable me to do it successfully."

The opinion which Dr. Wayland expresses, that the Wednesday evening services in the lecture-room were more productive of good than the public and formal utterances of the Sabbath, is probably correct. Some, at least, of the reasons for this fact, every person accustomed to public speaking will appreciate. The audience-room of the church is very large (the house having been built, in part, to accommodate the college Commencements), and is not filled on any ordinary occasion. The pulpit is high and massive. The singing, during most of the period of his labors, was performed by a choir, the congregation being listeners. There was as little as possible to bring speaker and hearer into sympathy. The whole service suggested decorum and propriety. The lecture-room, capable of holding perhaps four hundred persons, while large enough for comfort, is no larger than a speaker can easily fill, while retaining his ordinary conversational tone. The desk is low, and does not remove the speaker from the audience. The singing was united and heartfelt. The speaker could readily watch the faces before him, and mark each varying shade of emotion. Every one felt at home. The walls had been vocal with prayer, and the sob, and the falling tear, were familiar. In the vestry his language was unpremeditated, but the *matter* was the result of prolonged and intense meditation and feeling. When he stood before the audience in the lecture-room, looking into the eyes of those, many of whom had been his neighbors for thirty years, of those whose parents he had known and loved, and, filled and inspired by the divine wisdom, poured forth all the emotion of his soul, he probably reached a point of impressiveness that he never elsewhere attained.

A few years previously, Dr. Wayland resumed the ladies' Bible class, referred to in Chap. XV. of Vol. I. But this exercise, with the needful preparation, consumed the greater part of a day. As his labors increased, he found it impossible to spare so much time, and was compelled to suspend it, until the cessation of his pastoral cares left him more leisure.

To Rev. Dr. Anderson: —

"January 11, 1857.

"My dear Anderson: Our brother Granger has been called up higher. . . . As our circle of intimate friends grows smaller, let us draw nearer together. I wish you and Mrs. A. could come, when it is pleasant, and see us. We have labored together a good deal: may we not, like the apostles, 'rest a while' here 'in a desert place'? In the midst of your business you have 'no leisure so much as to eat.'

". . . Come and see us if you can. You, Anderson, are one of the very few men left whom I knew intimately thirty years since, and our intimacy and love remain undiminished."

To Mr. and Mrs. W., on hearing of the death of their son: —

"March 22, 1857.

"My dear Friends: It was not until yesterday that I learned of your sore affliction. It is sorrowful beyond expression, and I can only think of you as crushed and overwhelmed. Of the dear and most lovely child I dare not speak. Were I with you, I feel as if I should, like the friends of Job, sit down for days without uttering a word.

"Yet still, there is a word that may be spoken — one word, which alone is sufficient to quiet the soul in the most frenzied agitation. It is God. In the immeasurable depth of his perfections we may find repose even in the tumult of the deepest sorrow. The God of infinite wisdom and goodness, so good that he gave his only begotten Son for us, is surely a Being to be trusted, even though everything created fades away. Nay, may we not surrender a child to Him who gave his only begotten Son for us? Try and creep under the shadow of his wing; you will there find peace, and it is nowhere else to be found. Earthly helpers fail in all real sorrow; God alone can sustain us when support is truly needed."

To a minister: —

"March 4, 1857.

"You know I have undertaken the pastoral office *pro tempore.* I have preached twice, and am beginning to do some visiting. I intend to give myself to it as much as I can. The appearance of things is interesting. We hope for a revival.

"I am now laboring with the *church.* I want, by consecutive sermons, to fan the flame. I am preaching and visiting, and I have some faith that God will bless my labor. If he does not at this time pour out his Spirit upon us, we may almost despair."

"April 10, 1857.

"I am rejoiced to perceive, by your letter, that you are reading the New Testament with sufficient attention to see the difference between the teachings of Christ and those of his apostles. Keep on studying it. Bring your own heart to it. Preach your sermons first to yourself. Realize them in your own soul, if you would realize them in the hearts of your people. An intellectually prepared sermon will reach the intellect; a spiritually prepared sermon will reach the spirit. May the good Lord make you faithful in all things. I am preaching as well as I can, but without much visible result. I endeavor to say with entire plainness whatever is given me. I do not know if the people will bear it. I must, however, deliver my message.

"I wrote to Mr. Finney a few days ago, and received a reply. It is remarkable that two men almost ignorant of each other should see things so much alike."

To his son: —

"I pause in the midst of a sermon to congratulate you

on the anniversary of your birth. How old you are, I do not remember,* but at all events old enough to make me feel like an aged man. You are rapidly approaching the maturity of your intellect. You are now as capable as you will ever be, or very nearly so. Some things you will be able to do better, some more rapidly, and some more wisely; but for efficiency you are approaching very near to the table-land, the water-shed of your life.

"The ministry is a great work. Homer's highest conception of a man was, that he was *αναξ ανδρων*, or else a tamer of horses. The Christian conception is a converter of men. This is better than to be a political leader, or an eloquent orator, or anything else after which men may aspire. Try to be this in simplicity, and may the Holy Spirit lead you into all truth.

"I bless God especially for the unity of spirit and affection which he has given us all. That we are an undivided family is one of his richest gifts. I rejoice that I have entire confidence in the principles and in the affection of my children, and that, as I believe, they have confidence in me. May God increase and perpetuate it, so that when I am called away, they may be always on the side of truth, and abound in love to each other. I am glad that you come here when you can. Always do so when it is possible without neglecting any duty. I have always regretted that it was not in my power to visit my parents more frequently.

To a minister: —

"April 20, 1857.

"I have kept steadily at work since I commenced here, and have done nothing but labor for the First Church. There is, I think, a little improvement. I visit all I can, and have preached twice on Sunday and once in the week, without intermission. Frequently I write two and always one sermon for the Sabbath. I am, however, more and more satisfied that this is a useless labor, and I hope soon to begin to preach once a day without notes.

* This was one of his idiosyncrasies. He never remembered the ages of his children or other relatives, and probably could not have recalled his own age without calculation.

I see that I am in danger of becoming confined to them, and the writing consumes valuable time.

"There are some small indications of good."

To the same: —

"June 25, 1857.

"I am only pretty well. I have closed my Bible class for the summer. This will be some relief. I found that the services of Sunday oppressed me on Monday. My brain is growing old, and will not do as much work as it once did. I cannot well press it. I feel more and more that my opportunity of doing good to any one is short.

To the same: —

"July 6, 1857.

"I see with great pain, in to-day's paper, the death of W. L. Marcy, one of our best and ablest men. I rather think that as a negotiator and diplomatist he was superior to Webster, though most men would laugh at me for saying so. The fact is, that a large portion of Webster's mind was occupied with the thought of the presidency, and what was left was not superior to the minds of other able men. This shows the importance of having the eye single. Ministers fail more frequently from a want of this than from almost any other cause."

To his sister: —

"Poor, dear Marcy has been continually in my mind since his death. I had a very sincere regard for him. May it be, that he had been reconciled to God! Perhaps this is bad theology, yet I cannot but feel it."

He writes, —

"My labors were, at first, mainly confined to the church. I endeavored to set before them the character of the disciples of Christ, and the offence caused to the world if professors of religion manifested their godliness only on the Sabbath. I urged upon all, repentance and a return to the first works. The congregation increased, but for some time there appeared little change. At last there seemed some thoughtfulness. A few were baptized. This had a quickening effect on the church, and Christians became more prayerful. The female members, especially, were awakened, and abounded in prayer. To their efforts and prayers the progress of the church must, under God, be principally ascribed. As two or three were, from time to time, added by baptism, the flame which the Holy Spirit had kindled was kept alive, and became more intense and pervading. This was, however, very gradual; and, at the best, it was but a smouldering fire, leaving a large part of the church very little warmed." — *MS.*

In the latter part of July, 1857, he went to Saratoga Springs; but, after a few days' absence, he was recalled by the circumstances of the parish, and especially by the death of his friend, Mr. Moses B. Ives.* At the request of the corporation of the university, Dr. Wayland prepared a discourse on the services of Mr. Ives, many passages in which afford a touching insight into his own character.

"Again am I called upon, after too short an interval, to commemorate the virtues of one of my friends. The men who, on my coming to this city, received me with a kindness which has never abated, and with whom, for thirty years, I have labored in the cause of education and

* There were few of the citizens of Providence for whom Dr. Wayland cherished a stronger attachment than for Mr. Ives; on the other hand, no one was more untiring than Mr. Ives in his public-spirited regard for the interests of the university, and in his acts of personal friendship to Dr. Wayland. It is not too much to say, that without his large-hearted munificence, the subscription of 1850, and the reorganization of the university could not have succeeded. A single circumstance illustrates the spirit in which he discharged the office of treasurer, which he held from 1825 until his death. He had invested six thousand five hundred dollars of the funds of the college in a note of the Bay State Mills, indorsed by Lawrence, Stone, & Co. The investment was regarded as not only good, but eminently desirable. In course of time the makers and the indorsers became bankrupt, and the paper was worthless. Mr. Ives at once assumed the indebtedness, and put into the treasury his check for the whole amount. He never spoke of the act, and it was only by accident that it became known to the president, by whom it was communicated to the writer.

benevolence, have, for the most part, passed away. The good and the great, who were then the guiding lights of this city, have sunk beneath the horizon; and the memory of many of them is already fading from recollection. I seem to myself almost the representative of a bygone generation. And now another link that bound me to the earth is severed. The man who has so often cheered me in disappointment, and counselled me in success, lies low beneath the sods of the valley, and I shall meet him no more until the resurrection of the just. If Mr. Ives supposed a man to be honest and well intentioned, difference of opinion never arrested, for a moment, the genial flow of his kindly regard. On this subject I can speak from experience, as well as from observation. During the long period of our acquaintance, many questions arose in which our views were widely dissimilar. We were constitutionally unlike, he naturally looking upon the past, and I as instinctively turning to the future. Hence the lines of conduct which we pursued were sometimes divergent. I know that, for the moment, it pained him, that I should act, as he believed, unwisely; but I never perceived that these differences chilled in his bosom an emotion of kindness, or modified, in any respect, the friendship which so long subsisted between us." *

While the financial distress of 1857 was pressing upon the country, Dr. Wayland preached, on the 11th and 25th of October, two sermons, designed to impress and deepen the moral lesson of these disastrous days. Though prepared in the discharge of his ordinary parochial duties, the discourses attracted marked attention, from their singular adaptation to the wants of the public mind, and were published in compliance with the request of many citizens.

To a minister: —

"You speak of consecutive discourses for Wednesday

---

* Before opportunity offered for the public delivery of this discourse, the pecuniary embarrassments of 1857 had pre-occupied the public mind to the exclusion of every other topic. It was therefore published without having been pronounced.

evening. Some men succeed in such a thing. I never did. I would rather each week preach what seemed to be given me. And I would take less pains in *making out a discourse*, than in *imbuing my own mind with it, and feeding upon it myself*. We err in relying on our own intellect, rather than on the Spirit of God. . . . The prospect for winter is gloomy. There is danger of famishing among the poor. We are trying to economize all we can, to have something to give to the needy."

To a minister: —

"December 3, 1857.

"I am greatly rejoiced to learn that your mind is drawn in the direction you mention. You may be assured that we shall not receive the blessing of the conversion of men, unless we are wholly given to it. If we do a little in politics, a little in philanthropy, and a little in preaching, we shall accomplish but little in anything. The philanthropy which we need for our souls' good can be found in our daily duties. The more of this a minister does, the better, if it be personal; but these associations I think less and less of. Try to forget yourself and the fear of all but Christ. If we have reputation with the Master, it is all that the servant can desire. Strive for the conversion of souls, strive for it wholly, looking not for the conversion of the rich and intelligent, but of all men, especially the poor. And you may be sure that the less you honor yourself, the more Christ will honor you."

To the same: —

"December 14, 1857.

"I am encouraged by your letters to hope that you will soon see the fruit of your labors. May God give you a simple desire to glorify him, and that he will certainly gratify. Get out of yourself, and, like Paul, be willing to be a fool for Christ's sake; that is, let nothing connected with yourself prevent you from preaching so as to reach the consciences of men. Ask the Spirit of God what you shall say, and say it without regard to anything but the will of God. This will be the sure way of attaining a blessing. I am glad that you are carrying the gospel to the poor. This is the field which Christ cultivated, and on which his blessing is most apt to rest.

"There is little new here of any moment. There is some more earnestness in other congregations. On the first Sabbath I baptized two converts; and a few other cases promise well. An old and leading church, or one so esteemed, can hardly stoop low enough to receive a blessing."

In June, 1858, he was invited to become permanently the pastor of the church, but did not accept the invitation, though he continued his ministerial labors.

CHAPTER IX.

THE REVIVAL OF 1858. — CORRESPONDENCE. — DR. WAYLAND IN THE REVIVAL. — PERSONAL SOLICITUDE. — CARE FOR THE YOUNG. — PRAYER MEETINGS. — PREACHING. — RELIGIOUS ENTERPRISE. — CONGREGATIONAL SINGING. — THE GREAT SOURCE OF HIS INFLUENCE. — CLOSE OF HIS LABORS.

FOLLOWING the commercial reverses of 1857 came the revival of 1858. We resume the narrative of Dr. Wayland.

"In time, the revival which had overspread most of the cities and towns in the Northern States, through the power of the Holy Spirit, visited Providence. Prayer meetings in the morning, noon, and evening were attended by multitudes. On one or two occasions, when these were held with us, the lecture-room could not accommodate all the the people. Persons of all beliefs, and of no beliefs, and of all classes in society, attended. The solemnity was deep and affecting, and I believe that the impression was universal, 'This is the finger of God.' It was quite common for persons to rise and ask for the prayers of the congregation. Still more common was it for those who had, as they believed, given their hearts to the Savior, to express their new-found hope, and their reason for it, and to narrate the exercises through which they had passed. The congregations on the Sabbath and on Wednesday evenings were increased, and the solemnity which attended them was so great as to be by many persons distinctly remembered up to this time. Several of those converted with us joined other churches, being here only temporarily for the purpose of education. During my connection with the church I baptized fifty-one.

Several were baptized by the present pastor immediately after his coming. I think the number ostensibly benefited was not less than seventy."

To a minister: —

"I rejoice with you at the appearance of good among your people. God hears prayer, and blesses those who honor him.

"But you do not want any help from abroad, and I would not say that I did. You can do all the work yourself, with the aid of your best brethren and sisters. It will be a noble opportunity to develop the talent and piety of your church. As to yourself, all you need is the guidance of the Holy Spirit, which will be given abundantly, if you humbly seek it. Encourage the people to prayer, self-examination, conversation with sinners, abstraction from the world, and looking up to the Spirit alone for all the blessing. Do not aim at a great and temporary excitement; but pray and labor for a continual revival. The spirit of a revival should always be the spirit of the church. In a word, cast yourself on God for all, and read nothing but the Bible. Use this time specially to study the New Testament with the aid of the Spirit of God.

"Again I say, do not go to Egypt for help. Go to God with everything, and keep in his presence. You will learn more in this manner than in any other. It is not pleasing to the Master that we should ask others to do what he is willing and able to do for us.

"Try to keep your people low in the dust before God, prayerfully laboring for him. This will insure the greatest blessing. Have no revival expedients, that is, devices to commit people; to hold them up before the congregation for effect. Be perfectly true, and do nothing for any other motive than you profess."

To the same: —

"I rejoice greatly in your prospect. God grant that the heavens may gather blackness, and there be a sound of an abundance of rain. I want you to gain all the good of it in your own soul, and therefore wish you to derive all your aid directly from the Holy Spirit. There is no opportunity for becoming acquainted with him like a revival. We had very bad weather for our Fast Day meeting on Wednesday. The attendance was small, but the aspect solemn. There is, however, no revival here, unless, perhaps, one is beginning in Mr. Bixby's church.

To his sister: —

". . . I want much to see you, but I am let hitherto. My practical duties and responsibilities occupy all my time and thoughts, and, thus far, all to very little purpose. A few have been added, more come out to hear, and this is almost all that can be said. The church has called me to be the pastor. I have taken time to think of it, but I, as yet, see no light in that direction. I think I shall be guided aright, for I believe it is my desire to do what the Lord would have me. . . . There is considerable attention here among several of the churches, but nothing, as yet, of a powerful character. May God grant us some souls. Mr. Bixby, the missionary, has a greater blessing than any other of our ministers. The character of the persons converted is quite remarkable — mostly heads of families and those who will be very useful. He has simply proclaimed Christ, and God has blessed his labor. God will honor the preaching of the Cross. O that I knew how to preach it, so that he would bless it!"

To a minister: —

"A church must be in fault when there are not additions every month. I am glad that you are receiving accessions to your congregation from the poor. . . . Try to preach in entire simplicity: philosophical discussions in theology, which magnify ourselves, have little favor with God. Let us forget ourselves in striving to serve him."

To the same: —

"Were I visiting a place, and attending such meetings as we have had, I should have said, 'This is a time of revival.' But no apparent effect is produced, and there is no increase of attention. It looks as though all would pass away without result. . . . There seems something peculiar among our old churches here. Nothing moves them. All is dry as the mountains of Gilboa. It may be to illustrate the sovereignty of God that he withholds a blessing, or it may be because of our sinful formality and conformity to the world."

To his son: —

"I am now in my sixty-third year. Not many more birthdays await me. I have, on a few occasions, used my brain pretty hard, and I sometimes fear that it will never be wholly restored to its former power. But this is all as God wills. I have nothing to do with it.

"The attention here is on the increase. We had a solemn meeting on Wednesday evening. The morning prayer meeting to-day was encouraging. I have written to Deacon Lincoln to suggest united prayer for members of Congress. A revival in Congress would be a blessing to the world, and would show to all people what God could do. I feel just now more encouraged than ever before to hope that God is near. May you and I both do our duty here, and, bringing many souls to glory, meet with joy before the throne."

To a minister: —

"March 25, 1858.

"The interest here is increasing slowly. God evidently means to do it all himself. Attention is very general. All the prayer meetings are well attended. Conversions are few, and grace is not largely poured out. The most signal fact is the repentance of —— ——. At our meeting on Tuesday evening he was present, and made a most humble confession, which dissolved the meeting in tears. At the business men's meeting on Wednesday he did the same thing. He seems a real penitent. It is producing a great impression. It is all encouraging, but we hope for greater things, commensurate with the universality of the attention. Last evening our vestry was full. God will, I trust, be glorified."

To his son: —

"April 2, 1858.

"I have had your letter lying on my table in full sight ever since it came, watching for an opportunity to answer it. Every evening of the week has been occupied, and the day fully employed. I have read hardly anything but the Bible, and have not had all the time I wanted for that.

"There is, I think, some progress with us; but the characteristics remain the same — very general seriousness, but, comparatively, a small number of conversions."

"April 7, 1858.

"With us the work has assumed a somewhat new aspect. The interest in the general meetings has declined, I rather think, though I have not attended any since Monday. But there is more interest in the church. Confessions of sin, and mournings over departure from God, are of daily occurrence. We have had several meetings for this purpose, and there was not sufficient time for all that would have spoken. This is most encouraging. Conversions, however, do not as yet multiply. A few are brought in, — some of the young, some old and hardened sinners. What is to be the end I do not know; but if the church arises in the beauty and power of religion, sinners will be converted."

Probably there was not another minister or Christian in Providence who would have written the reminiscences and letters above quoted, and made no allusion to Dr. Wayland's labors in the revival of 1858. During the year preceding its appearance, the tone of spirituality in the church under his ministry had been deepening. Members of other churches would not unfrequently come to listen to his fervent utterances, and carry back to their several congregations something of the sacred flame.

His letters indicate that he had begun to grow conscious of waning vigor at the commencement of 1858; but no sooner did there seem a deeper interest, that offered more than usual encouragement to labor, than he forgot everything but the salvation of his fellow-men. He had completed the pastoral visiting of his charge, but he now recommenced it. If he heard of a case of inquiry or interest at the north end, or out on the borders of Olneyville, he at once set out to visit and converse with the inquirer, declining (for the reasons we have given above) all invitations to ride. As he met his acquaintances on the street, or in shops, he was ever pressing on them the claims of eternity. Sometimes it would be only in a few words. Often, when he met young men of his acquaintance, he would address them tenderly, solemnly, briefly, and then pass on. A member of his family says, "I was walking with him down Thomas Street, when he said to me, 'There is a man who has been avoiding me for weeks. I want to speak to him;' and he left me standing there till he had done so."

His interest in the young was unceasing. However pressed with care, he almost invariably came into the Sabbath school for a little while before meeting, and usually said a few simple words to the pupils. At the young people's meeting, too, he was often present, though leaving the conduct of it to the superintendent, his friend, pupil, and associate, Professor John L. Lincoln. When it was over, he would often offer some suggestion of practical significance. "John," he would say to Professor Lincoln, "did you see that boy in the corner? He wanted to speak. He ought to be encouraged." And when not himself present at the meeting, he never failed to inquire how it went on, and who took part. The superintendent did not feel that he could go through with the work without consulting him as to the means to be adopted for increasing the interest in the school.

Many of the members of Mrs. Buel's Young Ladies' School, who attended the church, will always remember the paternal tenderness and wisdom with which he spoke to them of Christ. He called one day and asked Mrs. Buel to send to the parlor, one by one, those who were his parishioners. It was a memorable visit. The Spirit of God seemed to dissolve all barriers. One young lady was quite determined that he should not move her, nor even speak to her on religion, if she could avoid it. He seemed to have an insight into her feelings, and said to her, "My child, do you want me to talk to you about religion?" She at once burst into tears; her opposition was divinely removed, and he soon saw her a new creature in Christ.

It seemed as if the God whom he served gave him peculiar access to many persons not easily approached. His age, his station, and yet more the character which for thirty years had been patent to the community, entitled him to speak, without fear of giving offence, to men of whatever age and standing. He has related that in but a single instance was he repulsed. A young man replied to his appeal, that free-masonry was all the religion that he wanted.

In the business men's meeting, and in the other prayer meetings, he often charged the person presiding to apply to him the five minutes' rule; but the expressed wish of the audience often constrained him to complete what he was saying. As he rose, he looked, as he was, a tower of strength. His aspect, and voice, and manner were those of one who was living in intimate communion with heaven. All about him conveyed irresistibly the impression that to him spiritual things were a reality, more vivid and palpable than the objects of bodily sense; that he looked not "at the things which are seen, but at the things which are not seen, for the things which are seen are temporal, but the things which are not seen are eternal." His massive frame seemed fitly to body forth the momentum of his spirit and his words. To men of business he spoke with peculiar plainness. "You believe that there is a God; that you have a soul which must live forever. Is it not the plainest dictate of prudence now to secure its eternal happiness? Is it not the greatest madness to neglect it?"

Again he would take up the complaints urged against religion, and would so turn them as to make them the ground of a new and more urgent appeal. After alluding to the objection founded on the lives of many professors of godliness, — after stating it in its strongest form, and sorrowfully conceding all that could be said of the worldliness, the avarice, the sharp-dealing by which often the professions of piety are deformed, then, — "Gentlemen, did I ever ask you to become such Christians as this? This is not Christianity. We ask you to be something unspeakably better; to be the very reverse of all this; to be followers of Christ." How many persons in these meetings received impressions that changed their character for eternity, cannot be known in time. The following incident is one of many. Deacon K. says, —

"I was going out of the hall one day, when I chanced to look around, and saw an aged man, bowed down, and Dr. Wayland leaning over and speaking to him. I went back, and found that it was the venerable Judge P., overwhelmed with anxiety and sorrow. He was expressing his fear that for one so old, who had lived so many scores of years without God, there was no help. Dr. Wayland was most tenderly pointing him to the boundless mercy of God in Christ Jesus."

A few days later, Judge P., in one of the meetings, feelingly spoke of his change of heart and his hopes for eternity. The hoary head became a crown of glory; and he has since finished his course, and entered into rest.

Meanwhile, Dr. Wayland's sermons became even more direct than before, — more affectionate and solemn. He gradually relinquished the practice of writing his discourses. Indeed, it was a necessity. How he could find time for even the most imperfect preparation, when his days and evenings were so engrossed with meetings and conversations, it is hard to conceive. But his unwritten speech did not discover any falling away in continuity of thought, in terseness, and clearness of expression. Men of mature age, strong character, and high mental endowments listened eagerly; and a boy of nine years old said to his mother, with delight, "Why, mother, I can understand every word he says." Not all the proprieties of the sanctuary could exclude the bowed head and the weeping eyes of men not used to tremble or to shed tears.

In the crowded vestry, upon Wednesday evening, he spoke as he had never done before. An atmosphere of heavenly solemnity seemed to pervade the room. From the moment that he rose to open the service with prayer, every heart seemed rapt in devotion. "We have come to meet *thee*," was an expression that he rarely failed to use in the opening petition, and every heart expected to hold communion with Christ. During the period of the service, every worldly thought was excluded. When he pronounced the benediction, it was not a form; it was a tender, affectionate prayer that the favor of Jesus Christ might rest upon all who were present. And then they separated silently, reluctant to speak, lest they should mar and dissipate the heavenly spell.

"Those sermons were scathing to a man's conscience," said a constant and most intelligent hearer. "When he preached from the text, 'Escape for thy life; look not behind thee, neither stay thou in all the plain,' we seemed to see it all, — the burning city, the descending flames, — and we scarcely dared to look behind us as we returned home." Once he spoke from the words, "How shall we escape if we neglect so great salvation;" and "it seemed," says a hearer, "as if he knew what was in the heart of every one there. He appeared to be unconscious of himself, and to speak merely as the Spirit spoke through him." At another time, preaching from the words, "that like as Christ was raised from the dead by the glory of the Father, even so we also should walk with him in newness of life," he said that the contrast between the old unregenerate life and the new divine life is so great, that the Scriptures compare it to the contrast between Christ lying dead in the tomb of Joseph and Christ exalted, glorified with the Father. As he spoke of the gloom of the tomb where the body of Jesus lay, it seemed as if the darkness could be felt; as if one could see the words falling from his lips, so real, so palpable were they. Again he spoke from the words, "This day shalt thou be with me in paradise." He described what it must be to be with Christ in paradise, "and it seemed as if all the sweetness of all the poets was poured into his lips, so unearthly was his delineation of the heavenly state."

His reading of the Scriptures on these occasions, as always, was marked by a depth of feeling such as none of the schools could impart; such as nothing could give but his profound realization of eternal verities. One felt as he read, If a man really believed these to be the words of the living God, he would read them just as Dr. Wayland does. In the vestry he did not always select a long passage. He was guided by his feelings. One of the peculiar felicities of the place was, that he could rise above propriety — the grave of power. Once he read only three verses: "So, when they had dined, Jesus saith to Simon Peter, Simon, son of Jonas, lovest thou me more than these? He saith unto him, Yea, Lord; thou knowest that I love thee. He saith unto him, Feed my lambs. He saith to him the second time, Simon, son of Jonas, lovest thou me? He saith unto him, Yea, Lord, thou knowest that I love thee. He saith unto him, Feed my sheep. He saith unto him the third time, Simon, son of Jonas, lovest thou me? Peter was grieved because he said unto him the third time, Lovest thou me. And he said unto him, Lord, thou knowest all things; thou knowest that I love thee. Jesus saith unto him, Feed my sheep." While he was reading, there had been an attention, a suspense, almost breathless; no one thought of *him* at the time; but in remembering it afterwards, it seemed as if he were inspired while reading. The feeling could hardly have been more profound if the repentant apostle had been visibly present. When he closed the

Bible, there was plainly to be heard a sigh of relief from the fixed and almost painful interest.

In these meetings the tenderness of his heart was as affecting as his boldness of speech was heroic. One evening, when a person, who had been a backslider for twenty years, was speaking of his wandering, and of his repentance, Dr. Wayland sat in the desk, the tears flowing down his cheeks; and when presently he arose to pray for the returning penitent, some moments elapsed before he could command his utterance.

During the closing part of his pastoral care, two movements greatly interested Dr. Wayland, connected with the greater efficiency of the church, and the higher spirituality of its worship. He had but a very slight estimate of the religion that is emotional only, and that ends in no practical efforts for the salvation of mankind. That every disciple should be constantly seeking the increase of piety in his fellow-disciples, and the conversion of the worldly, was a lesson which he ever endeavored to impress by his example, by his private conversation, and by his public teaching. The existence of a church which is doing nothing more than to enjoy the means of grace for itself, and is in no way extending to others the blessings of the gospel, seemed to him a monstrous contradiction in terms. He often alluded to the fact, that one evening in the month is devoted to hearing an account of the labors of Christian people in *heathen* lands for the conversion of souls, and that this is usually the most interesting meeting. "Why," he asked, "do we not meet to hear what we are doing for the cause of God *at home?* Why do we not, at least once a month, learn from our own members what labors they have engaged in to save their neighbors, to reclaim the vicious and wandering, to comfort the forsaken?" Realizing that what is left to hasty impulses, is usually done but imperfectly, and in time ceases to be done at all, he proposed to the church to establish the following system of visitation: —

"The church and congregation shall be distributed, according to their places of residence, into twelve districts.

"A committee of two brethren and two sisters shall be appointed annually to the watch care of each district.

"It is expected of the committees, —

"1. That they will make it their great object to call the unconverted to repentance; to encourage their brethren and sisters to lead a holy and consistent Christian life; to caution them against conformity to the world; to urge them to labor and self-sacrifice for the cause of Christ; and to suggest to them appropriate fields of labor, so that every one may be a living member of the body of Christ.

"2. That they will be in frequent communication with the pastor, and keep him informed of all matters in the several districts which require his special attention, particularly where there is sickness, affliction, or religious thoughtfulness and inquiry; also that they will seek out strangers in the congregation, introducing them to the pastor, and promoting their acquaintance with others.

"3. That the committee, or one of them, will visit every person committed to their charge at least once in six months.

"4. That the several committees will meet on the evening of Tuesday after communion in October, January, April, and July, to confer upon the state of the church, and to devise means for its increase in piety and usefulness, the pastor presiding.

"5. That they shall make report of their doings as often as the church shall direct, with such suggestions as they think proper for promoting the piety of the church and the advancement of Christ's kingdom.

"It is recommended that the members of the church in each district, if practicable, meet once a month, or from time to time, at some private house, for conference and prayer."

The plan was adopted, and continued for a number of years in active operation, with results (alike to those who put forth these Christian efforts, and to those in whose behalf they were exerted) the magnitude and the beneficence of which, eternity alone can reveal.

Nor was he satisfied to have the religious efforts of Christians limited to the single congregation with which they are associated. He was of opinion that every church should maintain mission schools and preaching stations in localities destitute of the gospel. He often dwelt upon the blessing which had attended such a system of evangelical effort among the German Baptist churches, who, beginning in feebleness and poverty, and under the positive prohibition of the civil magistrate, have increased almost beyond parallel. He felt, too, that every church, as soon as its numbers justify the step, should send out a colony, which would soon become a self-supporting interest; and he was equally of opinion that, in any such enterprise, those who feel moved to leave the spot endeared to them by many associations, in order to enlarge the facilities for preaching, and for hearing the gospel, ought to receive the cordial sympathy and aid of those who remain behind. These sentiments he often expressed, and he exemplified them in his own practice.

He had also long desired to see a reform in the service of sacred song. Though himself without any scientific acquaintance with melody, he knew what effect certain styles of music produced on him, he knew what belonged to moral impressiveness, and he thought he knew what manner of conducting this portion of worship was most conducive to devotion. That four persons, perhaps destitute of all pious feeling, should have in their hands this part of the service of God's house, introducing music utterly incapable of arousing a single religious emotion, holding themselves independent of all control, and rejecting any suggestions from the body of Christian worshippers, seemed to him utterly monstrous. He fully acquiesced in the remark of the late venerated Dr. Sharp, that the singing, as practised in most of our churches, is an abomination to God. He sometimes said, while acting as pastor, that often, when he had read a solemn and impressive hymn, the moral and devotional effect would have been greater to spend the time in perfect silence, than to have the hymn sung according to the prevalent method.

Holding these views, it will readily be understood that he was an advocate of *congregational singing;* and he ardently wished to introduce this mode of worship into the church for which he was laboring.

In urging the desired reform, he was not unfrequently met by the objection that there was not volume enough of voice in the congregation to carry it through. "So," he said, "one afternoon I gave out Old Hundred, and made the particular request that all would join in the singing; and you could have heard them at the top of Angell Street. That settled the question of the volume of voice." Finally, as the result of his repeated appeals, and no doubt in a great degree from personal regard to him, and from a desire to afford him gratification, the measure was adopted. Wishing to insure the successful inauguration of the reform, he invited Dr. Lowell Mason to come and address the people upon the method of carrying on this portion of worship. Dr. Mason accepted the invitation, and by his eminence in his profession, and his profound knowledge of the science of sacred music, removed many objections to the proposed change, and offered several most useful suggestions. Dr. Mason writes, —

"I well remember a remark which he made to me, after long and repeated conversations on sacred song, in reference to which we were fully agreed. 'Is it not strange,' he asked, 'that I, who am ignorant of music scientifically or artistically, should so exactly agree with one who has devoted half a century to its study, practically and theoretically, under such great advantages?' My answer was, in substance, this: 'Sir, your good common sense, and quick, intuitive perception of right, have done more for you than much study, experience, and observation can do for one less favored in these respects.'"

A few Sabbaths before the close of Dr. Wayland's labors with the church, the voice of the whole congregation was heard praising God.

In thus attempting a narration of Dr. Wayland's pastorate, we are aware that we have presented a most inadequate view of the sources and channels of the virtue which went forth from him. The chief influence which he exerted during those sixteen months of labor, during those months of universal revival, was that of his own character. "The great feature of his ministry," says a hearer, "was not this or that particular measure; it was his absolute and undivided consecration to the work." Another, an eminent practitioner of law, says, "It was the most wonderful exhibition of goodness that I ever saw or conceived of."

Since his death, two members of the bar were conversing, one of whom said, "I do not know how it is; I never felt so towards any one else, but I always had a strange sensation of awe whenever I met him, or saw him. I do not know what it was owing to." "Do you not know?" said the other; "why, you felt the influence of his almost superhuman goodness."

It was his *character* which afforded to men a demonstration of the divineness of the faith he preached. It was this which gave power to his words, and to his tone, as he read the Scriptures or gave out a hymn; to every movement of his hand as he closed the Bible, or as with a wave of his arm he seemed to put aside the excuses of the procrastinating, and the objections of the caviller; and this it was which both exhibited to the Christian the true standard of the religious life, and animated him to its attainment.

"There is a force in the natural world which has received the designation of catalytic. It is sometimes called the power of presence. Bodies in which it resides have the marvellous property of transmuting other bodies by mere contact into their likeness. The force is too subtle for analysis, and has hitherto defied all attempts at explanation. Philosophers have contented themselves with simply noting and naming it. The fact has its analogy in the moral world. There are men who possess a similar power of presence. An influence goes out from them equally controlling and alike incapable of analysis or philosophical explanation. President Wayland presented a most striking example of this. It was felt by all who came near him. His power as a speaker and as a teacher depended largely upon it. The same utterances might come from others, but how slight, comparatively, their effect! The same truths might be impressed by others, but how unlike their moulding influence! The same principles might be inculcated by others, but how different their transforming power! Behind the utterances, back of the teachings, was a living soul, from which proceeded emanations entirely distinct and separate from ideas, and quite independent of language. The subtle influence poured through the eye. It streamed from the features. It flowed through the voice. Gesture, posture, and form were its silent vehicles. It emphasized thought. It energized expression. It vitalized ideas. It awoke aspiration. It kindled enthusiasm. It evoked power. It was the direct efflux of spiritual energy by which a great nature transformed other natures, in proportion to their capacities, into its own likeness. It is the want of this incommunicable power which is most felt by his pupils in the perusal of his writings, and which makes them unwilling to admit that he has produced anything equal to himself." *

But his ministry had one defect, a defect remediless and daily increasing. It was the ministry of a man past threescore. In accordance with his life-long principle, while he was charged with responsibility, he could not see anything remain undone for want of effort on his part. His ideal of the work of the ministry was most exalted, and was perpetually advancing. He toiled after its realization with an earnestness which was enkindled by the constraining love of Christ, and which, not improbably, was intensified by his growing consciousness that the twelve

* Professor Chace's Address.

hours of the day in which he might work were far spent, and that night was at hand. It was a most instructive illustration of his estimate of the character of the work of the ministry, that while at the head of the college, he was always able, however engrossing his official cares, to find some time for outside work, for authorship, and various addresses. But after he assumed the care of the church, he had not an unoccupied hour, and did not even attempt anything outside of his strictly ministerial work, with the single exception — if it be an exception — of the address upon the occasion of the death of Mr. Ives. "His labors," says one gentleman, a member of the church, who observed him very closely, who is himself accustomed to intellectual toils, and eminent for industry, "were arduous beyond the power of expression."

And it became painfully obvious that while the inward man was renewed day by day, the outward man was inadequate to the demands of the soul. He grew visibly more wearied and feeble, and his physician again urged his speedy release from toil. Indeed, it is doubtful if he could have survived another year of such exertions.

Rev. Dr. Caldwell, having accepted the pastoral care of the church, Dr. Wayland preached, on the 30th of May, a sermon with which he designed to close his labors, from Acts xx. 32: "And now, brethren, I commend you to God, and to the word of his grace, which is able to build you up, and to give you an inheritance among all them which are sanctified."

"More than a year and three months have elapsed, my brethren and friends, since I commenced my labors among you. Neither you nor I, at the beginning, anticipated so long a continuance of my services. The providence of God, however, directs all events in infinite wisdom. For a long time you have waited patiently and prayerfully for the coming among you of a pastor in whom you would all be united. Your prayers have been answered; your patience rewarded. You have called to minister among you a brother beloved, whose praise is in all the churches, wherever he is known. You have done this, so far as I know, without a single dissenting, or even a reluctant voice. And he has informed us that very soon, perhaps on the next Sabbath, you may expect him to come among us to break to us the bread of life. My pastoral labors with you close, therefore, with the present Sabbath, and, in the words of the text, commending you to God and to the word of his grace, I commit you to the care of another."

The arrival of the pastor being delayed, he prepared and preached, on the following Sabbath, one more sermon, from the word (touchingly appropriate to his circumstances, and to the history of the past year), "He that goeth forth and weepeth, bearing precious seed, shall doubtless come again with rejoicing, bringing his sheaves with him." With this discourse, his services as pastor of the church were ended.

To a minister: —

"May 8, 1858.

"I am obliged, for the present, to continue laboring here, though I hope we shall soon have a pastor. I have next week meetings for private conversation on Monday afternoon and evening; Tuesday, meetings at the Hospital and State Prison, and a meeting in the evening; Wednesday evening, lecture; Thursday, church meeting; and meeting on Friday evening; besides preparation for Sunday. I am rather jaded."

To his son: —

"June 1, 1858.

"I intended to write to you before, but I have not been able. On Thursday I had people calling upon me all the morning; in the afternoon to attend a meeting of the committee; in the evening a church meeting, to receive fifteen converts; and on Friday and Saturday I wrote two sermons. On Sunday I baptized and preached twice. On Monday I called, as is my custom, on those baptized the day before, and attended meeting in the evening. To-day I have made a few needful calls. I feel that my work here is almost completed."

To the same: —

"June 15, 1858.

"Mr. C., the new pastor, preached last Sabbath very well, and the people are universally pleased. The church was never, since I have known it, in so hopeful a condition. This, so far as I have had anything to do with it, has been accomplished by steady *days' works*, and by putting aside everything that interfered with it. A year spent thus is worth ten of irregular, vacillating work, without plan or steadiness."

Exhausting as were these toils, consuming as were his solicitudes, and perceptible as was the draught on his strength, yet never were his consolations more abounding. In the "Letters on the Ministry of the Gospel," he observes, in allusion to this period, "I can truly say that no part of my ministerial life was so full of enjoyment as this; and upon no part of it do I look back with so much satisfaction." It was with a radiance brighter than that of noonday that the sun declined towards its setting.

CHAPTER X.

"SERMONS TO THE CHURCHES." — "SALVATION BY CHRIST." — CORRESPONDENCE. — WORK UPON THE MORAL SCIENCE. — VIEWS OF EUROPEAN AFFAIRS. — EXPOSITION OF EPHESIANS. — ATTACK OF ILLNESS. — BUST OF DR. WAYLAND. — ANNUAL REUNION OF HIS PUPILS. — HIS FEELING TOWARDS HIS PUPILS. — INSTRUCTION TO CANDIDATES FOR THE MINISTRY. — LETTERS.

DR. WAYLAND'S retirement from the pastoral care was succeeded, not by rest, but by change of labor. He immediately began to prepare for the press the volume entitled "Sermons to the Churches," which was published in August, 1858. It contained eight sermons, two of which had been previously published. The work is appropriately named, for the discourses were addressed peculiarly to professing Christians, and were designed to lead the people of God to emancipate themselves from subservience to the principles and examples of the world. A singular unity pervades the book; indeed, the several sermons might have been chapters in a single work. But its most marked characteristics are overwhelming earnestness and the absolute simplicity of its appeals. It would seem impossible to use language with greater plainness. The preacher takes up courses of action which are all the more likely to escape observation, because they are so universal; he exhibits them with such vividness that they appear novel, while yet the reader is compelled to confess that they are common — that they are his own. In none of his works has he excelled the presentation and enforcement here made of the ethics of the gospel.

In the following December was published, "Salvation by Christ," a collection of discourses, in the main, identical with those issued several years previously, under the title "University Sermons." Two, suggested by the revolutions in Europe, were omitted, and several new ones inserted, which had been prepared during his recent pastoral labors. A comparison of these with the sermons composing the original volume will substantiate the views presented in a previous chapter, of the change which the past few years had wrought in the character of his preaching.

In 1858 he was invited to accept the presidency of a university just established under circumstances of peculiar promise. He was informed that he would not be expected to put forth any large amount of personal labor, but only to give the weight of his name, and such supervision as he could exercise. We have alluded to the invitation only as introductory to the following extract from his reply: —

"I beg leave to express to the Board of Trustees my grateful acknowledgment for the honor which they have conferred upon me. I could not, of course, pretend to decide such a question without deliberate reflection. I have taken time for this purpose, and am obliged to say that it is not in my power to accept the appointment. I have overworked my brain, and it is not as good a servant as it used to be. I find that the labor of the pastoral office, which I occupied for sixteen months, has had an effect upon me from which it will take some time to recover. By manual labor and release from responsibility I am gaining ground; but were I to embark in such an undertaking as that which the university of —— presents, I should break down in twelve months. I do not think I could have continued my former presidency a year longer. There is not, I am persuaded, a physician who has known me for ten years, who would not, on this ground, forbid my going. It might be said that I need not do much labor; but I cannot connect myself with such an undertaking on such terms. To see a cause of this nature fail from want of anything that I could do would be impossible. Nor is such a man the man you want. You cannot succeed unless he who has the office of leader performs, in fact, the hardest work. If I have had success in any undertaking, it has been simply from hard labor, and I could not act otherwise; but such labor I am not now able to render."

Extracts from letters to a minister, a former pupil: —

"I apprehend that when we give up the account of our ministry, one of our greatest failures will be found to be that we have so often neglected the Word of God. It looks strange that the Son of God has left heaven to teach us, and has promised his Spirit to accompany his Word, and has set us to preach it, and that we should have anything to preach that we like better, or that we should merely take a start from the Bible, and go on with our own imaginings."

"I have been astonished at the effect of a baptism on the spiritual condition of a church. If administered religiously, as a solemn thing, and not as a spectacle, the moral effect is most salutary."

"Above all, remember that you have accepted from the Savior the care of these souls, for whom you have engaged to give account. This is a very different idea from supplying the pulpit. It is not pleasing to God to have his service made a convenience of. Do your own work well, in the fear of God, and what is left, use for other good things; but do not cut off a piece of God's work to make anything else out of."

"A man, to succeed, must have a fort — some place where he stands strong, and is impregnable. This, to a minister, is his church and people. If he stands well there, he may laugh at everything else. . . . The Spirit of God is jealous; and if we do not receive his presence with thankfulness and renewed effort, he will withdraw. In spiritual things, make hay while the sun shines."

". . . I heard yesterday Mr. ——. It was, I think, an attempted imitation of Mr. Beecher, but an unfortunate attempt. A sinner would hardly have been led to the Savior. I was saddened, for he used to be considered a very earnest and pious preacher. My dear ——, there is nothing but the glorious truth of the way of salvation by Christ that God will bless to the salvation of sinners. This is what Christ sends us to preach, and this alone he will bless."

"I have thought several times of the sermon you are to preach before the Association. The discourse will take its character from its object. What is that object? Is it to prove the truth of the text? I presume not, to ministers. Is it to confirm them in the belief of it? Hardly. What, then, is it? Here is a company of ministers, exposed, without knowing it, to the danger of being ashamed of the cross. You want to point out to them this danger, and so to affect them that, for the year to come, they may preach Christ more simply, earnestly, and effectually than ever before. Should they do this, no one can predict the result upon the churches, or the number of conversions that God would grant. It is possible that, with the blessing of God, from your sermon a revival may extend over the whole Association. I would labor and pray, and preach directly for that object; and it would, I doubt not, receive the blessing of the Savior, and cause joy in heaven over many a returning penitent."

"I have been reading several sermons in Spurgeon's new volume. I am struck with several things; first, the manifest truthfulness of the man, arising from his perfect belief in all that he says. The truths of religion are as much a verity to him as his own existence. Second, his intimate acquaintance with the whole Bible. It bubbles up everywhere as soon as he begins to speak. He uses it with great power to express his own ideas. Third, as a result of this, is his manner of making a sermon. He does not draw an abstract truth out of the text, but expands and illustrates the very text itself. It opens to him a train, or several trains of thought, which he illustrates from everything around him. It is owing to this that he has so great variety. Were he to deduce abstract propositions, he would of necessity often repeat himself. Fourth, he takes the very range of the thoughts of his hearers. They, therefore, all follow him. And then again, while he is accused of egotism, he seems to me to forget himself and his reputation more than any man I know of. He seems not to care what people say of him or do to him, if he can only convert them."

Upon the completion of the volumes named above, Dr. Wayland resumed his work upon the Moral Science. It had been his design entirely to reconstruct and re-write it, making it, in all but the general subject and spirit, a new book. With this view he prepared several hundred pages of manuscript. But he became satisfied that it would be a hazardous experiment to reconstruct a book, which, on the whole, had been so well received by the public in its original form. He therefore decided to revise it, re-writing only such chapters or passages as seemed susceptible of marked improvement. This labor engrossed him very constantly throughout the year 1859 and the early part of 1860. To his son he writes, —

"I am working at my book — sometimes doing a day's work, often only a fragment."

"I will try to come and see you; but it is difficult. I want to do something every day at my book, which is now advancing. If I leave it, even for a little while, I get cold in it, and it takes time to begin again."

"I am much engaged in my book, and am getting along slowly. I give up everything to it, and must do so in order to accomplish anything. I am thinking through a book at a time before I begin to write it, and it consumes more time than you would suppose. I sometimes come to a chapter which could, as it seems, be thought through in a day, and it takes a week or a fortnight. But this is no more than my ordinary experience."

". . . My health is, by the blessing of God, very good. I am rarely sick, but I feel that age is beginning to do its work upon me. I am not able to labor as I once could. My brain does not bear so long application. It is possible that I see as clearly, but my mind does not act as rapidly as formerly. I suppose I need recreation occasionally, but I have never learned to amuse myself, and have never had many intimate friends. I presume I must be unfortunately constituted in this respect, or else I have formed bad habits. I, however, keep on with my work, and am happy in it. Perhaps some good may come out of it."

The passages just quoted show, if we do not mistake, the singular control which he possessed over his powers. One who knew him for more than thirty years, and who is himself very observant of mental phenomena, has said, "I never knew any one who had such command over his mind. He made it obey his will perfectly." His mind had no freaks, no caprices. What he set it to do, it did, so long as the power to labor remained. When it failed to obey him, the failure was not the effect of insubordination, but of exhaustion and powerlessness.

During a part of the years 1859–60, his oldest son, with his wife, was in Europe. Many of Dr. Wayland's letters to them exhibit alike his comprehensive views on passing events, and the tenderness with which his heart yearned over those whom he loved, and from whom he was separated.

To his son, just previous to his embarkation: —

"And now, my dear son, I commend you and M. to God. I have a confident trust that he will watch over you, and return you both in safety. Keep it ever in mind that the first of all your relations is with God; that he is ever near to them that love and serve him; then try to make this journey a spiritual blessing to you both.

"I trust that I shall see you again. It may be otherwise. You know all I have so very imperfectly tried to teach you. You know that I have, first of all, desired that you should serve God, and be a high-minded, noble, disinterested benefactor towards man. God grant that you may be all this and more. May God bless and preserve you both to his heavenly kingdom."

"Strange as it may seem, things have gone on during your absence very much as usual, only a few families are always thinking of you, and frequently looking up to our common Father for his blessing upon you."

"Napoleon III. is almost a miracle. Having twice made himself the laughing-stock of the world, he has, at a single leap, shown himself the foremost man in it. His uncle said there was but a step between the sublime and the ridiculous. He, for the first time in history, has shown that there may be but a single step from the ridiculous to the sublime. He has astonished the world by his ability in war. So far as I can judge, in every case, the Austrians had the advantage before the fight, and in every case have been decidedly beaten by a man who had never seen a battle before. Every thing in Europe seems now to turn upon his moral character. If he should be true to principle, faith, and honor, and, after driving out the Austrians, should establish human rights in Italy, and then unite with England in promoting the best interests of man, he will overshadow the fame of his uncle. . . . Should he organize a great nation in the north of Italy, he will be able to attack England if he chooses. Their weakness is in their aristocracy in the army. Merit cannot rise. The very ablest men in India and the Crimea were discovered by accident and by the death of those above them. Aristocracy is good for many things, but it will not make great generals. War is a real business, and not a conventional arrangement. Skill and talent must command their proper position, or the requisite energy never will be developed. Napoleon III. has shown an unusual common-sense talent for it. He has commenced by making the individual soldier, whether officer or private, as distinctive a being as possible, and has given him, in the next place, the best means of distinction, and then has adopted the motto, 'The career open to talent.' If war is to be carried on, it is on these principles that it must succeed. If the English had learned the lesson taught them at New Orleans, they would not now be using the muskets of Ramillies and Blenheim."

"The news of the peace took us all, as it did the rest of the world, by surprise. No one knows how to understand it. It may be that the emperor tells the truth (not a common thing with emperors or diplomatists), that he was afraid of encountering all Germany, and of carrying on the war in the marshes of the Mincio and Adige in midsummer. But this he must have anticipated; and he says himself that he commenced the war in the face of all Europe. The other view taken — though I have not seen it fully stated — is this: He got the English into the Crimean war, and withdrew from the contest in order to secure the gratitude of the Emperor of Russia. He has played the same game with the King of Sardinia, and made the Emperor of Austria his friend. Here, then, are the three strongest military powers united, and the man of the greatest ability and boldness will use them. But still more: here are the three despotic powers, embracing the Greek and Catholic churches, together with the Pope, united as one man. Civil and religious despotism was never so powerful. There remain to Protestantism and liberty only Prussia and England. It looks as if a war of opinions would ensue, and the spirit of liberty triumph; or else despotism must press on the human race, how long, O Lord, how long? Protestantism may have the aid of the free spirit of Italy and Hungary; but they are weak in opposition to such tremendous forces, united and upheld by the religious spirit of the Greek and Roman churches. I incline to this view, and I should be alarmed, were it not that God reigns, and that he is able to make the wrath of man praise him, while he restrains the remainder. He frequently allows his enemies to bring forth all their power for the sake of rendering his victory the more impressive. The view which I have taken corresponds with the gigantic ambition of the chief agent, and the love of glory and domination so characteristic of the French."

"Since I wrote you, I see new reasons given for the peace. It is said that Napoleon saw, that though the Sardinians were profuse in demonstrations, they did nothing in aid of the war, and he would soon have to meet Europe in arms, alone. This, however, is contradicted by all the previous accounts of the war, and of each battle. The only thing certain, I presume, is that, for reasons known to himself, he thought that he had carried on the war far enough, and made up his mind to put an end to it. The reasons will probably transpire in time. The Villa Franca convention is a very hurried and loose document, fixing hardly anything, and meaning simply, 'We will stop fighting.' I am glad they stopped, but care little about their reasons."

"I hope you will spend as much of your time in England as possible. There are brighter prospects and finer mountains elsewhere, but the men and women are in England, and at present it is the culminating point in modern civilization. . . ."

"You will have read in the papers all about Harper's Ferry and old Ossawottamie Brown. The results are yet to be seen. I believe they will be much greater than is anticipated. Every one perceives the madness or insanity of the attempt, and, so far as is known, the want of plan or forecast in the movement. But every one admires the bravery, coolness, and evident sincerity of the old captain. It will oblige millions to think of the subject, and will raise the tone of anti-slavery feeling several degrees higher throughout the North."

"We are greatly interested in your account of the revival in Scotland. Every one must say, with the magicians, 'This is the finger of God.' It is the work of the Spirit, as in the day of Pentecost; and it is sent, not to accompany preaching, nor to make much use of it. I sincerely hope that this power of the Holy Ghost is to be a general feature of our times, and that it will work a change in the minds of men as to the way of laboring for souls. All the recent manifestations have been in the direction which I have intended to indicate, so that I hope that I have not erred in my attempt to point out a more excellent way. But I seem to tread in the steps of that excellent old spinster, Cassandra, whom no one would believe. I have tried to be useful to my brethren, and have stood up for the rights and duties of the laity of Christ's people."

"I repeat what I said before: Make yourself acquainted with England. There is now, in their best circles, perhaps the highest state of civilization on earth. But more than this, in a general uprising of the human race, which is not impossible, Great Britain and the United States must stand together for the rights of mankind."

"Louis Napoleon is evidently a political economist and a statesman. His decrees are despotic, but they are wise and suited to the building up of a nation. If he would abandon the absurd idea of war and conquest, he would show wisdom. But this, perhaps, is impossible. France, largely intellectual, but wholly irreligious, can be governed by nothing but a military despotism. With a strong desire for liberty, they have no moral instincts to direct them how to secure it. A despot is therefore a necessity, and Louis Napoleon supplies that necessity. Rigid as is his rule, it is better than anarchy, and the majority uphold him. But granting a despotism, government is not a very difficult thing. It is all reduced to *Sic volo, sic jubeo.* The government of France by a despot does not require as much talent as the government of England by the prime minister, if we consider the complication of obstacles to be met and overcome at every important movement."

"Every one in the civilized world is now looking towards Italy and the French emperor. Whether he intended it or not, his course has been directed with, apparently, great wisdom. He went far enough to give the Italians room and space to develop themselves, organize governments, and get that taste of freedom so fatal to oppression; and now, united with them, his word can control Austria. He has let the Pope amuse himself until the course of events has rendered the return to the papal dynasty impossible; and now the Holy Father is in his power, and must really ask of him leave to exist. At precisely the right moment he has strengthened his alliance with England, not by a treaty of combination, offensive and defensive, but by the tie of mutual interest, which will make them in a few years almost one people. There were never two nations, highly civilized and so near together, whose products were so dissimilar, and who would gain so much and be so cemented by freedom of trade. All this looks well for the liberty of man. Napoleon III. is a political economist, which his uncle was not. It looks as if he was determined to free France from the papal despotism. His letter to the Pope is such a one as has never been sent before to the Holy Father. It is plain, forcible, and ingenuous. If he can control the priesthood of France, he will succeed. I do not doubt that he will succeed if he has the people with him, and I think he has. Priests are not so purblind as not to know on which side their bread is buttered, and few of them will prefer exile to a good benefice. If you and M. make the acquaintance of the emperor and empress (and they will of course call as soon as they hear of your arrival), I hope you will treat them with every respect, and present them with my sincere regards, assuring them of the pleasure it will give me to have them visit us when they come to Providence. I think I shall not invite Cardinal Antonelli."

"I am glad that you have seen the 'city of the dead,'* as Scott calls it. It is worth a volume of history, and has shown you what the most cultivated nation on earth was at the time of Christ's appearing. Had he not appeared, what would have been the condition of the world? There was nothing to arrest a downward tendency to the deepest abyss."

"It now appears from all we can learn that both our friend Napoleon III. and Victor Emmanuel are held up before the world as being by no means such enthusiastic admirers of truth as we should wish to see. The latest information is, that the cession of Savoy was arranged from the beginning, although both of these excellent men had most steadfastly denied it. No one can henceforth trust either of them. It is, however, no disgrace for a Frenchman to lie. Louis Philippe would hardly shrug his shoulders when detected in a flat-footed falsehood. How it will affect a man in Italy, I do not know. It will, however, damage him in England. The Protestant religion forms a vastly superior national character to the Catholic."

"You can attend courts wherever you are, and will acquire new views by observing how other people than Yankees look at questions of right. Have you seen Macaulay's prophecy respecting this country? I confess it has made me tremble. It is according to all the wisdom of the past, and unless there are elements of safety in us that do not yet appear, or there be some wonderful display of divine power in our behalf, it will be fulfilled. A nation where everything can be bought and sanctified with money, is on an inclined plane, and nothing can arrest its progress."

"The Pope's bull has been issued, and it seems to have fallen to the ground, perfectly innocuous, — the thunder

* Pompeii.

without the lightning, — and that in Italy itself. The world has certainly advanced since the middle ages. This will give courage to Napoleon, and he will probably emancipate himself. This will be the beginning of the end of the papacy; for, if left to its moral power, what has it to hope for? But what then? It will make a struggle, and if a war of opinion is waged, it will be war to the knife, over every acre of that land. The French revolution will be child's play to it. The more, however, I look at these things, the more I am impressed with the vanity of human plans and the folly of human combinations. There sits upon the circle of the heavens One to whom all the nations of the earth are as the small dust of the balance, who is working out his own purposes, and will overthrow all wickedness, and bring out right and justice triumphant. Men's plans are all turned to dust, but the plan of God moves on, slowly, steadily, overturning nations, to establish a single principle, and making the wrath of man to praise him. You possibly may ask, When will all this be done? I answer, at the time appointed. God has plenty of time; a thousand years are with him as one day, and he, without regard to our calculations, takes a thousand years to accomplish what we would have done, if we could, in a day. The insects on a leaf, if the leaf dries up and falls to the ground, might think that the universe was coming to an end. They know not that the drying up of that leaf was to make way for a fruit-spur, and that from that fruit-spur will arise the seed of a mighty tree, that will furnish ten million such universes as their single leaf. Thus is it in the government of God. I reluctate from all plans, especially all wise ones. I incline to believe that our safest course is to do our personal duty, leaving all the planning to Him who sees the end from the beginning. I rejoice that over all this turmoil the Lord reigneth, and though clouds and darkness are round about him, justice and judgment are the habitation of his throne. It may be a geological epoch before all that is promised will be accomplished, but it will assuredly come."

"July 2, 1860.

". . . There is a great deal of humbug about art. Not one in a thousand is willing to confess what he feels, but makes believe feel what he is told he ought to, and then sneers at those who do not repeat his words. They say when you put a pail of boiling water in a yard full of pigs, if one puts in his nose, and is scalded, and goes off grunting, another will follow, and do the same thing, and so on till every one has his snout scalded. So it is of pictures, and all this talk of high art. I know that there cannot be a greater number of pictures and statues than there are of poems and orations, that are worthy of commanding the admiration of all ages.

"Your letter of July 7, from London, gave me occasion to remember many of my own experiences. I am very glad that you saw Mr. Ingham. He is a very fine fellow, and was peculiarly kind to me. He has great weight of character from his honesty, intelligence, and disinterestedness. I was greatly pleased to find that the impression produced on your mind by the courts of justice and by Parliament were so similar to my own. The courts, I visited, as you did, with Mr. Ingham, when you were somewhat of a youngster. They presented to me the idea of a company of men, of the highest intelligence and most thorough learning, devoting themselves, in their different positions, to the simple purpose of administering justice. The decorum was perfect, as became men engaged in such a business. While the utmost deference was paid to the court, the court manifested almost fraternal courtesy to the bar, and seemed really to consider them as gentlemen who were aiding them to execute justice. One felt that he was in an atmosphere where slang, *ad populum* harangue, or personal altercation, could not breathe for a moment.

"*Mutatis mutandis*, the same remarks apply to Parliament. There was a collection of highly-educated gentlemen who had made statesmanship, not politics, their study, and had taken pains to render themselves acquainted with every subject that would come before them. As the subject opened, each one presented his views briefly, pertinently, in remarks rich in information, and bearing directly upon the point. Each sat down, when he had contributed his part to the discussion, to hear and learn from others. It was an appropriate national council for a great and free people.

"I want you to see all you can in London. What you see and hear there, will not greatly gratify the senses, but it will furnish you with facts, and principles, and recollections, that will build you up as a man of sense, and furnish you with matter for future judgments. Neither a view of a picture or a temple will aid you in conducting a difficult case, or give soundness to your opinion in an important political crisis; and who knows how soon such crisis may come!"

It had been the not unfrequent practice of the church of which Dr. Wayland was a member, to suspend the Wednesday evening service during the most oppressive portion of the summer, and more particularly during the vacation of the pastor. As the summer of 1859 approached, he expressed his opinion that it was undesirable to deprive those who remained in town of this means of grace, and he consented to bear the responsibility of the service. He accordingly gave, upon the Wednesday evenings of this summer, a series of expository discourses on the Epistle to the Ephesians. These expositions were characterized by his wonted simplicity of language, and secured a full attendance, even during the extreme heat of August. But those who remarked him closely could but observe, with pain and solicitude, the evident effort which these services cost him — the falling away from the abundant and unconscious power of other days.

Meanwhile he continued to labor upon the revision of Moral Science. In the winter of 1859–60, he wrote to his son, —

"I have just completed the first or theoretical part of my volume, and I think it is in straight lines, but I do not know. I have now but one heavy article before me — that on slavery. The rest is all familiar."

And again in March, 1860, he writes to his son, —

"I thank you most truly for all your expressions of affection. . . . I cannot express the yearning desire I feel for all my children, that they should accomplish their destiny, and return to the Master the talent which he has committed to them, improved and greatly increased. I fear that this interest sometimes carries me too far, and that I seem more earnest about your success and improvement than is proper. If I do, I trust you will pardon me, for you know my motive. I want you to be perfect in every good work, and I may seem to express myself to you in words much more direct than I should to any other person. . . .

"I am this day sixty-four years old. What remains to me, and how much, is known only to Him who will do all things aright. I should like to bear my testimony fully on human rights, and to labor at some other things that may be useful; but if I do not, some one else will be commissioned, who will do it better. I am in the midst of that subject now, and I ask your prayers that I may be enabled to treat it properly. I proceed slowly. It is difficult to state articulately truth that is so simple, and to state it so as to impress men. However, I make some progress. I hope I have been directed to do it, so as to aid Christ's little ones. The more I think of it, the more inextinguishable is my abhorrence of oppression, especially of our own slavery.

"God bless you, my dear son, and make you abundantly useful, and give you a bright crown to cast at his feet."

"I had labored for several years without any relaxation, and when I resigned, those who would have been most anxious that I should remain, were convinced that it was my duty to relinquish the position. My brain was tired out, and there was nothing to be done but to give it rest. I did not, however, long remain idle. My work as pastor, following so soon after my labors in college, had a bad effect on my brain. It kept up continual thought in one direction, without relaxation or diversion. During the period of my pastoral work, my strength had begun to fail. In fact, it had been so severely tried during my connection with the college, that I could no longer do what I had formerly done with ease. After publishing two volumes of sermons, I commenced re-writing my system of Moral Philosophy, and continued it until May, 1860. I wrote steadily, but not intemperately, — working every day, both morning and afternoon, and doing, as I supposed, no more than I could do with ease. I wrote in the attic room, away from noise. The room is small, and the roof of the house forms the ceiling. In the summer it was very warm, particularly in the afternoon, and in the winter it was very difficult to regulate the temperature. It was not easy to heat it sufficiently without rendering it too warm, and of this increase of temperature I could not readily be aware. I mention all the circumstances of the case which I can remember, not on account of their absolute importance, nor from senile garrulity, but because the knowledge of them, though apparently needlessly minute, may serve to guard my children from a similar misfortune."

As he proceeded with the chapter just alluded to, his soul became more and more deeply engrossed in the effort to vindicate the rights of man, and to exhibit the violation of personal liberty in the case of domestic slavery, until, unconsciously to himself, he had overtaxed his already strained energies. In his reminiscences he writes, —

"My habit in regard to sleep was to retire at eleven P. M., or a little later, and to rise in summer at half past five, and in winter at six. This did not give me sleep enough. I should have had one or two hours more. I found, when I put myself to work, that my mind did not act well in the morning. I was drowsy, and did not think readily or clearly. This was quite unlike my previous experience. I took exercise enough, but still did not improve.

"About the middle of May, as I was writing, I found my mind unusually dull, and not easily controlled by my will. The subject on which I was writing was one with which I was perfectly familiar; yet I composed with unusual difficulty, hardly finishing one page when I should have finished three; and on looking it over I found it badly done. I did not know what could be the cause, but I perceived that my thinking powers were in some way disordered. In the afternoon I attended my Bible class, without observing anything peculiar in the action of my mind. The only circumstance that seemed unusual was an incessant gaping, which I could neither control nor account for. So remarkable was it, that I was strongly inclined to apologize to the members of my class for the apparent rudeness.

"I retired to rest, and slept as usual. When I arose in the morning I found that my speech was affected. Some words I could not pronounce without effort, and my organs would not obey me without a special act of the will, and even then only imperfectly. My right leg was weak, and seemed to share in the general derangement. I went as usual to my dressing-room to shave, and my experience there was singular. Ordinarily, shaving is with me almost an automatic process, which proceeds regularly after it is commenced. But I found that this was not the case now. I had a sort of dialogue with my hand. It asked me, 'What shall I do next?' or, 'How shall I do it?' and I was obliged to answer by a distinct act of the will. I, however, completed the operation, though in constant danger of cutting myself.

"After breakfast it was necessary for me to answer a note. I found it impossible to write as usual, or in fact more than barely legibly. I could not keep on the line, nor command my hand so as to form the letters distinctly. My first attempt could not, I think, be understood. I tried a second time, and by writing slowly, and with constant attention of the will to every letter, succeeded a little better, but only a little. I at once perceived that something was the matter with my brain. I took medical advice. My pulse, and all that belongs to my physical system, was found to be in perfect health. I was advised to use entire quiet for the brain, moderate exercise, and patience. These I at once put in practice; and, indeed, they were necessary. I could not use my brain. It refused to work, and seemed to say to me, at the least attempt, 'I cannot do it.' I soon saw Dr. Jackson, of Boston. He told me, contrary to all my expectation, that it would take eighteen months or two years before I could be restored, and recommended the treatment just mentioned, with the additional prescription of a diet almost exclusively vegetable.

"I endeavored to conform to this medical advice, and very slowly improved. With regard to vegetable diet, I am not quite certain of its effect. I pursued it for a long time, and then returned to my usual diet, and have, for a season, again fallen back upon it. I think, in both cases, I have derived benefit from change. Which would be best for a permanent course I can hardly determine. I observe that medical writers of late, in general, advise, in similar cases, a full rather than a spare diet. I say a full, but of course not a feasting diet; merely generous living. It is now nearly three years since this attack, and I have only within a few months recovered the power of writing with my usual rapidity.

"One symptom that accompanied my disease, I have not seen noticed by physicians. It was disordered action in the sense of feeling on my right side (which was the most affected). Cold objects seemed to me warm. A glass of ice water, when held in the hand, had a tepid feeling. This symptom has not left me entirely at the present time.

"For a while I could read almost nothing; then easy narrative. What seemed impossible was original thinking — that is, thinking out a train of thought on any subject, or even following such a train of thought written by another. I have not yet regained the power of doing this. Perhaps it is only fancy; but my brain apparently refuses to do it, and says, 'I am not able to do it.' I do not like to pursue a train of thought in conversation, and in any given case had rather have the facts, and form an opinion spontaneously, than go through a process of reasoning to reach it.

"I have found it necessary to avoid all excitement. To become deeply interested in anything deprives me of sleep. I have been obliged to give up reading newspapers. I dare not attend public meetings, especially in the evening. It would be difficult for me to write a sermon, — so at least it appears to me, — or to think out the plan of a sermon. I can expound a passage of Scripture much more easily. Here the plan is laid out before me, and I can take up every separate point as it is presented, without thinking out the whole range of thought for myself.

"I am, however, through the mercy of God, slowly recovering. For some time (as I have said) I could read but little of anything. Afterwards I read that which required more thinking, but was obliged to use much care. On one occasion I read Macaulay's Essays with great pleasure, and pretty continuously. I found, however, that I had transcended my limits, and for a considerable time could read nothing of that character.

"After a while I attempted composition. The first thing which I undertook was this scattering collection of reminiscences. I was obliged to write but little at a time, say, for instance, two or three hours a day. If I did more than this, I was obliged to intermit for a number of days the work of composition. On several occasions I wrote too much, and was compelled to lay aside my pen for weeks together. I observe that I commenced these reminiscences in October, 1860. It is now April, 1863, and they have constituted my principal work, at frequently long intervals, since that time. It is a poor way of occupying one's self, yet I found the need of some mental exercise. I think that I improve by gentle use of the brain, but I suffer unless that exercise be confined within very exact limits.

"My means of recovery have been few and simple. I have devoted, during the summer, a large part of the day to labor in the garden. My diet has been simple, and almost entirely confined to two meals a day, at first with no animal food, and latterly with but little. I have taken more sleep, and find that I work more effectively the more I sleep."

In the account above quoted, the reader has undoubtedly remarked, if not the actual presence of paralysis, yet the evident tokens of its imminence. It was in this light that Dr. Wayland interpreted the symptoms he has delineated, although, probably from regard to their feelings, he rarely expressed to his family or to his friends his full apprehensions.

In August he wrote to his son, —

"I am gradually improving, gaining strength, and having a more natural mental feeling. I do not try to use my mind, but I think, with the blessing of God, I shall soon be able to do so. I have work to do which I should like to accomplish, if it be the will of God. But if he is pleased to devolve it on others, I am content; I think entirely so."

In September he wrote to Rev. Dr. Hoby, —

"You have me in your debt, as well as your excellent wife. I must confess it, but also add, that it has not been without reason. Since the spring I have been interdicted from mental effort and writing. Some time in May I was attacked with symptoms of overwrought brain, showing danger of paralysis, and demanding, most imperatively, rest; and rest I have taken. My illness was not severe, but only premonitory; and I at once laid aside my papers, and have not even looked at them since. So, you see, the troubles of advancing years affect us both. Soon the last will arrive — how soon God only knows; and I would not wish to ask him."

He was, of course, compelled to abandon many undertakings involving mental exertion, and to defer the execution of others. He had promised to deliver an address at the Andover Theological Seminary at the ensuing anniversary, and to give a course of lectures before the Lowell Institute. Both of these promises he was compelled to recall. And the Moral Science was laid aside for several years. In the fall of 1860 he prepared the Introduction to the "Life of Trust" (a condensed narrative of the dealings of God with George Müller).

This Introduction was written at the rate of six or eight pages a day, and was subsequently re-written.

The immediate effect produced on his mind by the attack lately referred to was seen rather in the diminished rapidity of his mental action, than in any want of accuracy in his judgment. He found himself, in time, able to think, and to express his thoughts, as clearly as heretofore. But he could not labor as continuously, nor as intensely. When formed, however, his conclusions were as just as they had ever been. Yet the attack acted, it is probable, indirectly, by abridging his physical power. He found it not easy to walk, and he grew more and more averse to travelling. He felt himself, he said, too clumsy for much motion. From this circumstance, and from the fact that he was compelled to avoid anything that excited him, may have resulted a greater degree of isolation than was favorable to his spirits, or to the soundest mental action.

During the summer of 1860 a circumstance occurred

which appropriately expressed the sentiments entertained towards Dr. Wayland by the successive generations of his pupils. For the following narrative we are indebted to Professor Gammell, who was active in the series of transactions of which he speaks.

"A desire to secure and transmit some memorial of President Wayland had long existed in the minds of very many of his pupils, and the matter had often been talked about among the graduates as they met each other; but it was not until April, 1860, that any move was made for carrying into execution what was known to be a common wish. At that time a meeting was held of graduates residing in Providence. At this meeting, which was fully attended, it was determined to ask Dr. Wayland to sit for his bust, to be executed in marble by the best artist that could be procured. Several of those present were in favor of a statue in colossal size, either of marble or of bronze; and they expressed a desire to see such a work placed in a conspicuous position on the college grounds. It was, however, believed that he was not likely to consent to this, even if it were solicited; and it was at length generally agreed that a marble bust would be most appropriate, and on the whole most acceptable to his pupils.

"As soon as Dr. Wayland had given his consent, Mr. Thomas Ball, of Boston, was selected as the sculptor; and he very soon came to Providence to commence the requisite preparations. This eminent artist was at the time just commencing his studies for the equestrian statue of Washington, ordered by the city of Boston, upon which, I believe, he is still engaged, while residing in Italy. He entered with great interest into the spirit of the work to which we invited him, and there presently sprang up a warm sympathy between him and his subject — a circumstance that, no doubt, contributed its full share to his ultimate success. The likeness has always been regarded as very excellent.

"It fell to me to conduct much of the correspondence with those of the graduates who lived at a distance, and I recall very distinctly the warm expressions of personal respect and admiration which often accompanied their contributions, and the evident pleasure which they felt in having an opportunity to unite in this testimonial. These expressions were particularly marked in the letters received from members of the older classes, and they often came from those who had scarcely seen him since they left the university, but who had felt his influence as a perpetual presence along all their way in life.

"The subscribers were all gentlemen who had graduated at Brown University under his presidency, with, I believe, but a single exception, that of Hon. William H. Seward, at that time a member of the United States Senate from New York. He had been a pupil of Dr. Wayland when the latter was a tutor at Union College, and, chancing to hear the matter spoken of by some of the graduates of Brown University in the Senate, he insisted on writing his name in the list of those who were thus expressing their gratitude to our president.

"The bust was formally committed to the custody of the corporation at Commencement, 1861."

As the Commencement of 1860 approached, Dr. Wayland conveyed, through the Providence Journal, an invitation to his former pupils to call upon him, after the usual annual dinner. In response to this invitation, many of the graduates changed their plans of business or of pleasure, that they might visit him in compliance with his request. The invitation was renewed, with one or two exceptions, during each of the succeeding years of his life.

It was a source of peculiar gratification to Dr. Wayland to meet his former pupils, in an unofficial way, on the ground of friendship; and he felt grateful to any who afforded him this opportunity. It was a matter of regret and of mortification to him, that he was unable in every case to recognize them by name, particularly when the progress of years had both effaced something of the vividness of his recollections, and had changed their lineaments of countenance.

A gentleman of deserved professional and literary eminence writes, —

"For several years, as I afterwards learned, I entirely

misinterpreted Dr. Wayland in one respect, and I am quite sure that others, at one time or another, made the same mistake. During my college course I had no *special* occasion to come in contact with the president. I was always regular in my performance of college duties, and never asked permission to be absent for a single day, nor needed to be excused for any delinquency. It was only in the presence of others that I saw him, in the chapel, or the recitation-room, until the very close of our course, after the last lesson had been recited. Of course I had had very little opportunity to know him as a personal friend. For three years following my graduation I had been unable to attend Commencement; and in the mean time, although I had seen him several times, he had not spoken with me. On one or two occasions he *seemed* to pass by me without recognition, as if not wishing to know me. When I remembered that no student had ever passed through college with a fairer record as to attendance and a faithful performance of college duties, I was grieved by this apparent slight. More than once I put myself in his way, and saluted him respectfully, that he might be sure of my desire to be recognized. But, although he always returned the salutation, he did it as if he did not care for me, and in no instance uttered a word. Subsequently, I made a more deliberate attempt to attract the president's notice, but failed utterly. He cast a glance at me, and then passed on, as if he could have no concern with me. This troubled me not a little. I did not like to be so completely ignored by a man whom I respected so highly, and to whom I had sustained such a relation. I could not help believing that he thought me guilty of some wrong, which made him unwilling to recognize me.

"But on the day on which he retired from the presidency of the college, you remember, perhaps, that he said he should be glad to have his pupils take him by the hand, if they felt any interest in his welfare, and that there was not one among them all for whom he did not cherish a feeling of fatherly kindness. I resolved at once that he should have no reason to doubt my confidence and respect. Seizing the earliest opportunity, I extended my hand, reminding him, by way of apology, of what he had said in the tent after Commencement dinner. What was my amazement on his asking my name, and seeming to be surprised when I gave it. He spoke pleasantly, cordially, and evidently knew my name and history much better than my face. I had abundant confirmation afterwards of his personal good will, and have no doubt that he supposed he had not seen me since the day of my graduation.

"I afterwards learned two facts, which were unknown to me before; first, that his memory in reference to facts and incidents was not good,— that he was utterly unable to tell in what year he was baptized; and, second, that he had far more personal interest in those who had been his pupils than he seemed to them to have. He knew where they had been; he rejoiced in their prosperity; his great heart was glad when they were honored. Most of his pupils never knew the depth of his affections, nor suspected the warmth of his generous nature. Those who went to him in trouble — especially if they sought religious counsel — learned how tenderly he could speak to them, and with what loving earnestness he could pray with them. But most of the students knew him only as the stern president, whose imperial presence awed them, and whose commanding spirit claimed their respectful obedience. Repeatedly, during the last years of his life, I saw the most convincing evidence of a warm and generous nature under his somewhat severe exterior, and in the assurance that he was my friend, and recognized me as his friend, I found ample compensation for years of apparent, but not intended, neglect."

It has already been said that Dr. Wayland was, for a time, prevented from any composition requiring exact or original thinking. He could, however, converse without difficulty upon subjects which were familiar to him, and this single talent he as heartily consecrated to the service of the Master as he had done the fulness of his powers. Two candidates for the ministry, who had known him through his works, requested him to give them some stated instruction suited to their future work. He consented to do so, and accordingly, during the summer, they met him twice a week for this purpose.

One of the gentlemen referred to writes, —

"During the revival of 1858, while Dr. Wayland was

pastor of the First Church in Providence, I attended his meetings, and watched his course very closely; for I saw that a new way of doing things had come over that conservative church, and that I could learn much which would be of great use to a minister. I read also his book on 'The Principles and Practices,' &c., which produced a strong impression on my mind. . . .

"After he consented to give us some instruction, it was decided that, as our time was so limited, our attention should be given wholly to the matter of homiletics and pastoral work. I remember well his first remark to us at the opening of our brief course. I have never seen it in any work on homiletics. 'When you have selected your text, spread your Bible before you, and, kneeling down, ask God to show you just what the Spirit means in the words.' That came in his mind before the consultation of commentaries. How many times have I thought of his direction, given, not to save research in the original, or hard mental toil, but that a minister's mind might be brought *en rapport* with the Spirit, and might find the glow and unction so much needed in preparing for the pulpit, which nothing but prayer will bring; that he might experience the insight which a young convert feels when he first opens the Bible after his conversion, and reads again familiar passages. No better sentence for the title-page of a work on sermonizing could be given, than his opening remark to us on the first Thursday of July, 1860.

"How often he charged us to stick to our text, and to the exact shade of thought in the text — advice which has been of incalculable value to me, and has always provided me with fresh subjects for my people. He had given me this text, on which to present a plan — 'The love of Christ constraineth us.' I brought in a plan which pleased me somewhat, and which he thought would make a good sermon. He took his Greek Testament, and looked at the original, and remarked on the word translated 'constraineth.' 'Brother ——, you could make a sermon that would be admired from that plan; but you have no συνέχει in it. Try again, and put in a large charge of συνέχει.' I did try again, and heard his 'Admirable!' His remark has put the συνέχει into a great many sermons of mine since, and I have asked myself again and again, as I have come from the pulpit, 'Did I aim to have some one *do* something, as well as admire the truth and enjoy its presentation?'

"This leads me to mention another remark of his concerning sermons, which I often think of when I am writing my text. Reading my plan, he would ask, 'Now, ——, what is the precise thing you are aiming at in that sermon? What is *the* thing you wish to accomplish?' I would state it, and then he would go on with his criticism. I think it a remarkable test to apply to a sermon. Is it not true that very many sermons are preached each Sunday in evangelical pulpits that are as aimless as the lives that are lived about us? 'What do you want to accomplish? Are you driving at anything?' he would say. If I have in any degree the power of driving at one thing in a sermon, I owe it to him.

"You cannot conceive how invaluable were his suggestions concerning the pastoral work of the ministry. He had lately been putting his own principles to a practical test as pastor of the First Church, where they had proved themselves to be powerful in upholding God's cause, in converting souls, and in giving him access to men whose hearts had been closed.

"Over and over again he insisted on the value of a personal application of religion to the individual soul. I remember his saying, 'There will be no time when you cannot drop a word for Jesus. In the social gathering of your church, a word in the ear of the sinner will not be lost.' He insisted that it was ever my duty, as a minister of Jesus, to have the souls of my people always before me, and to be ever planning, as well as praying, to bring the truth to bear in the right direction. Always I was to remember that souls were going to hell, and many of them through the neglect of the Lord's people. I cannot forget an illustration which he quoted from a shrewd minister, much to my, as well as his own, amusement. It was to exhibit the character of the minister's work, according to the circumstances under which it is performed. A man sits down to fill a large number of bottles, which are ranged before him on the floor. Taking up a water-pot, he waves it over them; but much more water falls upon the floor than into the narrow mouths of the bottles. Tired of that, he takes a bottle at a time in his hand, and just pours the water in; and soon the bottle is filled, for the water must go in. So take a sinner, as it were, by the neck, and the truth must go in. It is not lost.

"'And then, when you visit them, remember that you are a minister, and that conversation on other topics, *to the exclusion of religion*, is wicked. Your business is religion, and men, as well as God, expect you to attend to it.'

"When I was settled, it was his intention to preach my ordination sermon; but he was prevented. I used to write to him occasionally, though not so often as I wished to; for his time was so much occupied that it seemed presumption in me to be always asking questions. I sought to make an application in practical life of the principles he so closely held, and I found them wonderfully powerful in moving men and influencing the churches. The Association was composed of a number of weak churches, almost too weak to live; and among them I was accustomed to do much of the work of an evangelist. I never visited Rhode Island without reporting to him, and spending three or four hours in his study. I remember calling once when he was busy with some distinguished visitors; but he would not let me retire, and I apprehend that his guests thought me something more than a simple country minister, from the reception he gave me.

"It may be well to sum up what I consider to be his influence upon my ministerial work.

"First. He led me to feel that the ministerial life which is not saving souls, is, in the view of the gospel, a comparative failure. In this balance he weighed us all, and it was here that he first began to doubt the faithfulness of the ministry. He realized, O, how intensely! the value of the soul, and the danger of its eternal loss. In August, when I last saw him, I was telling him of a letter which I had just received, informing me of the very sudden death of one of my friends, occurring only one week after the man's conversion, during a visit which had long been contemplated—a visit which had almost persuaded him to delay attention to his soul's salvation until his return. Dr. Wayland's eyes filled with tears, and his voice trembled, as he said, 'O, how near that man came to losing his soul!' It was this feeling that made his great heart burn with holy indignation as he saw so many of God's ministers engaged in everything besides saving souls.

"Second. I felt the influence of his estimate of the importance of the work of the ministry. I refer to his opinion that the Christian ministry was exalted above every other calling under the sun.

"Third. I have very decidedly sympathized with his views concerning the ministry as a mere profession. Under the influence which I brought away from my repeated conferences with him, I have endeavored to look upon my work, not as a way of getting a living, but as God's way of saving men, and building up his cause.

"Fourth. I have been greatly influenced by him in my preaching. Tempted at times into the use of a word or phrase which I knew that very few of my congregation could understand, I have drawn my pen across it, as I have thought of his remark, 'Say what you mean in language that the commonest mind will not fail to understand.' And as I already remarked, he helped me incalculably by his homiletic instructions.

"Fifth. He gave me new views of a Christian church, and of its duties, which have been of great benefit to me. He longed to see the unused talent of the church brought out, and the inactive members led to duty and earnestness. I have tried to accomplish this, and have been so far favored that in my young church I have a hundred whom I can depend on in a prayer meeting. I have sought, too, to impress each one with the duty of laboring personally for the salvation of others, so that our weekly reports are full of interest, and souls are constantly coming to Jesus.

"A word as to his views of the ministry of the present day. Some have said that he seemed to be growing sour in his old age; that he was querulous, and in his dotage; whereas I know that during the five years of my acquaintance with him — which, I hope, it may not be presumption on my part to call an intimate one — he seemed to grow even more tender and more affectionate, to yearn with more depth of piety for the salvation of souls, to sigh with more heartfelt pain over the languishing condition of Zion, and to speak of the Baptist ministry with more and more concern. And his family knew how false the charge that his heart was growing acrid, when every month showed him increasing in love to Christ, and to those whom he loved as his own.

"He had no prejudice against the ministry (why should he have?), and no desire to be a fault-finder or accuser. He did not believe that the ministry was a failure; that all, or that any, utterly failed in the performance of their duty. He was met with the declaration of faithfulness, of devotion, and of the possession of all that he thought wanting in the ministry, from those whose congregations were waning, and whose people were dissatisfied and complaining. He was very forbearing, and went away to pray when some men would have taunted and tried the *argumentum ad hominem*, with an effect that would have closed many mouths that had been loudest in condemnation.

"His views of the ministry, which have excited the most severe comment, may be expressed in one sentence: The ministry of the day is wanting in a passion for the salvation of souls. In details he was at times in error, — I mean in appearing to charge all with neglect, when some felt that they had been peculiarly faithful. But in the general charge — absence of the flame, the fire, the zeal, the συνέχει — he was, alas! too true.

"May God speed the day when all of us shall realize that we build up and edify the church and all believers, when we are on fire for the salvation of souls. Whoever takes this stand-point, will admit all, and more than all, that Dr. Wayland has said of the failure of the ministry in earnestness."

To the same: —

"I am glad you had a pleasant gathering of your parish. I would have them at your house as often as they will come. People like society; it is natural, and they will have it. Society of this kind is innocent, and it binds them together, and may be made an instrument of good. When we had our gathering here, I had a very good and long talk about religion with a person whom I should not have seen elsewhere."

To the same: —

"You write about faith. It is manifest, if we suppose the existence of an all-perfect Creator, and a dependent moral creature, that there must be a feeling required from the creature towards the Creator. This is evident from other cases. You have certain feelings, it may be to a rock, to a brute, to a good or to a bad man, to a relative, a son, &c. So, in the same way, there is a feeling towards the Creator, properly called forth by the exhibition of his perfections. Power in the Creator calls for the feeling of dependence; holiness, for the feeling of awe and adoration; goodness, for that of love and confidence; and, in general, paternal affection calls for the feeling of filial love. Now, this feeling, which is due towards God, in what form soever exhibited, is faith. Sin broke up this feeling, and sinners look upon God without any responsive emotion, unless it be dread. Hence sin is often spoken of as death; that is, a state in which the natural moral causes produce no effect, as ordinary agents that move the living exert no influence on the dead body. And this death is eternal without some power to new-create.

"Repentance is an accidental affection, for sin is an accident not provided for in the original constitution, since that was made for a holy world. It is merely a true sorrow for what is past, and a surrender of the heart to God on the part of one who has rebelled against him. In virtue of the atonement, when a sinner does this, God receives him back again, and puts a new life in him, by virtue of which this responsive emotion begins to act again, and a man is rightly exercised in view of the perfection of God.

"Faith in Christ is a similar feeling towards the Redeemer, God manifest in the flesh. To man, in his fallen state, Christ is a root out of a dry ground; but when the soul is vivified, he is the chief among ten thousand, and every manifestation of his love creates a corresponding action in the soul.

"This all shows the necessity of the work of the Holy Spirit, without which no soul could ever be converted. This agency is taken for granted.

"You see I have here merely sketched out the thought; by reflecting on it you will easily fill it up for yourself. Faith is thus a temper of mind, varying with every attribute of God to which it responds. Hence the variety of ways in which it presents itself. *I am not sure* that God does not always recognize it even in unregenerate men. Samson may have exercised it in a certain way by trusting to the word and promise of God, without any other emotion; so of Rahab and others."

To a minister: —

"There is no reason, that I can see, why it should not be given to Christians to work miracles. Miracles are variations from the ordinary laws of cause and effect. Is not Müller's establishment a miracle? The conversion of a soul is a standing miracle, which nothing but omnipotence can effect. It is God's witness, and will always be, to the end of the world."

To his son, after the election of 1860: —

"Since the evening of the 6th I have breathed more freely. It is plain that the only constitutional party is the Republican. Nothing would be acceptable to the south but our entire submission — that we should become slaves. This we are not yet ready for. It is a question, not of black, but of white slavery."

To a minister: —

"About the day of fasting and prayer [for the country] let me say, I would have it a real day of fasting and prayer, as solemn as I could — as if I really believed in prayer. I would not preach politics, but, looking on this as a day of trouble and danger, would ask God to help us. I would set the people's sins before them, and ask for forgiveness and deliverance; that God would overrule all things for the glory of his holy name, for the spread of the gospel, and the overthrow of oppression; that he would give oppressors better minds, would forgive and bless them, and would unite all our citizens in love of liberty and right. I would not discuss, but honestly strive to lead the people to pray. If I preached in the morning, I would have a prayer meeting in the afternoon. It is a crisis in which nothing will do us so much good as real prayer."

To a minister: —

"Seek for simple reliance on God, and trust him. Was any one that trusted in him ever confounded? Strive to go beneath the mere exegetical view of a text, and realize in your own soul the whole depth of its meaning. The Spirit will grant you this."

To a young man, a relative: —

"As to your being distinguished or great, my dear ——, I have no wish about it. I want you to do your duty, and the rest I willingly leave. I would rather, immeasurably, have you a God-fearing, honest man, doing your duty, than have you Choate or Webster. If I could make you such as either of them by dotting an i or crossing a t, God forbid that I should do it."

To Rev. Dr. Withington: —

"You ask me about Müller and his book. The book has, I think, many imperfections: cases are set down as answers to prayer which can as well be accounted for in other ways; and some things are published which might better have been left between God and his own soul. My son (and I agreed with him) did not feel authorized to do anything else than condense the book, leaving it to make precisely the impression which Mr. Müller intended.

"But leaving out these doubtful cases, as we should do when a new law is to be set forth, there is enough to turn a thoughtful man's mind in a new direction. The question is simple. We go to God in all special cases, and ask for, and believe we receive, an answer. Why not in every case? for we can never tell whether the most trivial thing may not be special. Or, in general, what is the relation of Creator and creature, and especially of the creature to God in Christ? Is it not that of a *little* child to a kind and wise parent? Is not that a model child who will do nothing without asking the parent's consent, and confiding itself always to his care? Is not this the type of the most exalted piety? Is not this the fruit of the indwelling Spirit which the Savior promises? This would be living as though God were everywhere present, and to be called upon, not by an outcry like that of the priests of Baal, but addressed to one so near that he could hear the faintest whisper."

CHAPTER XI.

DR. WAYLAND'S VIEW OF WAR. — FEELINGS AT THE OUTBREAK OF THE REBELLION. — TRUST IN GOD. — THE HAND OF GOD RECOGNIZED. — MEEKNESS INCULCATED. — WEST POINT. — GENERAL MITCHELL. — LOVE, THE UNIVERSAL SOLVENT. — THE ELECTION OF 1864. — CONDUCT OF ENGLAND. — THE ASSASSINATION. — THE CHARITIES OF THE WAR. — FREEDMEN. — THE CHRISTIAN COMMISSION.

THE reader of these pages will, perhaps, be interested in observing the impression made on Dr. Wayland's mind by the series of unparalleled events which crowded closely upon each other during the war for Liberty and Union.

Of war he entertained the opinion which, as we suppose, prevails among the great body of enlightened Christians. He thought it an evil of enormous magnitude, destructive of wealth, life, happiness, and prejudicial to morality. He sought to promote the bloodless settlement of all international disputes. He was, for several years, president of the American Peace Society. We have already remarked the abhorrence with which he regarded the invasion of Mexico by the United States.

But he did not look upon war as universally and absolutely wrong. To be enslaved was, in his opinion, worse than war.

In 1861 he writes to a minister, —

"Your question admits, I think, of an easy solution. Civil government is an ordinance of God, and its object is to punish evil-doers, and to protect the innocent. It has authority to do this. The magistrate beareth not the *sword* in vain. The sheriff is the organ of society in the county, and he arrests and hangs evil-doers. He acts, not for himself, but for society; and has the right and authority to summon to his aid the whole community. When the violence is done or intended by a part of a community, the sheriff cannot act, but the community must act for itself; in other words, it must resist iniquitous force by innocent force, that is, there must be war.

"Such being the case, a Christian may exert himself for the support of a just government. He is called on to do it. He prays for it, and, as in any other case, must act in accordance with his prayers. He cannot ask other men to do for him what he cannot properly do for himself; and if he neither acts nor encourages others to act, no government would stand against wicked men for an hour.

"—— ——, I believe, is going as chaplain to one of the regiments, and I have advised it. Here are men who need the consolations and principles of religion. It is our duty to offer them to both parties alike, and to aid Christian men in resisting the influences of the camp. Religious men may, I think, do great good by going."

Some months before the actual outbreak of hostilities, he wrote to a friend who was deeply interested in the issues at stake, —

"I advise you to make yourself fully acquainted with the principles of military science. A knowledge of these often enables a commander to accomplish his objects with the smallest possible waste of life."

From the firing of the first gun, the struggle, in its various aspects, took precedence of all else in his thoughts. He found it impossible to read the accounts of battles. They affected him so painfully as to deprive him of sleep. Once, after receiving from a son a letter describing an engagement, he kept it, for several days, unread. He could not, he said, endure the thought that one dear to him was exposed to such peril. But there was no such bar to his carrying every issue to God in prayer. He regarded the war as an event in the moral history of man and in the providential government of God, and hence he looked upon it perpetually in its highest relations. He prayed incessantly for the country, for the soldiers, and for the enemies of the republic. He searched the Word of God for promises, for revelations of the divine character, which might strengthen his own faith, and which he might use in pleading with the Hearer of prayer. He perpetually sought, by every form of private and public appeal, to extend and intensify the spirit of supplication. In anticipation of the national day of fasting, September 26, 1861, he prepared, at the request of the executive committee of the American Tract Society at Boston, a tract, appealing to all the disciples of Christ to unite, upon the approaching day, in persevering intercession for the country.

The following extracts from his letters in 1861–5, copied nearly in the order of their dates, require, we imagine, no introduction or explanation: —

To Senator Foster: —

"January 18, 1861.

". . . It is one of the most wicked things, I fear, that God ever looked upon. It is a legitimate effect of slavery. The prostitution of conscience in one thing leads to its universal prostitution. . . . Well, what is to be done? I dare not pray for any one thing, only that a just and holy God would glorify himself, and deliver the oppressed, and show himself in favor of justice, by giving strength to right and to those who preserve it. In looking for this I have not forgotten you. . . .

"Can it be doubted on which side God will declare himself? Can we doubt that, if we look to him in faith, he will bring forth judgment unto victory? If you want to see how God looks upon oppression, read the ninety-fifth psalm. I hope all our friends will continue firm, and sacrifice no principle for a present advantage. The best place to meet a difficulty is just where God puts it. If we dodge it, it will come in a worse place. May God grant you wisdom. Look to him, and lean upon him in confidence and earnest faith."

To his son: —

"January 5, 1861.

"... God is about to bring slavery forever to an end. He has taken it into his own hands, and allowed the south to have their own way. They proclaim slavery as a most religious thing, for which they are willing to die. God is taking this way to free us from complicity, and to let them try it by themselves. Greater madness never existed. But 'the Lord is known by the judgment which he executeth; the wicked is snared in the work of his own hands.'"

To the same: —

"January 8, 1861.

"The slavery question is all in a nutshell. 1. No one can establish slavery unless he makes it the law of humanity. This will authorize the intensest oppression, and will justify any man in enslaving any other man; this would destroy society.

"2. No one can affirm that Jesus approved of slavery, unless he affirm that he approved of it as then practised in Rome and elsewhere; how that was we all know.

"3. No one can affirm that Jesus approves of it now (so as to be of any use in the argument), unless he affirms that the Lord approves of it as it now exists in the Southern States, — which would be blasphemy. It is horrible. I wish I could get out my Moral Science. I go into the subject thoroughly. But I must wait the decision of Providence.

"Slavery all falls into fragments before generalization. Just say, 'If this is true, it is universally true,' and see where it will lead you."

To a friend: —

"I have been this afternoon to two flag-raisings; on Wednesday I addressed the troops, and marched with them to the wharf; our flag goes up to-morrow or Monday. Mrs. Wayland cannot sew, but she and I have been making bandages. The state of the country was the theme of every sermon yesterday. At this moment, probably, seven hundred Rhode Island troops are in the presence of the enemy."

To his son:—

"I should be glad to take the journey you speak of, but I fear I cannot meet the expense. I will pay my debts, and then I can decide better. I have been trying to secure a little money, but the sale of my books is very small, and I must have something for my country and her defenders besides my regular charities. I must, therefore, hold the journey in abeyance, until I see my way more clearly."

To a member of Congress:—

"I have thought frequently of you of late, in connection with the subject which agitates every bosom; and specially do I think of you now, when the destinies of this country, and of the race, are so palpably in the hands of you and your brethren in Congress. It is a time when, if ever, you need the wisdom which Omniscience alone can confer, and which every one of his perfections is pledged to grant us abundantly, if we ask it. . . . Do your duty, my friend, and humbly look to God for the wisdom of his Omniscience and the strength of his Almightiness. Live and think as ever in his sight, and plead his love for our race in becoming incarnate to save sinners.

"Why could not you, and one or two whom you might know, meet in private for prayer? I do not think much of prayer meetings for such objects, in such a place, where it may be for Bunkum, though I would encourage calling upon God in every reasonable and devout form; but for myself I enjoy such things most with a congenial few in a private chamber, the doors being closed."

To a chaplain in the army:—

"I think of you and your comrades almost constantly. I read the papers but little; I strive to ask our Father in heaven to overrule all to his glory and the good of mankind, to preserve you from evil, and to bring to confusion all the devices of the adversary. . . . The wrath of man worketh not the righteousness of God. Our Master loved and prayed for those who were murdering him, and committing the greatest crime in the history of our race. Try to imitate him, and to cherish no feeling that would prevent you from praying for those whose wickedness you abhor."

To the same, at the sailing of the Sherman expedition: —

"Your officers are well spoken of. These things give me a little comfort, for God is more likely to use wisdom than folly in the accomplishment of his purposes. But I strive to commend you, and the expedition of which you form a part, to his care. You are safe only in his hands. There I, without ceasing, commit you.

". . . War is intensely demoralizing. Doing nothing in the intervals of the strongest excitement can hardly continue long without something to occupy the attention. Gambling, licentious conversation, and profanity spring up naturally in such a soil. . . . The grace of God, however, can go anywhere, and can bless the faithful proclamation of the message of salvation to any sinners under any circumstances. When we see the amount of wickedness perpetrated by man in a day, and think of the elements of atrocity in a single sin, and remember the centuries during which this earth has raised to heaven the smoke of awful transgressions of a holy law, how it shows us the magnitude of the atoning sacrifice, which is sufficient to change this whole race, to expel sin from the earth, and to justify God in pardoning the ungodly! May you be able to present this truth in such a manner that hundreds may receive it, and be rescued from eternal death."

In allusion to the wedding of a relation, he writes, —

"We stay at home for a very vulgar reason. We cannot afford the journey; we could not go without taking the money from charity, already so small that I think of it with pain. However, the blessed Lord accepts according to that a man hath, and not according to that he hath not."

To a chaplain: —

"I think that you do right in having the communion whenever it can conveniently be arranged. It is of great consequence that Christian men, under such circumstances, should learn to testify publicly for Christ, and that all who are disciples should unite in the service. . . . I would also form Christians into a sort of church, an association, for the purpose of watching over each other, and building up the cause of Christ. I would unite together all who seem to love the Lord Jesus, and they will form the leaven to leaven the whole lump. They will be the more energetic for being thus associated."

To his sister: —

"If we look upon God's dealings, as recorded in the Old Testament, there is great reason to tremble. I do not suppose that Israel did worse things than surrounding nations. Yet they alone knew God's will, and were the more guilty. 'Thee only have I known of all the nations of the earth; *therefore* I will punish you for your iniquities.' There has been, I think, too much confessing other people's sins, and not enough confessing our own. Slavery is a very wicked thing; but I know not that it is any worse than idolatry, and shutting God out of his own universe. I do not feel guilty on account of slavery, but I do on account of my forgetfulness of God, and disobedience. He has made use of the slavery question to bring about his judgments. He will chastise and humble us; and then he will pour out his wrath upon those who, in addition to sins in common with us, must answer for the sin of slavery, and for laying it at the door of the Holy One"

To a chaplain: —

"Let no opportunity escape you to learn and record every fact respecting the condition of the slaves — physically, intellectually, and morally. . . . My impression has been, that a fair and true photograph of slavery, just as it is, would deprive it of the support of all moral and honorable men, to say nothing of Christians. . . . I derived more material for the formation of a judgment on our relations with the south, from Olmsted's volumes than from anything else I ever read. I came deliberately to the conclusion that the opinions and civilization of the south must change, or we must of necessity separate before many years; but I had no idea that the thing was so nearly upon us.

"May God give us success in bloodless victories, change the minds of our deluded fellow-citizens, and restore peace to our once happy land. And, what is of more consequence than all, may he so order things that his great name may be glorified, and that his perfections may be displayed as never before. It is surely a time in which we may expect God to work. Moral issues of the most signal kind are at stake. His truth and justice, his hatred of sin, of lust, of oppression, of treachery, are all involved in the termination of this struggle. I cannot but hope that he will appear for us in such a way that all may see his hand, and, above all, that his Spirit may be poured upon all our land as never before. This is my only prayer."

"February, 1862.

"The temper of the south in this war has been about as bad as it can be, and in the professors of religion worst of all. If they were hungry, I would feed them; if thirsty, I would give them drink; if sick or in prison, I would visit them; but beyond this, *I eschew them. Selah.*"

To a chaplain: —

"... A great step has been taken in the right direction by the abolition of slavery in the District of Columbia. The number of the enslaved was small; but this is a declaration of the sentiments of the north, to go before the whole world. And it will change the character of Congress. ... Let us thank God and take courage. I believe that he will remember us in mercy, in that we, as a nation, have done and suffered something for disobedience to his commandments. This is all we hope. Almost everything takes place contrary to our calculations."

To his sister: —

"April 9, 1862.

"... As to public matters, I have very little to say, except it be to bless God for his repeated appearances in our behalf. I dare hardly read newspapers; in fact, for several years I have not seen the time when I read them so little as now. I am always apprehensive of defeat and slaughter; or, if victory is given to us, the death of men who have made themselves enemies, but to whom I have no feeling of enmity, is sad beyond anything that I can express. I cannot get these things out of my mind, and they prevent me from sleeping. I say, 'Lord, how long? Shall the sword devour forever? Say to the destroying angel, It is enough; put up thy sword into its sheath.' I beseech you pray without ceasing for this beloved country, for friends and enemies; that God would give these latter better minds. . . ."

To a chaplain: —

". . . But in order to accomplish this, we must be filled with the love of Christ, and strengthened with might by his spirit in the inner man. We must strive earnestly after a deeper, more pervading, spiritual life; we must gain victory over the world in all its forms, and not let it get inside of our hearts. The danger is imminent in your case. The army, and the victories and operations of the army, are liable to enter in and possess the heart, and to drive the Holy Spirit out of it. This danger is increased by the necessary association with men who do not know the grace of God, and by the imperfect opportunities of being alone. God must be *first*, and other things will then assume their proper position. The country may be loved, the army may be loved, but God must be loved before all. These are small things in comparison with the love of Christ, and are really valuable only as they promote the cause for which he took upon him our flesh. What is this whole war good for, but as it prepares the way for the reign of Christ, by removing various forms of evil which oppose his cause? He was manifested to do away with, or overthrow, the works of the devil, and I trust he is thus doing it. If we are carried safely at last through this trial, what glory will God have conferred upon our country!"

To the same: —

"I have lately seen two colored people from Virginia. They represent that the negroes have very generally been praying for this event, at least for deliverance; and when their children were taken away and sold, they quelled their natural vindictiveness, and left their judgment with the Lord. . . . This forms, in my view, a most important feature in the case. If they are laying aside the weapons of the flesh, and taking hold on the promises and faithfulness of a God of holiness and truth, everything in the book of God teaches us that at some time their prayers must be answered. I know that we are an ungrateful and wicked people; but prayer in faith, without wrath, breathing the breath of forgiveness, waiting solely upon God, never, since the morning of creation, failed of entering the ear of the Lord of Hosts. God will help us, and that right early. Events of every kind, prosperous and adverse, all turn to the same end. God will be glorified, and will rebuke the foul slander which asserts that he is the author of this system, that he loves oppression, and approves of shutting up the Bible from our fellow-men, that we may make them the more profitable beasts of burden. But this destruction of human life weighs on me.

". . . I do not see how the war could have been averted, except by surrendering ourselves and all we hold dear to the rule of men who have displayed nothing less than the heart of demons. Under such a government as they would establish, we could not have existed. God has called us to this conflict, sad as it is, and I trust and believe he will carry us through it."

To a chaplain: —

"I have great faith in the prayers of the poor, downtrodden Africans, held in bondage, deprived of the privilege of reading the word of salvation, who cry day and night unto him. Fenelon asked a person in affliction, whom he was consoling, to pray for him, adding, 'I have great faith in the prayers of the afflicted.'

"Duty is ours. Success, in just the way he sees best, is God's. He can keep us in safety amid the greatest peril, as he kept you, through mercy, in that disastrous battle. I think of you and look up for you many times in the day."

In the summer of 1862, Dr. Wayland was appointed a member of the Board of Visitors to the West Point Military Academy.

In his reminiscences he writes, —

"I accepted the appointment with some reluctance, for I doubted whether I was able to discharge the duties. I found, on reaching West Point, that the members of the board had delayed their organization until my arrival. They immediately elected me chairman. I could not, under these circumstances, decline the office, although it imposed on me additional duties, especially the labor of writing the report. I discovered, to my surprise, that the mental exertion did not oppress me, but that I was really better for it. Indeed, my health perceptibly improved while I remained at West Point. . . .

"My visit was agreeable in many respects. The gentlemen associated with me were all moral, and a large proportion of them religious, men. I am happy in the belief that nothing was said or done that would tend to set a bad example to the young cadets. There was not a member of the board whom I should not be glad to meet again. Mrs. Wayland and my son were with me for a few days, and this added greatly to the pleasantness of the occasion.

"Some of the visitors were very able men. Of these I cannot forbear to mention the name of Judge Christiancy, of Michigan. I formed very agreeable intimacies with Judge Biddle, Mr. Knox, Dr. Batty, Rev. Dr. Scott, Mr. MacPherson, General Rodgers, and others of the board. We separated with mutual regret; such, indeed, on my own part, as I have rarely experienced after so short an acquaintance. Immediately before our final adjournment we united in prayer. Every member of the board appeared to join fervently and solemnly in this religious service."

That the friendly feelings which Dr. Wayland entertained for his associates were warmly reciprocated, will appear in the following letter from Judge Christiancy, dated November 11, 1865:—

"I had known President Wayland by reputation for many years prior to 1862. I was familiar with his writings, and esteemed them very highly. But much as I had revered him, I discovered, on personal acquaintance, that I had not half appreciated the excellence of his character.

"Our intercourse at West Point was as free and familiar as if we had been members of the same family. With a powerful and massive intellect, he combined the frank simplicity of a child and the tenderness of a woman. His whole bearing exhibited the transparency of truth, and we felt as much attracted to him by the purity and amiability of his character as by the greatness of his mental powers.

"Although our acquaintance had lasted less than two weeks, I left him with a greater reverence and a warmer attachment than I have ever felt towards any man I have met in the course of my life. No one could be in his company without acquiring higher notions of the dignity of human nature, and its susceptibility of progress and improvement. When I heard of his death, I felt as though I had lost a father."

To his son Dr. Wayland writes, —

"This morning has brought to us the news of the death of General Mitchell — to human appearance an irreparable loss. We must turn to the Lord and be devout, and open not our mouths, because he has done it. General Mitchell's last letter to me breathes the spirit of a Christian soldier. I have had several long talks with him on the subject of religion, and believe him to have been a truly pious man."

To a home missionary, laboring at the south: —

"I imagine that your position is one of peculiar difficulty, one in which you will especially need the presence and direction of the Spirit of all wisdom. Try to keep near to him, and rely, not on your own wisdom, or on that of any one else, but simply and earnestly trust in him. One thing I would suggest: the universal solvent is love. This can melt the hardest hearts. It was this that God used to bring back to himself our lost and ruined race. I would try the effect of this in the position in which you are placed."

To a relative in England: —

". . . As to public affairs, I try to think of them as little as possible, except to pray that God would deliver us. One of the worst trials we have to bear is the conduct of England. The kind, fraternal feeling that welcomed the prince a few years ago, may have been extravagant, or even childish, but it signified the good will of our people to England, and our respect and love for your queen and her consort. That kind feeling will never again be seen by any man now living. To think of your welcoming Semmes, of the Alabama, who, after fitting himself out in British waters, had done nothing but burn and destroy non-combatants, and had thus put the carrying trade into your hands!"

To C. G. Loring, Esq.: —

"September, 1864.

"As to the coming election, to beat the Copperheads is nothing. They ought to be crushed. We have all the argument, the honesty, the character, the patriotism, and power of appeal to the American heart. God grant us success. All is in his hand, and I look up to him with confidence and hope."

To George Bemis, Esq., Boston: —

"I have re-read with deep interest your article, which you have enlarged from the Advertiser, on our relations with England. I thank you for it in my own behalf and in behalf of our country. I hope that you will, from time to time, give us the results of your investigation and logic upon this great question. It is a source of unmingled joy that our own record is so clear, as you have shown before, and that now it holds that of Great Britain in so disgraceful contrast. It looks as if we should defeat them in diplomacy, as we have defeated their friends, the rebels, in the field. But this is not all. We are making laws for the nation, and establishing the principle, that nations, as well as individuals, must submit to justice. And it is a great thing that we ourselves set the example and hold to the principle.

"It is most astonishing that men who have a reputation and who are supposed to have a character, should be as reckless of dates as you have shown them to be, and of facts, as Mr. Adams has demonstrated. Earl Russell must, with true aristocratic spirit, have relied more on his blood than on facts. If he were not of the house of Bedford, I should suppose that he would be mortified. But the same stigma rests on their most eminent jurists. It looks as if there were a selfish meanness lurking in the national character, which believes in the rights of others only where their cannon cannot reach."

To Senator Foster: —

"March 22, 1865.

"I sympathize with you entirely on the question of retaliation. It is awful to know that our fellow-citizens were starved to death. It is abhorrent to every feeling to visit the same treatment on mere brutes. I hardly know what I should do. But how thoroughly are the southern people doing all in the power of men, or devils, to eradicate from our bosoms every feeling of respect or kindness!"

On the morning of the 15th of April, Dr. Wayland opened his paper, and read, as millions were reading at the same moment, the tidings of the murder of Abraham Lincoln. Late in the afternoon of the same day, a gentleman called, in behalf of the citizens of Providence, to request him to attend and address a public meeting in the evening. Dr. Wayland was compelled to decline this invitation, feeling his strength at that time inadequate to the effort. The committee then said, "Will you address them if they will come to your house." This request he could not refuse. Accordingly, not far from nightfall, a body of citizens, numbering about fifteen hundred, proceeded in order, to the sound of appropriate music, towards his residence. Regardless of the pouring rain, they gathered silently about a platform which had been hastily erected near the corner of the house. Prayer was offered by Dr. Caswell. Then, —

"Dr. Wayland arose to address, for the last time, as it proved, his assembled fellow-citizens. It is the same noble presence which many there had, in years long gone by, gazed upon, with such pride and admiration, from seats in the old chapel. It is the same voice whose eloquence then so inflamed them, and stirred their young bosoms to such a tumult of passion. The speaker is the same; but how changed! That hair, playing in the breeze, has been whitened by the snows of seventy winters. That venerable form is pressed by their accumulated weight. The glorious intellectual power that sat upon those features is veiled beneath the softer lines of moral grace and beauty. It is not now the Athenian orator, but one of the old prophets, from whose touched lips flow forth the teachings of inspired wisdom. The dead first claims his thoughts. He recounts most appreciatively his great services, and dwells with loving eulogy upon his unswerving patriotism, and his high civic virtues. Next the duties of the living, and the lessons of the hour, occupy attention. Then come words of devout thanksgiving, of holy trust, of sublime faith, uttered as he only ever uttered them. They fall upon that waiting assembly like a blessed benediction, assuaging grief, dispelling gloom, and kindling worship in every bosom. God is no longer at a distance, but all around and within them. They go away strengthened and comforted." *

To his son: —

"April 18, 1865.

"The event is overwhelming. The crime is atrocious beyond expression. It seems as if God has given over the south and their friends to work all iniquity with greediness, and to make themselves an insufferable abhorrence to the civilized world. The moral sense of mankind rises against them. They stand without a defence to meet the condemnation of humanity.

"But I never felt more sure that God has taken all this work into his own hands. He has left the rebels to work out the wickedness of the human heart, intensified by the practice of slavery. And he will glorify himself out of this overwhelming disaster. The mind of this whole people, even of the thoughtless and irreligious, has been brought to acknowledge God, and to believe that he has done it. They have never before wept or prayed so much or so earnestly.

"Is not God thus preparing us for a universal revival of his work? He has swept over the whole land in a few hours, so that all men had but one thought. Now, why should not his Holy Spirit, as a rushing mighty wind, visit the soil thus prepared for his influences? How would God be glorified, and all heaven rejoice! Cease not to pray for this. Urge others to pray for it.

". . . Let us lay aside all malice and all revenge, and let us firmly *do justice* to the high as well as the low. Let the moral principle of this people be strengthened. God has made us the leading nation in the world. Let us act as it becomes us. Let our example lead other nations in the way of peace and holiness."

---

* Professor Chace's Address.

To Rev. Dr. Hoby:—

"All is now swallowed up in the overwhelming news which, before this letter arrives, will have reached you. For some months past the Almighty Ruler of nations seems to have made bare his arm, and to have moved like a God. Our presidential election was most astounding; in an election among more than twenty millions of people, from the Atlantic to the Pacific, over the whole country, there was not so much *rowdyism* as you have at the election of a single member of Parliament. Such an election, after four years' war, was never heard of; and what is remarkable, the people seemed with one voice to acknowledge it as the work of God. Then came victory after victory. At last Richmond itself was abandoned; and in a week after, Lee, with his army, capitulated. The entire country was in a frenzy of joy; the burden and anxiety of four years were cast off. Then, on Friday, April 14, Lincoln was assassinated, and the nation awoke on Saturday morning to a grief that has rarely, if ever, had a parallel! I have not since seen a smile on the face of a man. Old men in the streets wept like women, and women sobbed at home. All loved him for his kindness, revered him for his patriotism, honored him for his honesty of purpose, and rejoiced in him for his success. He was emphatically the man of the people."

It will readily be believed that Dr. Wayland's whole soul was enlisted in the grand charities which grew out of the war. In the efforts for the elevation of the emancipated negroes he sympathized profoundly; but his benevolence was as wise and discriminating as it was sincere.

To E. L. Pierce, Esq., then at Port Royal, he writes, in 1861,—

"To free the negroes, and pay them wages for their labor, will be hardly a blessing, unless you teach them the responsibilities of freedom. If they begin by having such wages as they never dreamed of, and besides this, have their clothes *given* to them, they will be ruined. They will expect it, and be idle, loafing beggars, without an atom of self-respect. I would not give away a rag except in cases of sickness. I would make every one pay for his shirt, or her petticoat; if not able at once, at any rate by weekly instalments. No one knows how long this war will last; and we shall want so much for real destitution that it is not best to bestow charity in such a way as to render the necessity perennial."

To Rev. S. Peck, D. D., Beaufort, S. C.:—

"I look upon Beaufort District, just now, as one of the most interesting spots on the face of the earth. There, under our own eyes, is going on an experiment which may either confirm, or consign to universal contempt the statements which southerners have made concerning the character and capabilities of the colored people. They have said that the negroes are incapable of being taught, or of taking care of themselves, and are unwilling to work except under the stimulus of the lash, and that efforts to change this character were entirely thrown away.

"Now, if it can be practically shown that they are just like all the rest of Adam's children; willing to work for compensation; capable of taking care of themselves, if they only have an opportunity; as eager to learn as any others who have for years been forbidden to use their brain; willing to give every effort to the acquisition of some little learning, — they will stand forth before the world, calling, with a voice that must be heard, for sympathy and aid from every philanthropist and every Christian. . . .

"You must teach them the responsibilities, as well as the blessings, of freedom. This is absolutely necessary to the success of the experiment. . . . If we pay them fair wages, and begin by giving them clothing and schooling, they will expect it as a part of freedom. It has been found, by the most successful laborers among outcasts in London, that it is of the most questionable benefit ever to *give* to a person who is able to work. The dresses, shoes, &c., are all paid for, and in advance; the poor person paying the price by the day or week, in instalments, as best able to do it, and the account being kept and the article delivered when its price has been received. The prospect of obtaining it at the end of a stated period quickens the disposition to work; thus the labor bears visible fruit, and the association is at once formed between the sweat of the brow and the convenience which it brings. All this is new, and needs to be established in what some philosophers call the 'negro mind.' Labor and the rewards of labor have never before had any connection. I would extend this to schools, and everything else. Of course moral laws are not cast iron, or unsusceptible of variation. There may be sick persons, widows with children, and orphans, whom God evidently casts upon us for support. A man, however, with full health and plenty of work, may need a loan, but never charity. It will be no fair experiment, and of no value to the south, unless we carry it on upon sound political principles. I beg you to think of this. I would let them pay for everything, schooling included; I do not say that they should pay the full price at first, but something, that they may see that all their blessings are the result of their own labor. Nothing will do more to elevate them into self-dependent men."

To a chaplain: —

"It seems to me important that the negroes should be taught to instruct each other. This will spread education indefinitely, and will give it the habit of spreading. If you teach twenty men A, B, C, D, you have twenty teachers of these four letters, who can teach them as well as you can. If each of these teaches ten others, you will thus teach two hundred, each of whom might be a teacher in turn. They would thus impress the lesson on their own minds, and would be proud of their office.

"Of one thing I am pretty sure — that the black people need, more than anything else, good superintendents, to keep them at work, and to show them the connection between labor and comforts; to explain to them that without work they shall not eat, and that the more they work the better shall they eat, and the more desirable things there are in possession or in prospect. We are in danger of relying too much on book learning. I doubt if any book learning, such as it is possible for them to acquire, would elevate and expand their minds so much as a good superintendent, who would set them steadily at work, show them the reasons of things, and teach them their duty, *viva voce*. I think that nothing would make them desire reading so much. . . . I fear the government err egregiously in supporting them in idleness."

Dr. Wayland was filled with sympathy for those who were exposed to the hardships of war. To a member of one of the regiments stationed on Morris Island he writes, —

"I have thought of you much in respect to the weather, and when it has been unseasonably cool here (the thermometer at 50°), I rejoiced that, although it was unpropitious for us, it was a source of relief to you all on Morris Island. It is a most merciful providence that you are so well, and have been able to endure your unparalleled labors."

To Senator Foster he writes, —

"December 10, 1863.

"This note will be presented to you by Lieutenant-Colonel Palfrey, late of the Massachusetts Volunteers. Colonel Palfrey visits Washington on an errand of mercy, justice, and humanity. He wishes to promote the views of those citizens in this vicinity who desire the organization of a competent ambulance corps. He will explain our views to you. But the thing is at once beyond argument. Our fellow-citizens go into battle in defence of all that we hold dear. The result of battle is death or wounds of the most terrific character. How can we answer it to our own consciences, if we do not provide every alleviation in our power?"

But it was for the souls of those who were exposed to peculiar temptations and in hourly peril of death that he felt most deeply; and accordingly his whole heart was enlisted in the work of the Christian Commission, which sought to promote the bodily comfort and the eternal salvation of the soldier. Mr. Stuart, the noble apostle of this grand charity, writes, —

"During the four years of work of the Christian Commission, I met few men who took such an *intense* and abiding interest in that organization. When I was in Providence, he came to see me repeatedly, with respect to the work in which we were engaged, and expressed, with every evidence of heartfelt sympathy and love, his earnest desire for its success. He presided at our last public meeting in Providence, and also at a meeting held for the organization of a Ladies' Christian Commission. I was deeply impressed with our last conversation, when he said to me, 'I am looking forward to the most glorious revival of religion, at the close of the war, that this country has ever seen. In all efforts to secure it, your Christian Commission work will be largely instrumental. I may not live to see it, but I hope you will.' "

CHAPTER XII.

"HOW TO BE SAVED." — A LAWSUIT. — "LETTERS ON THE MINISTRY OF THE GOSPEL." — CORRESPONDENCE. — MEMOIR OF CHALMERS. — NEIGHBORHOOD PRAYER MEETING. — CORRESPONDENCE.

WE have said that, during the continuance of the war, the welfare of the country had the first place in the thoughts and prayers of Dr. Wayland. But he did not withhold his hand from any duty which the providence of God seemed to indicate.

He prepared, in 1861, a tract entitled "How to be Saved," which was published by the American Tract Society, Boston, and was widely circulated. A year or two later, an honored minister, residing at the west,* wrote to him, —

"I was lately at B., Ill., on a Sabbath, when a man and his wife were baptized, and united with the Baptist church. I learned that they owned a farm out upon one of the prairies, and attended no place of worship, feeling no interest in religion. Our excellent sister F. gave the woman a copy of your tract 'How to be Saved,' and it was blessed of God to the conversion of herself and her husband. I have heard of many similar cases."

During the years 1861–3, probably for the first time in his life, Dr. Wayland was involved in a lawsuit. Miss Eliza Angell, a benevolent Christian lady, residing near Providence, having no near kindred, had bequeathed her property to trustees (of whom Dr. Wayland was

* The late Rev. L. Porter, D. D.

one), for the erection of two Baptist meeting-houses. The will was contested, and three trials were had before the jury agreed upon a verdict. The needful preparation for these trials, and the attendance upon the daily and protracted sessions of the court, — held at the court-house which has since been indicted by the grand jury for its wretched accommodations and its want of ventilation, — were a severe draught on his time and health. He constantly carried the cause to the throne of grace; and at the family altar — and no doubt in his secret devotions — he pleaded with God that justice might prevail, and that the humane and pious purpose of a Christian woman might not be frustrated. After the conclusion of the trials, and the overthrow of the will, he writes to his son, "Personally it is a relief to me, but I am sorry to have lost so much valuable time."

He had been gaining in strength ever since the attack of 1860, and found himself gradually becoming able to apply himself to original composition. His mind continued deeply impressed with the need of a revived spirituality and an increased efficiency among the ministry. Fully convinced of the power of the gospel of Christ to regenerate the world, yet seeing that in a country blessed with absolute religious freedom, it failed to produce its legitimate results, he was compelled to believe that there was need of much searching of heart on the part of those charged with the proclamation of the gospel, to learn whether the responsibility lay in any degree at their door. The result of these impressions was his little work, published in 1863, entitled "Letters on the Ministry of the Gospel."

This volume was, by some persons, severely criticised as a distorted picture of the state of religion, and as proceeding from a morbid condition of mind. On the other hand, it was welcomed by Christians of eminent piety and wisdom, members of various denominations, as truthful, and urgently demanded by the aspect of the times.

The work may be open to criticism in some incidental features. When Dr. Wayland believed anything, he believed it fully. When he arrived at a view, or embraced a general truth, he sometimes may have overlooked the exceptional cases and the modifying circumstances. Yet, when all just concessions have been made, as to the incidental and superficial defects of the book, must it not also be said that its excellences are radical, are essential, and that no one can read it, candidly and seriously, without being aroused, quickened, and profited?

In one of the "Letters" he expresses his conviction that he had erred in leaving the work of a pastor for that of an educator. Probably very few persons, and perhaps none of his pupils, would agree in this view; yet it strikingly illustrates his candor and his exalted estimate of the work of the minister. It is certain that no one of his writings was the result of a deeper conviction of duty; never did he less than on this occasion seek to please men, or to confer with flesh and blood.

He writes to Rev. S. Peck, D. D., —

"I wrote the 'Letters' under a solemn sense of responsibility. I did not dare to do otherwise. I endeavored to say the truth, and I labored faithfully to avoid giving unnecessary offence. . . . I look back upon my ministry with pain. I tried to preach the truth, but I did not proclaim the whole truth as it is in Jesus. If I should ever be able to enter the ministry again, I hope that I shall preach Christ and him crucified, and nothing else. Is it not true that our orthodox preaching is frequently such that you would not read the sermons on the Sabbath, because not sufficiently religious? Is it not the fact that a sinner might attend many of our churches, and never learn what he must do to be saved?"

We may appropriately quote, at this point, from a letter written in October, 1865, to the St. John's (N. B.) Christian Visitor, by Rev. William L. McKenzie (pastor of the Friendship Street Baptist Church), a much valued friend of Dr. Wayland.

"As I was sitting with him one day, not long since, in his study, he conversed very freely, with the tears rolling down his face, concerning the ungracious reception which had been accorded by the ministry to his honest and earnest attempts to raise the type of piety among his brethren, and to bring about a more thorough preaching of the gospel. Never can I forget the tone of amazement and sadness in which he raised his voice, at the same time lifting his clasped hands and tearful eyes heavenward, and exclaimed, 'My God, thou knowest *all* things — thou *knowest* I have spoken the *truth* in regard to the condition of religion among us; but my dear brethren will not receive it from thy unworthy servant.' Then suddenly turning to me, with the smile peculiar to him, he said, 'But, my son, we must not expect to be above our Lord. Perhaps, when I'm in my grave, God will show them that I was right.' He was charged with painting a gloomy picture of the present piety and activity of the churches and the ministry. But they are not few in number, nor weak in influence, who fully concur with Dr. Wayland in his view of the condition of the ministry and the churches in this land. Instead of attempting to deny, or to explain away the statements of this holy man and devout servant of God, we had better look facts in the face, and pray God to roll upon our souls the burden of sorrow which *oppressed* the great heart which has now ceased to beat.

"It is true, as it has of late been frequently and emphatically asserted, in order to weaken the force of his statements respecting the condition of religion in our churches, that Dr. Wayland had not mingled much in actual life. But he nevertheless knew all that was going on, far and near. And his estimate of the degeneracy of this age was formed in a region of purer air and light than is to be found in actual life. He was preëminently a *praying* man. He walked with God. He dwelt under the shadows of the eternal throne, and measured human life by the exalted standard of divine revelation. It was in his habitual and intimate communings with God in prayer that he opened his eyes and gazed out upon the field around him, and saw, with a vision clarified, the real condition and necessities of that field. It was from the *mount of prayer* that he looked down into the vale below, and saw the disciples, destitute of faith and independent of prayer and fasting, attempting to exorcise demons from human hearts, but ever failing, and bringing into disrepute the power and glory of the religion they *proclaimed* as divine and efficacious.

"I have said that Dr. Wayland was a man of *prayer*. In this service he was as simple as a child. Any one who has heard him pray, can never forget the *pleading* intonations of his voice and the simplicity of his language. His *public* prayers were like those which Christians are wont to offer in the privacy of closet devotions. During the past year he has frequently sent me notes through the post office, requesting me to meet him in his study, for special and mutual supplication at the throne of grace for the descent of the Holy Spirit. To the latest day of life shall I remember that great frame bending at my side, and that *beseeching* voice, and that *importunate* pouring forth, from the depths of his soul, such prayer as he only could frame. How humble, how earnest, how familiar, he was, not only in his study, but when he prayed in public! He *talked* with God. But not one tone of his voice, not one syllable of his supplications, indicated any of that lack of reverence which we sometimes hear from human lips addressing the Majesty of heaven."

The following letters are taken from a considerable body of similar correspondence, called forth by the publication of the "Letters on the Ministry of the Gospel."

From the late Rev. J. H. Kennard, D. D., Philadelphia: —

"I read your letters on 'the Ministry of the Gospel' with the deepest interest. On closing the book, I gave thanks to the adorable Head of the church, that your attention had been called to the subject, and also for the fearless but kind spirit that pervades its pages. The book cannot fail to do good. Our churches and ministers have occasion to consider the whole matter seriously and prayerfully. You do not speak too strongly of the growing departure from the simplicity of New Testament churches and their Christ-like ministers.

"For forty-six years, I have aimed to live and labor in accordance with the views you have so ably presented. I began preaching when very young, and without the advantage of a liberal education. This led me more earnestly to read the Word of God with prayer, and to depend on the Master's aid with a child-like faith. I believed that he would help me, and he has helped me. Allow me confidentially to speak of the last twenty-five years of my ministry, the period of my labors in the church I now serve. Our twenty-fifth anniversary occurred in January of this year, we having been dismissed from the Fourth Baptist Church in 1838. Our number was one hundred and sixty-one; we had little wealth, but there was a mind to work. A plain house was soon erected, capable of seating more persons than several recently built at double the expense. The Lord, from the beginning, prospered the work of our hands. Revival succeeded revival, to the praise of his grace, for many years. A narrative read at our late anniversary showed the following results: —

"'Our number had increased from one hundred and sixty-one to twenty-three hundred and seventy-five, of whom fourteen hundred and fifty have been baptized, or an average of fifty-eight each year. Five churches have been successfully established in this city, and twenty brethren sent forth to preach the gospel, many of whom are now useful pastors. Your plan of outpost labor and visitation has been our plan from the first. The five churches planted grew out of Sabbath schools, accompanied with preaching. We have also had meetings of the church to revive our spiritual state and labors. The pastor has a report on the general state of the church. Other reports follow, on the Sabbath school, on collections for benevolent societies, &c., accompanied by prayer and praise. To encourage the church to abound in such labors, I read a few pages of your book, and they were much pleased with the agreement between your plan and our practice.'"

Dr. Wayland to Bishop McIlvaine, of Ohio: —

"September 7, 1863.

"I thank you much for your Charge on 'Preaching Christ.' I have read it twice, and should be reading it the third time were I not writing to you.* I have read it

* Dr. Wayland circulated the Charge among his friends, and those who, he thought, would sympathize in its devout sentiments.

with great pleasure, and I hope, spiritual profit. You have succeeded in striking at the very point of divergence from the simplicity of the gospel of Christ, which has led New England, and I fear our whole country, so far from the great truth of God manifest in the flesh. This is really the great effect of Unitarianism and its kindred errors. It has made the Cross, the great work of the Son of God, an offence, and men want to preach so as not to disaffect the rich. It has created a desire among ministers to appear as members of the *élite*, and not subject to such old-fashioned dogmas as *Christ crucified, the only hope of a perishing sinner.* Hence we have *societies*, rather than *churches;* handsome buildings, but few conversions; sermons which might as well be preached in one place as in another; and the truth so disguised by generalities that no one understands it. I unite with you in prayer that God will make your Charge greatly useful; that it may be an arrow that shall reach the heart of every one who shall read it.

"I do not know whether you ever come eastward. If you do, it will give me great pleasure if you will visit me. You and I are both growing old, and I should like very much to see you while we are on this side Jordan."

From Bishop McIlvaine:—

"Reverend and dear Sir: I had no doubt that the views in my Charge would find a most cordial response in your heart and mind. I read your late book on the ministry with great pleasure, and more especially because it points out evils and departures from the 'old paths,' which I have long marked with great pain. The impression of sad decline in the real preaching of the gospel as identical with the person and work of our Lord Jesus, within the

---

He sent a copy to an eminent layman of a Congregational church in Boston (Abner Kingman, Esq.), who was so impressed with the value of its teachings, that he caused to be printed and circulated four or five thousand copies. Is it not thus, by Episcopal prelate, and Baptist minister, and Congregational layman, uniting to spread the knowledge of Christ crucified, that the prayer of our Redeemer is fulfilled, "that they all may be one, as thou, Father, art in me, and I in thee, that they also may be one in us"?

last thirty years, has long been a burden on my mind. When the 'truth as it is in Jesus' is substantially preached, there is so often a dress put on it, robes of philosophy, trappings of man's speculation, language studiously as far from the simplicity of the Scriptures as possible, that one gets the impression that the preacher is rather a lecturer on Christian abstractions, a sort of baptized philosopher, than a follower of St. Paul, a seeker of souls for Christ, a sower of seed taken from the Scriptures. Sensational preaching, the overwrought inculcation that ministers must be intellectual according to the demands of an intellectual age, all fostering the ambition of men to be thought wise, and learned, and great, rather than simple teachers and preachers of Jesus Christ, have perverted and effeminated much of the work of the pulpit in our time.

"Be assured, dear sir, that, should I be in Providence, it will give me sincere pleasure to visit you. As you say, we are both nearing the end of our work and of our days on earth. We are closing our pilgrimage in awful times, and most affecting as concerns our country. One would like, if God please, to live to see this wicked rebellion put down, and peace and union restored. But we must leave such things with God. It is sweet to think of being so near the rest, and holiness, and glorious communion of the people of God in their everlasting home, and in the immediate vision of Christ. May grace be given us to become more and more meet for that inheritance."

A Presbyterian clergyman presented a copy of the "Letters" to each member of the graduating class at Princeton; and a layman of the same denomination (Hon. William E. Dodge, of New York) sent one to each member of the Auburn and the Union Theological Seminaries, accompanied by the following letter: —

"NEW YORK, September, 1863.

"My young Friend: In presenting you with a copy of 'The Letters of President Wayland on the Ministry of the Gospel,' let me request you to read and carefully ponder each letter, and prayerfully ask yourself if you have properly considered the importance of the work you have undertaken. I have felt for years the need of just such a book as this. I fear that many enter the ministry who have little idea that the great object is to rescue souls from hell by leading them to Christ.

"Each Letter is full of valuable suggestions; but let me call your especial attention to the sixth, 'On the Manner of Preaching,' each part of which I commend to your careful consideration.

"I might suggest, that while I approve of all the author says about extemporaneous speaking, yet a carefully written sermon once a week might be best for a few years; but if you would reach the hearts of your hearers, they must feel that your own heart is so full of the love of Christ that you can tell them of it without a written manuscript.

"For many years I have made the subject of the *voice* and *manner* of public speakers one of especial interest, and have been pained to see how little attention has been given to it in our theological seminaries. Many of our students come out good scholars, can write well, are fervent in spirit, and are anxious to be useful; but having neglected the cultivation of the voice and the manner of delivery, they enter upon their work sadly deficient in grace and ease of action, and in well-developed, clear intonations; and for lack of these they never attain any considerable standing as preachers, and much of what they have acquired avails but little, for want of ability to present it with attractiveness.

"When a youth, I resided in a New England village, where there was no place for evening meetings but a school-room, in which we held frequent meetings, and enjoyed several revivals. At times we would have, perhaps, a Methodist preacher with but little theological education, but good natural talents, and a fine, full, clear voice, who, without notes, would deliver a plain gospel sermon fresh from the heart, and secure the attention of all present; and I was often ashamed at the contrast when one of our young men from New Haven or Andover would come along to preach, and I would have to take a bandbox and cover it with a towel, and place it on the table with candles, that he might read off his sermon, generally to a sleepy and inattentive audience.

"I hold it to be the duty of every man, who is preparing to deliver God's message to dying sinners, to see to it that in tone and manner it be done in the best way to secure attention.

"A person intending to make public singing a profession will study for years to cultivate the voice, to give it strength and volume, so that, if necessary, he can interest the largest audiences. Let me beg of you to consider the vast importance of a full, clear, pleasant voice, properly modulated, and without any unpleasant tone. A beautiful piece of music, performed upon a harsh, discordant instrument, loses all its effect.

"The man who becomes confined to his notes can never make an attractive speaker. The times demand an easy, off-hand style of address.

"Don't wait until you can enter the pulpit before you learn to speak, but in the prayer meeting and Sunday school acquire an easy, familiar style of public address. If you would give the trumpet a certain sound, you must learn to use it.

"May God bless you, and prepare you for turning many to righteousness, is the earnest prayer of

Your friend,

WILLIAM E. DODGE."

During the winter of 1863–4, wishing to neglect no opportunity for religious usefulness that lay within the limit of his physical powers, Dr. Wayland taught a class in the Sabbath school of the colored church on Meeting Street, near his residence.

Shortly after the publication of the volume last alluded to, Dr. Wayland chanced to open the Life of Chalmers, which he had not read for several years; and becoming interested in it, he re-read it throughout. He was profoundly impressed with the fact that the life of this eminent servant of God presented a striking example of the earnestness and devotion which he had himself endeavored to awaken in his Christian brethren. Believing that an exhibition of his distinctively Christian and evangelical labor could not but be useful, he prepared for publication "A Memoir of the Christian Labors, pastoral and philanthropic, of Thomas Chalmers." The volume is, of course, drawn mainly from the large standard work of Dr. Hanna. It is not, however, an abridgment, but is made up by selecting, arranging, and, in some cases, condensing the portions which exhibit a single aspect of the life and character of Chalmers. This work was published in 1864.

If we are not mistaken, there is a striking resemblance between the character of Dr. Wayland and that of Chalmers. In power of commanding an audience, and of inspiring his hearers with his own enthusiasm, the Scotch divine stands alone. But in profound earnestness, and in consecration of large intellectual endowments to the unselfish promotion of simple Christianity, they were clearly akin. We apprehend, also, that Dr. Wayland sympathized deeply with the feelings of Chalmers, as thus delineated on pages 192, 193 of the Memoir: —

"With all his social cheerfulness and beaming joy, there were tokens not a few of an internal conflict — glimpses of an inward desolation — which told, unmistakably, that, like David, he felt himself to be a stranger on this earth. 'I would not live always' was a sentence which he often uttered. 'What a wilderness this world is to the heart, with all it has to inspire happiness! I am more conversant with principles than with persons. I begin to suspect that the intensity of my own pursuits has isolated me from living men, and that there is a want of that amalgamation which cements the companionships and closer brotherhoods that obtain in society. I have a great and growing sense of desolation.' These are perhaps the feelings which arise, in advanced life, from the necessity of the case, and belong to a mind of originality and independence, oppressed with that sense of responsibility which withdraws instinctively from all ambiguous or useless associations."

During the winter of 1864–5, Dr. Wayland invited his neighbors to unite with him, each Friday evening, in a prayer meeting at his house. His design was to promote the spiritual good of those who found it difficult to attend the evening meetings of the various churches, and also to engage his neighbors in prayer in behalf of the suffering and imperilled country. These meetings, which were often attended by thirty or forty persons, he conducted with his wonted, or even more than his wonted simplicity, tenderness, and devotion. One who was often present says, "Sometimes, as he sat with his eyes closed, his hands clasped, and the Bible open before him, while the words of eternal life were flowing from his lips, we knew something of the feelings of Peter, when on the Mount he said, 'It is good to be here.'" Many persons, who were not accustomed to frequent prayer meetings, attended these from personal regard for him. The young, even, won by his kindness and sincerity of manner, longed for Friday evening to arrive. Professors of religion who had lost the ardor of their piety were revived, and impressions were made upon the careless that proved a permanent blessing. Nor was the influence limited to those who were actually present. Months after Dr. Wayland's voice had ceased to be heard among men, a candidate for admission to a church in the city, relating her religious experience, said, —

"I was living in the neighborhood of Dr. Wayland, and he invited me to come and attend the prayer meeting held at his house. I did not want to go, and did not mean to; but I told him that I would come, and should be glad to do so. I did not go, however. Some time afterwards, he asked me again if I would not come; and again I told him that I would, but still without meaning to attend. As I thought of it afterwards, it made me feel wretchedly to think that I had *lied* to *Dr. Wayland*, and the more I thought of it, the more ashamed I felt; and I had no rest until I sought from God the pardon of that and of all my other sins."

In January, 1865, Dr. Wayland published in the "American Presbyterian and Theological Review" an article suggested by the celebrated letter of John Foster on the Duration of Future Punishment; and in the July number of the same Quarterly, an article on "the Ministry of Brainerd."

We quote from his letters written in 1861–5.

To Mrs. O'Brien:—

"1861.

"... Has God ever been unfaithful to you, even in a single instance? Then why should you ever distrust him? You speak of assurance. Why, what is the ground of assurance? Is it not the temper of our heart, the bias of our desires? Do you not want, above all things, to be holy? Do you not want to be like Christ? Does anything give you joy like the light of his countenance? Does anything torment you like sin? Who has wrought this in you? Man, yourself, Satan, or God? You know that these are the gifts of the Holy Spirit. You say your faith is weak, and that you have many imperfections. You will have them, as all others do on this side of Jordan. But take just such a soul, with just such desires, and tell me, was it ever lost? You think much about death. Is not this a conquered foe? I talked lately with a departing saint, who said, 'God has dying grace, which he gives only to the dying.' You have it not now, but you will when you need it. Why should we not trust Christ in advance?"

To Dr. James Jackson:—

"1862.

"I should have answered your letter immediately, but I had not a copy of my photograph in the house. I was able to procure one this morning, and I enclose it immediately. It is, I think, the best I have had taken, though much inferior to yours. This, however, is as it should be.

"In your letter you refer to the doctrine of original sin. I am not going into an argument, for you cannot dislike controversy more than I do. Permit me, however, to say that, in my view, the Scriptures fully teach the doctrine of the universal sinfulness of man. As to the mode in which the race became sinful, I am not sure that they teach us. It may be accounted for, or, in other words, referred to a general law, in either of two ways. It may be by hereditary descent. Much, both of good and of evil, comes to us in this way. Or, again, it may be owing to the entrance of such a being as an infant into a sinful world, at enmity with God. He would inevitably take the type of character which existed universally around him. The general law is, that much which we suffer, or enjoy, comes to us through those with whom we have no direct connection. You and I both know how much our probation has been rendered favorable by good parents. The contrary, also, we see every day. This law is necessary to our present state, or our race would be at a perpetual stand-still. I hope I make myself intelligible; but I do not know. My impression is, that the Bible deals with the fact, and this may be accounted for in either of these ways, or perhaps in others.

"May God, my dear friend, lead us into all necessary truth, and prepare us for his heavenly glory. To me, the plan of salvation made known in the New Testament seems evidently one of the ideas of God. Man did not frame it.

"I forgot to say how much I am obliged by your sun picture. I have given it an appropriate place in our album. It faces that of Florence Nightingale."

To a minister: —

"I will merely turn your attention to John viii., from the twelfth verse, and also John x. Has it ever occurred to you that nothing more sublime can be conceived than when that poor barefooted Jewish peasant stood on our earth and declared, "I am the light of the world; whosoever believeth in me shall not walk in darkness, but shall have the light of life"? He declares that whatever he does is done by God; that, like Him who appeared to Moses, he is the "I am," and that none shall pluck out of his hand those that believe in him; that he is the only way of access to the eternal God. What overpowering and astonishing words! a little too good and important for ministers to use as a theme for an essay, and people to hear for an intellectual diversion. O my Savior, has it come to this, that the message thou didst bring from heaven should be used as an instrument for building up a reputation among men! May God forgive us."

To Mr. Loring: —

"... I have read Mill on "Liberty" once, and had re-read the first half the second time, when I was taken sick. It is a strong book, and by an able thinker. Most of his points are good, though I think that they might have been stated more simply. His treatment of the rights of the individual might have been better by setting out with the simple principle, 'Every one has a right to himself,' and, of course, to all the legitimate use of himself, that is, of all his powers. As this belongs to every one, it excludes interference. His style is not easily understood, at least by stupid fellows like me. He does not believe in the Christian religion, as I do, but apparently thinks it of human origin; nor does he set forth the fundamental principle of its morality. He seems to consider absolute obedience to God as slavery. But such obedience is evidently necessary to the condition of a creature ignorant of the future. In my opinion he exaggerates the obedience to custom, and the want of independence in man; at least, I do not find it as he states it, in my own consciousness. Men do not commonly long hold to a custom, unless they find it, by practice, to be convenient. You wear pantaloons not simply because every one else does. I presume you remember when your father wore small-clothes. I know mine did. The reason of the change is, that pantaloons have proved more comfortable and convenient."

To his son: —

"I have read Herbert Spencer through, and some of the essays twice, and have read his volume on education. . . . His book will do much to change the opinions of the civilized world. I hope it will be widely read here and in England. . . . As to the worth of knowledge, he is very strong. Here, he and I are aiming at the same thing. I did not expect to see, in my day, any one with whose views I could so sincerely sympathize. . . . He speaks to the common sense of humanity, and hates sham; and he will triumph, though it will take some time first. The ruts are deep, the crust is old and strong, and a generation will pass away before a change comes. However, it will come. Democracy must prevail, but can be a blessing only by the intellectual and moral education of the people. This education must be a reality, and must not consist in spending years in hammering on Horace and Virgil, and Græca Majora. Revelation may follow revelation, each coming nearer to the truth, until the benevolence of the gospel makes every one the helper of his brother; and then democracy will stand."

To his son, — after alluding to the sudden death of his friend, Rev. Henry Jackson, D. D.: —

"March 10, 1863.

"My summons may be as sudden. When I am called to leave you, live in love; seek each other's best interests; bear with each other's infirmities, and strive to present each other faultless before the throne. Let each esteem the other better than himself. Live so as to please God. Think the same things. Contend lovingly for the faith once delivered to the saints."

To a former pupil: —

"... Is it wise to take so much upon one's self? After doing the things that you mentioned, what time is there left for things of at least as great importance? I have thought of this of late, frequently, in connection with you. You know that the word failed to bring forth fruit on some soil, being choked with the cares of the world and the deceitfulness of riches. You will say, I have no time to attend to my soul's concerns. But what was your time given for? If God gives it to you, and you use it for something else, on what principle can you say, I have no time? He gave you time for this very purpose."

To his son: —

"Have you ever seen the hymn commencing, 'I worship thee, sweet Will of God,' in the Plymouth Collection? I think it will be useful to you. I admire it very much."

The hymn referred to is from the Lyra Catholica.

I worship thee, sweet Will of God,
  And all thy ways adore;
And every day I live, I long
  To love thee more and more.

Man's weakness, waiting upon God,
  Its end can never miss;
For men on earth no work can do
  More angel-like than this.

He always wins who sides with God;
  To him no chance is lost;
God's will is sweetest to him when
  It triumphs at his cost.

Ill that God blesses is our good,
And unblessed good is ill;
And all is right that seems most wrong,
If it be his dear will.

When obstacles and trials seem
Like prison walls to be,
I do the little I can do,
And leave the rest to thee.

I have no cares, O blessed Will,
For all my cares are thine;
I live in triumph, Lord, for thou
Hast made thy triumphs mine.

In writing to his sister, Dr. Wayland alludes to the hymn just quoted, and says, —

"I cannot yet say that I have attained; but this is the spirit after which I am striving, and towards which I hope that I make some feeble approach."

To Hon. L. H. Morgan, Rochester: —

"Dear Sir: I have just completed reading, for the second or third time, your 'League of the Iroquois.' I cannot forbear the pleasure of thanking you for it. It is the most remarkable book of the kind I have ever seen. The plan of social organization is original, unlike any other I have ever known of, and exhibits a power of statesmanship such as I do not remember to have seen equalled. It was a great man who devised it, a most powerful man who persuaded men to adopt it at first, and a most self-governed and sagacious people who received it. And then their religion was the purest and best theism that men unblessed with revelation have ever arrived at. Their dresses show a refinement of taste such as a barbarous people almost never attain. It is in all respects, to me, a most surprising book, and ought to be in every public library in the world. Men ought to know that such a race as this has lived."

To Professor W. D. Atkinson: —

"I thank you for your discourse on the schools of Great Britain. I have read it with much interest. The lessons which it suggests are of great importance, but I fear they will not be heeded as they deserve. Your motto is significant—*Mutato nomine, de te fabula narratur.* We, I apprehend, are following in the same course. It is now supposed that the only way to build up a college is, not to teach well what it is important to teach, and thus make the success of an institution depend on the skill and power of the instructors, but to collect money, to found scholarships, and endow professorships, and thus make the teachers wholly independent of their own labor. . . . In this country public opinion may discover a corrective, but what it is I know not. I thank you for placing before us the facts in the case."

To Rev. Dr. Hoby:—

"... I have had some sad, very sad, hours and days: there was no refuge but God. A train of thought like this has given me consolation—God is omniscient! He knows everything about us, and is able to do everything for us. He is all love—such love that he gave his Son for us. He is as faithful to his promises as he is full of love and power. I know that nothing can happen to me that has not been appointed by the perfect will of a God of love. And more than this, he has promised that he will receive as his child every one who comes to Christ. Have I thus come? Do I now take him for my Savior? Do I long for holiness more than for anything else? Are the marks of a child of God upon me? I try myself—I must believe that Christ has given me new life, and that I am a child of God. All the promises are mine, and our God has never, through eternity, been unfaithful to his word. He will do all, and more than all, that he has promised. All things will therefore work together for my good—pains as much as pleasures, sickness as well as health. On these things I try to rely, and when I find my faith failing, I cry in anguish, Lord, increase my faith.

"I have lately read the Bible more than ever in my life, in the same space of time, and at every new reading I find more to love and admire. O, how much have I lost by not reading it more! I have reason to bless God for setting me apart, on a side bench, at school, alone, to read his Word and call upon his name. Sometimes I think how much better I might have lived, how much more good I might have done, if, eschewing everything but Christ, I had lived above the world, and laid myself a living sacrifice on his altar.

"It is a great comfort to me to know that 'The Life of Judson' has been a blessing to you. There is no labor which we perform that yields so delightful a result, as that undertaken to promote the cause of Christ, and do good to the souls of men."

To a clergyman: —

"I received a letter, some days since, from Mr. T., with a prospectus of the new monthly magazine [Hours at Home] which he proposes soon to issue, and to which he asks me to become a contributor. He mentions you as one of the stated contributors. It is not in my power now to engage in the undertaking; but it seems to me to be a matter of great importance. The social literature of this country is almost wholly in the hands of those whose religious opinions are entirely dissimilar to ours: the best are merely neutral on those points which we esteem of vital importance, and the others tend to a position at variance with the doctrines which we hold dear. It seems to be time to establish something which shall be popular and useful, and which shall maintain boldly, on all suitable occasions, the doctrines of the cross. I believe it can be done. Let us engage in it with our whole thought. We are liable to let the truth become obscured or forgotten by our silence. I am for uniting good men of all denominations in the effort."

CHAPTER XIII.

HIS HOME. — THE MORNING HOUR. — THE GARDEN. — THE STUDY. — THE TABLE. — VISITORS. — THE YOUNG. — THE DAY CLOSED. — THE SABBATH. — THE HOUSE OF GOD.

AT no time had the life of Dr. Wayland been diversified by startling adventure, or marked by sudden inspirations. One day greatly resembled its fellow. But during the latter portion of his life, his employment of time afforded a better index to his character than when his occupations were closely prescribed by his external circumstances and his official duties.

The hour before breakfast was always given to secret prayer and reading the Scriptures. During this hour he read the Bible for devotion, not at all for criticism. He highly estimated the value of communion with God before the mind has become pre-occupied or distracted with other thoughts. From his study he came, when summoned, to lead in domestic devotions, which were invariably brief, never tedious.

Breakfast over, he was ready for exercise. He seemed to take as much pains to provide himself with physical labor as many persons to avoid it. He sometimes walked; but this did not fully satisfy him. It was scarcely active enough; and moreover he wanted his work to have a result, to show what had been done. In the winter he shovelled the snow from the walks, if there was opportunity. If this could not be done, he continued his practice of sawing and splitting wood. There seemed something of heroism in his victories over the gnarliest logs; and beyond the tamer toils of the axe and saw, he valued the conquests won by the beetle and wedges.

But joyful was the season when he could lay aside the saw, and could take the spade and rake. Gardening was to him what pictures, statuary, travel are to another. He loved his garden, because it afforded him exercise diversified in character; because it was a productive form of labor, and because it combined thought with toil. He was never weary of working in it, of walking through it, of talking about it. He seemed to establish personal relations with all his plants. He would go out many times a day to visit them, as a fond parent would visit the chamber of a sick child. "I think that my garden knows me," he sometimes said; and it seemed as if every tree and shrub would put forth peculiar efforts, and at his instance would do what no one else could prevail on them to achieve. His tenderness was like the love of woman. Once, when the house was building, it was found that a cherry tree, then in full blossom, must be moved. He had it taken up with every care, and transplanted. He watched over it, watered it, sheltered it, and it lived for perhaps a year, though its constitution never recovered from the shock. He was training a grape vine by the porch, and a branch, about which he was very hopeful, had become cracked in the effort to give it a symmetrical curve. He at once made a sort of splint of sponge, and wound it around, and kept it moist for days, coming out from his study every hour or two to watch it.

He was keenly alive to his honor as a gardener. In the following, to Mr. F., of New Haven, he expressed the pleasure he felt at a compliment from a professional horticulturist: —

"I thank you for the line by Mr. H. I showed him all my plantation. He gave me a fair character as a gardener, with which I was much pleased. He is a rare man. I admire him exceedingly."

He did not like to be surpassed. When he was outstripped by those who could afford the luxury of a greenhouse, he was not perturbed, for that, he said, was capital. But he would not willingly be inferior to any who had only the advantages of sun and air, common to all. In gardening, as in all else, nothing satisfied him but perfection. Nothing was done so long as anything remained to be done. Wishing to gather wisdom from past experience, he kept, during the latter portion of his life, and after he felt that he could spare time for the employment, a garden diary. Some extracts, embracing a few weeks in the spring of 1863, will give an idea of its character: —

" *March* 22. Commenced labor in the garden. Sowed peas in A. 1, east of asparagus bed. Hoed spinach.

" 27, 28, 30. Scraped and washed trees. At the south end of the bed, sowed Tom Thumb peas. At the north end, early Philadelphia, for seed, if they prove good. The rest are Daniel O'Rourke.

" *April* 1. Prepared hot-bed.

" 2. Planted elm tree on Governor Street.

" 6. Sowed celery and lettuce in hot-bed. Planted elm tree at end of the lot.

" 8. Prepared another hot-bed.

" 10. Planted early June potatoes, put salt in three rows, lime in the others, with manure over all; salt in three western rows.

" 11. Buckeye potatoes treated as above, two rows east salt, others lime.

" 13. Uncovered rose-bushes and raspberries; sowed onions and some beets. Weather at night cold.

" 14. Warm and pleasant day. Treated raspberries with vegetable manure made from refuse rubbish of the last year. Planted more onions.

" 15. Finished raspberries.

" 16. Rained incessantly and violently all day.

" 17. Set out cauliflowers and lettuce from Mr. Nesbit. Warm and pleasant.

" 20. Hoed and raked strawberries — not hoed, but loosened with the hoe. Weather cold and cloudy.

"21. Sowed Champion of England peas.

"22. Planted white apple potatoes. Cold last night; white frost. Gathered spinach for the first time. Treated potatoes with lime.

"23. Raked the grass on plats.

"24. Rain.

"25. Rain, cold and dreary. Set out in the hot-bed plants from Mrs. Sprague.

"27. Raked borders. Cut spinach; it is growing well.

"28. Sowed carrots on upper border. Planted early beans and cotton seed. Raked borders. Loosened the ground round early peas. Weather warm and sunny. Strawberries show buds.

"*May* 1. Warm and pleasant. Asparagus begins to appear. Early potatoes are breaking ground.

"2. Very warm. Grafted Easter Beurre and St. Michael's, the former with the Glout Morceau, the latter with Belle Lucrative and Rostezer. Planted melons. Cut about half a pound of asparagus.

"4. Rained almost all day. No work done, excepting the setting out of Silesia and California lettuce.

"7. Rain continues. Easterly wind and cold. Nothing done in garden. There is fear lest the seed sown some days since may rot in the ground. Blossoms do not advance.

"8. Planted pole beans. Continued spading. Cherry blossoms begin to appear.

"9. Sowed parsnips and carrots. Set out tomatoes. Spinach gone. Cherries begin to bloom. Gooseberries in full bloom. Some blossoms on strawberries. Onions and beets, the first planted, are up.

"10. This and the two preceding days warm and pleasant. To-day cherries in bloom. Cut two and a half pounds of asparagus. Hoed peas. Planted melons. Finished spading upper side of C. 1. Sowed mignonette."

In writing to his friends, with whom he had any horticultural affiliations, he would always ask and give the news of the garden; thus, "Strawberries will be ripe in a few days; peas are well formed, but do not yet fill. Nothing else deserves notice but the gooseberries, which thrive finely." "Beans picked to-day, beets in a day or two; strawberries fail since the dry weather." And again, "I must acknowledge that you beat us in Hubbard squashes." He always delighted in the exercise of reciprocity among the craft, in giving and receiving plants.

We know not whether the cause was material or spiritual, but somehow, when he could not walk without fatigue, he could be on his feet in the garden, working from breakfast until two o'clock, and was not conscious of weariness. It was truly wonderful to see him, almost up to his latest summer, toiling under the sun of July, his hair drenched in perspiration, distancing his sons, and exhibiting hardly any falling away from the vigor of forty years.

His labor was not devoted to the useful merely. Perhaps he loved the beautiful quite as truly. He was exceedingly fond of flowers. Of a Wisteria in full bloom he said, "It is the prettiest thing in town." Especially he liked to combine beauty with use, to train his pear trees and grape vines in graceful lines, and to cultivate fruit that was fair to the eye as well as pleasing to the taste.

Self-control seemed to be powerless when he went into the garden. Here alone he did not keep his resolution. He often went out intending to stay only a few minutes; but, fascinated by the spell of nature, he would expand the minutes to hours. Sometimes Mrs. Wayland would urge him to relinquish his toils, and he would promise to work only half an hour more; but one moment led to another, until some imperative call summoned him to the house.

During one year only was his garden neglected. In the spring of 1858, he was so engrossed with gathering in sheaves from the Master's fields, that his grounds had little care. He writes in July, "I was so much engaged with the church that I put the garden off on the man, and nothing has prospered. Everything in gardening depends on the work in spring. If this is badly done, it is difficult to repair the damage."

The morning did not often pass away without the cows receiving a moment's attention. For horses he did not profess admiration, nor had he any thorough knowledge of them; but cows he understood and loved. He had studied the theory of Guenon, and knew the points of a good cow. He was much amused, and probably not at all displeased, when a stranger, who was proposing to exhibit some fat cattle or extraordinary stock in Providence, called to ask him for a line of commendation in behalf of his exhibition. He urged that "everybody told him that Dr. Wayland knew more about stock than anybody else in town."

When the work of the garden was over, he bathed, and soon was dressed for the remainder of the day. He then spent a little while in prayer in his chamber; and at this time he would lay before God any event affecting the household, any unusual care or embarrassment. If a servant were needed, he did not fail to tell Him who watches the fall of the sparrow, and he would say, "We must wait and see what God will do for us." He *believed in prayer*. He believed that God is a rewarder of them that diligently seek him. In one of his last years, when a young friend asked him, "Can you always feel, when you pray, that prayer is a reality?" he said, "Almost always I can; and the older I grow, the more fully I am convinced that it is a real thing to ask God for blessings, and to receive them in answer to prayer."

Then, if the morning were not already past, he went to his study. The view from this room is not marked. Its attractions were within. Upon the walls were two portraits of Napoleon, one as at Milan, in command of the army of Italy, and the other, as at Fontainebleau, on the eve of his abdication. Separated from these by a window, was Wellington. Elsewhere were Dr. Nott, and Sir Robert Peel, and Dr. J. M. Mason, and Humboldt in his study, and Algernon Sidney, and Cromwell, the Protector, conversing with Milton, the secretary of the commonwealth. On two sides were books; and on the study table were those in most constant use. Chief of these was the Greek Testament. Of late years he used Bagster's edition, on account of the distinctness of the type; but he found many misprints, and one page of the fly-leaf is covered with his errata. Robinson's invaluable Lexicon was ever beside him. He did not greatly affect commentators, but relied rather on prolonged meditation and on prayer for divine illumination. When a gentleman, about commencing a Bible class, asked him, "What is the best commentary?" he replied, "Your own eyes, first of all." The annotated Paragraph Bible of the Religious Tract Society he valued extremely, for its brief notes and its full references. Of exposition, he most enjoyed Dr. Brown on I. Peter, preferring him even to Leighton, his early favorite. Of the English Bible his reading was mainly in a very plain, leather-covered quarto, which he had procured in 1824. With each year he seemed to spend more and more time in reading the Scriptures. No sense of duty urged him; in the wisdom imparted, and the hopes revealed, he found a perpetual reward. Can his children ever forget, how, entering the study, they would find him in the rocking-chair, opposite the door, with his Bible open on his knee, and his eyes filled with a strange liquid light, and how, becoming conscious of earth, not without an effort and a perceptible lapse of time, bringing from heaven its gentle benignity, he would put his spectacles back upon his forehead, and, leaving his silk handkerchief as a mark in the Bible, would say, "Well, my son?" and then would flow forth the utterings of affection, of experience, of human counsel, and of divine wisdom, but all spontaneous, all natural, never preceptive.

On the table was the long, narrow note-book, in which he made minutes of the trains of thought that he wished to follow out. Sometimes he worked on a subject; not seldom a subject came to him, and he put down his spontaneous thoughts, to be used hereafter.

Thus the hours passed until dinner. He was usually an "honest eater," despising with all his heart an epicure, or gourmand, yet enjoying without disguise the blessings of Providence, particularly the fruit of his own labor. Scarcely less keen was his gratification when some product, redolent of the forest or the deep, or of the garden or orchard, served as a token of the remembrance of valued and perhaps distant friends. Thus he writes, —

"Yesterday a box of prairie chickens arrived, all in excellent order. To-day we invited a pair of them to dine with us, and they discharged their duty admirably. ——, who is here, pronounced them first rate. I thank you for your kindness. We shall be all the while wishing that you were with us."

And again, after an arrival from Florida, in 1863, —

"The box of oranges reached us, as you had foretold. We thank you very much. They are thinner-skinned than is usual, and are the most juicy I ever saw. They substantiate what you say — that we need not go out of the United States for oranges, or indeed for any tropical fruit. Besides being delicious, they are in remarkable preservation."

His readiness to be pleased with any well-meant kindness was always touching.

It is probable that, in his later years, from 1860, he erred on the side of undue abstemiousness. It seemed to escape his attention that an attack, like that which he had experienced, might result either from too high living or from too intense labor, and that the treatment, in cases so widely diverse, must needs be as different as are the two sources of the disease. He dieted, as if his attack was the result of excessive indulgence, and allowed himself by no means (in our opinion) the nourishment needed for his great frame and his protracted physical exercise — drawing upon his will to supply the needed energy.

After dinner there was often some public business to transact, or meeting to attend. If not thus called from his home, he spent the afternoon in reading, or in writing letters. After 1860 he confined his severe mental exertions to the forenoon.

His reading, during the most laborious portion of his life, especially during the later years of his presidency, had been very limited, embracing few books that were not directly in the line of his duties, or required for immediate use. He had, however, always read the leading reviews, particularly the English quarterlies, with regularity, and had thus "kept himself abreast of society." And his singular faculty of wise questioning, his power of extracting from others the result of their studies or experiences, made him well informed on many subjects that were apparently out of his line.

During his temporary pastorate, as we have seen, he relinquished all secular reading. He did not, of course, think this the duty of every minister, nor of himself under ordinary circumstances. He felt that the demands upon him were for the time so pressing that all his spiritual and mental energies must be turned into a single channel. But after he was released from official care, he read more, probably, than he had ever done since he entered public life. His intellectual sympathies were almost as broad as his moral. He read universally, in all departments.

Few days passed without some visitor, perhaps one of his old friends, — with every year growing fewer, — or one of his former colleagues in instruction, or a colaborer in benevolent enterprises. Not unfrequently one of his younger brethren in the ministry, always welcomed, came to tell him of the progress of the work of God, or to ask his counsel. Or perhaps some stranger, visiting Providence, would have a desire to see the ex-president, and the author of the Moral Science.

With many visitors, strangers till then, he enjoyed delightful interviews, conversing upon the great interests of the world, and the brighter glories of immortality. In

July, 1861, Dr. Tobey called with Mr. John Hodgkin, an eminent English barrister, and a leading member of the Society of Friends. Mr. Hodgkin had declined high station under the British government that he might engage in a religious mission to America and other countries. He had a long and deeply interesting conversation with Dr. Wayland; and their views of the spirituality of worship, and the duty of alienation from the world, were remarkably coincident. After leaving him, Mr. Hodgkin said, "That man has a *bruised brain*." Perhaps no words could more justly express the results of the violent strain to which Dr. Wayland had long subjected his mental powers.

On the following day Dr. Wayland met Mr. Hodgkin again, and they enjoyed a further delightful conversation. Not long before leaving town, Mr. Hodgkin said, "I must see Dr. Wayland once more." He went to the house, and found him in the study, alone and at leisure. After conversing a little while, they "fell into silence." Presently the spirit of prayer being given, Mr. Hodgkin knelt, and at once Dr. Wayland knelt beside him. Mr. Hodgkin offered a touching petition for the advancement of religion, for the welfare of the church of God, and especially for the aged disciple at his side. Tears were flowing from the eyes of each. Then Dr. Wayland prayed, asking peculiar blessing for Mr. Hodgkin; and then they separated, with the most tender Christian feeling, after Dr. Wayland had given to Mr. Hodgkin a letter of commendation to Christians in America, of all denominations.

From Mr. Hodgkin to Dr. Tobey:—

"August, 1866.

". . . How peculiarly does he live in my memory and in my heart! There was a grandeur, and yet a simplicity, about him that were almost apostolical. Rarely have I known a man in whom intellectual power and culture were so harmoniously combined with love, and faith, and every Christian grace. It was, moreover, a very unusual feature in one who had ruled and taught with chief authority more than a quarter of a century, that he was so totally devoid of all approach to dogmatism, either in thought, expression, or manner. Instead of laying down the law, he conferred, and reasoned, as one who sought to learn; and he held communion with those who were his inferiors, as showing that he and they sat at one table, where all are brethren, and where one is our Master even our omnipotent yet all-gracious Lord and Redeemer."

Often he received visits from some of his young friends, whom he had guided to the Savior. When perplexed in questions of duty, they came and confided all to him. He was often enabled to remove clouds, and doubts, and anxious cares. To one who was much troubled with the fear that she had assumed too great responsibility in the advice she had given to another, he said, —

"Did you ever see a person rolling tenpins, who, after he has rolled a ball, and while it is on its way, will sway his body and twist himself about, as if to influence the movements of the ball? But it all does no good. You are doing just so. But you acted in the fear of God. You have rolled your ball; now, dismiss it from your mind."

Sometimes religious inquirers would visit him, either brought by their Christian friends, or urged by their own feelings. He was remarkable for the simple directness, mingled with tenderness, with which he relieved them from all embarrassment. He would see, as by intuition, the errand which had brought them; and, "Well, my child, you have come to talk with me about religion — have you not?" he would say. In removing obstacles from their pathway, he was, as he has hitherto said, greatly aided by the remembrance of his own religious experience.

It was wonderful to see how the youngest and most timid found themselves able to talk without constraint with one who had often been regarded as the embodiment of all that was stern and awe-inspiring. While charged with the discipline of the college, and compelled almost always to stand in antagonism to something or somebody, he could not venture to exhibit the tenderness which was in his heart. Nor was the change merely in his aspect; but as he grew older, and drew nearer to the world of love, he was perpetually more gentle, more considerate, more patient, more ready to bear with everything, in the hope of being useful. Once in his later years, while he was visiting a friend for a few days, and had to see a good many rather commonplace people, a member of his family, when alone with him, said, "This must be very tiresome to you." He replied, "I am very willing to do it. Seeing people in this way is a means of doing good."

The thought of awakening a sensation of fear seemed painful to him. When one, who had known him very well, brought with her a young friend who knew him only by name, he walked with them a portion of the way home, and at parting said to his new acquaintance, "Now, I am not so very terrible — am I?" A lady, brought up in sentiments opposed to the evangelical belief, was invited by a friend to attend his Bible class. She says, —

"I continued to go for many weeks, and I more and more wanted to talk with him; but I did not venture to. At last I went to him one day after the class, and asked him if I might call and see him. He was exceedingly kind, and urged me to come. I went a great many times. It was very hard for me to understand about the doctrines of religion. I had never had any idea of such a thing as a change of heart. I could not believe in the atonement; and I told him so. I could not say that I saw, until I was more than sure that I did see. He was unwearied in his patience. I said to him once, that I at first believed that his kindness would wear out, when he found how slow I was in believing as he did, and that he would show his severer side. He laughed, and said, 'Well, S——, you haven't seen it yet — have you?'"

His parental care of the young disciples, for whom he had been interested, never ceased. Meeting one of them on the street, he said, "Who was that I saw you walking with the other day?" She replied, "That was Miss ——." He asked, "Is she a Christian?" "O, yes." "That is right," he said: "you know, if you put one coal of fire out on the hearth by itself, it soon goes out; but if you put a good many together, they keep each other warm."

He was walking by the High School, when he met a young girl, a pupil, who was on her way home. He asked her about her studies, and presently said, "When are you going to be a Christian?" She answered, "I ought to be now; I hope I shall be some time." He replied, "I am sure that you will be. I am praying for you." These simple, tender words could not be forgotten. His prayers were not in vain.

Persons sometimes wondered that he, with his broad experience, lofty ideas, and severe sense of duty, should awaken such confidence and attachment in the young, the ignorant, the impulsive, the often erratic, and that he should be able to make so large allowance for them, and to bear with them so patiently. It was owing, in part, to the unaffected benevolence of his nature, to which nothing of human interest could be indifferent; in part to his universal power of sympathy; and in part to the clearness of all his conceptions and the simplicity of his teachings. His singular power to attract the young, and to elevate them, in some degree, to his own spiritual level, was not the only feature in which he resembled the Man of Nazareth. It was not by humoring them that he won their regard. Rather he held them most rigidly to the one standard — the perfect law. Says one of his young friends, —

"I would tell him of some fondly-cherished ambition. He would listen patiently to the close, and then say, 'Well, my child, you have given yourself to the service of the Lord. Would the cultivation of this talent, the gratification of this taste, help you to serve him better? Would it tend to his glory? If you are sincere in your Christian profession, you must carefully consider, and abide by the decision.' He never would consent to a compromise. There were only two paths — one right, and one wrong. There must be a choice between the two. He believed that a Christian had no right to call anything his own. If he had truly given himself to the Lord, he could not say, 'Here, Lord, this proportion of my time, or wealth, or energies, shall be devoted to your service, and the rest shall be devoted to my own use.' And yet, the religion that he inculcated never seemed to me gloomy. Often he taught me self-sacrifice, which it was hard to make; but then he made the service appear so sweet and sacred, that the burden was taken away in the thought of the dear Savior for whom it was performed.

"Once when he asked me how I was employing my time, I told him of one of my occupations, at which a strange expression appeared in his face. I inquired, 'Do you not think it right?' I told him that it was with my mother's approval. He said, 'Then it is all right; but it seems trifling, when life is so short, and there is so much to be done.'"

He did not shrink from reproving; but as affection attended the motive of the reproof, so it governed its spirit.

The following letters illustrate the tone of his intercourse with his young friends, some of whom had been converted under his ministry, others of whom had been pupils in his Bible class.

"My dear ——: . . . The best of all, however, is what you tell me of yourself. You have done something for Christ, and he has rewarded you with his richest blessing, by giving you more grace. You must have acquired more government over yourself. You have learned to *swim* in the place of *drifting*. Go on in this strength, my dear ——, and he will aid you abundantly. . . .

"Seek for consistency of character; that is, let the love of Christ *rule* in your heart, and that will accomplish what I recommend. If the love of Christ does not rule, but only shares with other things your best affections, your likes and dislikes, your character will not be consistent. Never think, 'How far may I go? I will obey just up to the line,' as though you were a slave; but as a dear daughter, act from love, and think, not, How far may I go in the course of worldly pleasure without forfeiting my Christian hope; but, What can I do, or from what can I refrain, that will most please the Savior who died for me, who loved me, and whom I love. You know from experience that this is the happy way of living, and that we do not surrender anything for Christ without receiving abundantly from him. The reward for sacrifices for Christ is, you know, a hundred fold. Form your character on the highest and most noble principles, and you will be the loveliest —— in the world."

"... Your letter deeply interested me, and made me wish you could be here in my study for an hour or two, to talk over the things which concern our spiritual interests. How many hours we have spent in such happy conference, gaining strength to resist the world and to follow in the steps of the blessed Savior! I know it is pleasant to you, and, am sure it is to me, to remember those interviews, and to recall the hour when, at last giving up all the world, you surrendered your heart to the Savior, and felt in your own soul that he had received you, that he loved you, and had given you a new heart. And then remember the day of your baptism — that bright and beautiful morning in May, when you publicly took Christ for your Savior, when you died to the world, and rose again to a new life, and on the evening of that day, for the first time, partook of the memorial of that body which was broken and the blood that was shed for you. It is sweet to recall those days. Has the world ever yielded you anything so satisfying, so delightful in the recollection?

"Dear ——, I fear that you have changed somewhat from the 'little girl' of those days. I fear that worldly pleasure, and amusement, and society, have taken possession of a portion of your heart, and that it has become divided. The struggle is now going on between Christ and the world; and for some time past the world has gained strength, and the love of Christ has grown weaker. Is it not so, my dear child? But if it be so, you have made a poor exchange, and you feel it to be so. You long for the days when the candle of the Lord shone round about you, and when by his light you walked through darkness. If you have wandered from him, he has not cast you off; he still loves you; he still hears your feeblest cry for his presence, and is waiting to fold you again in his arms. Look back and see when, and where, and how, it was that you began to forsake his path, and resolve to return to him. Think how he followed you when you were determined to have nothing to do with him. He is grieved that you should cherish anything in comparison with him; and yet he loves you, and pleads with you to be reconciled to him.

"My dear ——, if I loved you less, I should not have written thus. But my time is short: soon I must give up my account, and it would be very wrong if I did not seek first of all your best good. You will know how to understand it."

"My dear ——: It gives me great pleasure to learn that you have marked out a path of duty for yourself, and are becoming decided to walk in it, and thus to be a consistent Christian. The Savior calls us to take up the cross, and follow him, denying ourselves. Sometimes the cross is in one shape, and sometimes in another. It may be in the form of persecution. Parents may persecute, brothers and sisters may be unkind, the world may sneer, imprisonment may threaten, nay, life may be in danger, for doing the will of Christ. Or the cross may take another form. The opera may open its doors, company may invite, balls and parties may induce, dress may attract, ease may beckon, intellectual vanity may whisper, — all tending to withdraw us from simple obedience to the commands of Christ. Pleasures sought for themselves appeal powerfully to the young, and do not allow them time to reflect that the pleasures which God has prepared are all blooming on both sides of the path of duty. My dear ——, remember that if we deny ourselves, and take up the cross for Christ, one form is as pleasing to him as another. It may be as hard a thing for a young person to bear the reproach of being too precise, as it was in old times to be whipped or imprisoned; and the blessing of the Savior rests on one as much as the other."

"My dear ——: . . . But what you say of yourself deeply interests me. You look upon yourself very much as I do. I have thought and told you that there seemed to me undeveloped powers of doing good in you, and that you would not be very happy until they were called into exercise. You are surrounded by the kindest of parents and friends, and seeing and loving them takes up all your time. You have not object enough to call forth and strengthen your energies. You need some active pursuit in which you can *labor* to do good. You are in danger of getting into a miscellaneous life; this is unprofitable. You say you love teaching. That is a beautiful and useful talent. God gave it to you for something: see that something comes out of it. Do not drizzle away your time. You tell me that you would like to go to the *west.* Do you not fix your eyes there because there is no prospect of your being wanted here? The world is round, and it is all west. You say that there are some ten or twelve young persons around you who ought to be taught. Begin and teach them. If this be a seed which God plants, he will water it; and who knows how large a tree it may become!"

When visitors called, if the weather was suitable, he often took them into the garden; using, like his Master and example, nature as a means of leading the soul to God and heaven. Many of his young friends, who were pupils at Mr. Buel's school, will remember the afternoon when, after he had shown them all that the garden contained, clothing its commonest features with attractiveness by the love he bore it, there was spread before them a table crowned with his own melons and grapes.

It was not easy to say whether he took more delight in the labor of cultivating his garden, or in bestowing its products upon others. When he heard that visitors had been at the house during his absence, "Did you take them into the garden," he would ask, "and give them some fruit and flowers?" Once, when he asked, "Did you give them some pears?" and received the reply that there were none in the house, and that there was hardly time to take the visitors into the garden, "You should have a plate of them always at hand," he said. "We do not realize how persons value these things, when they cannot raise them for themselves."

By five o'clock he usually went out again for exercise, walking or working in the garden. But walking became wearisome to him in time.

After tea he often sat a little while in the parlor with the family, conversing, or reading a magazine for a few minutes, or looking over some volumes of humorous sketches by Leech, extracted from Punch, in which he found great amusement. But after a few minutes, he would seem to hear the call of duty, and would return to his study.

He received many letters from persons quite unknown to him, often persons in remote places, propounding questions of conscience, of church discipline, of moral science, and of Christian doctrine.

How lovingly he wrote to his kindred, particularly when any anniversary awakened affectionate remembrances, or when their circumstances, temporal or spiritual, called for a word of cheer or of wisdom, need not be told to any one who has read the preceding pages.

Of his tenderness to the members of his immediate family, to his wife, to his children, we know not how to attempt any description. Perhaps in no instance was it more marked than in his relations to his youngest son, an invalid for many years. It might with truth be said that "whatever touched him touched the apple of the father's eye." As this son was rarely absent from his home but few letters were addressed to him. From those which have been found, we make the following extracts:—

"1852.

"I write to you the first letter with the pretty pen and handle which you gave me. I am much obliged to you for it, my dear boy, and shall think of my little son very frequently when I am using it. I hope that you may have a great many birthdays, and that you may grow every year wiser and better.

"... We thought frequently of you, my dear son, yesterday, and remembered that it was your birthday. We wished we could have been with you, and have made a little party for you. You are now in your thirteenth year, and getting to be a large boy. We hope that God will restore your health, and especially that he will give you a new heart, and make you a religious boy."

"1858.

"... I am rejoiced to hear of your good health and happiness during your visit. I hope you will return much stronger than you were when you went away. Nothing is growing much, and you will see but little change on your return. The cold rain keeps everything stationary. I hope, my dear son, you are improving in piety, as well as in health. All these changes are trials of our religion, which always gains strength with every effort to do right and to keep ourselves in the love of God."

He writes to the same: —

"The chapter of events in your department is as follows: —

"1. Jerry [the horse] is as well as usual.

"2. Ned [the terrier] has killed several rats; the last time, three in one morning.

"3. The top-knot pullet is dead.

"4. Eggs to-day, four; yesterday, six.

"5. Two mice caught in the trap this morning; one small, the other very large.

"I do not remember anything else of consequence."

Sometimes the little family circle was enlarged by the presence of relatives, always welcome to his home. At Thanksgiving, 1860, his family was united. His three sons were present, one just returned after a year's absence from the country, and with them the wives of his two older sons, whom he had taken to his heart, making them, not only daughters-in-law, but daughters in love. And in the third generation he saw his children's children, and peace upon Israel. His intercourse with them did not, indeed, afford any confirmation of the popular belief, that grand-parents are the ruin of children. Yet with what a wise affection he was endowed, the little grandson will not forget, who, while attending school for a short time at Providence, was wont to bring home his cards marked "Good boy," or "Excellent," and to receive from a drawer in the study-table a welcome reward if the report was favorable, and to meet a grave, grieved look if no approving testimonial was at hand; and who, at a later day, used to sob himself to sleep at the thought that he should never see his grandfather again.

On the Thanksgiving of which we speak, Dr. Wayland was in unusual spirits. He was recovering slowly from the attack of the spring. He had received an enforced release from toil. The country had just declared for liberty by the first election of Lincoln; nor did any one anticipate the madness that would take occasion from the election to reveal itself.

He was cheerful, even mirthful, keenly enjoying the humor of others, and contributing his share to the common hilarity.

Persons who knew the earnestness of his mind, and the grave character of his pursuits, often supposed him to be wanting in a sense of humor. We learn from Rev. Dr. Hoby, that while Mrs. Emily C. Judson was in England, on her return from Burmah, allusion having been made to Dr. Wayland as a suitable biographer of Dr. Judson, she expressed her entire satisfaction in all but a single respect. She feared that Dr. Wayland would not appreciate the lighter aspects of Dr. Judson's character — his refined sense of the ludicrous, his keen wit. Never was there a greater mistake. His humor was not, indeed, trifling and flippant. It was earnest and practical, like all his faculties. But his appreciation of wit in others was quick, and his drollery was often irresistible. It gleamed in his conversation, sometimes in his letters; not often in his public discourses or printed works.

Sometimes he went, at the call of affection, to visit his kindred in Boston, or one of his sons in New Haven or Worcester, or his sisters in Saratoga. As a guest he was the most easily entertained of mortals. In fact he did not want to be entertained at all. Nothing could be too simple for him, nothing too quiet. He made allowances for everything; the youngest, the most inexperienced housekeeper need not fear him. He would not permit any of the ordinary engagements of life to be neglected on account of his presence.

The few visits which he made he enjoyed keenly. He was exceedingly appreciative of the kindness shown him on such occasions, and added immeasurably to the pleasure of his hosts by his readiness to be pleased. After visiting a friend and former pupil, he writes, —

> "We both enjoyed ourselves extremely, and are quite invigorated. My mind, old as it is, is quickened by your conversation; and your constant kindness has brightened the links which bind me to humanity. It will be long before your home and its surroundings grow dim in my recollection. It is all delightful to think of, as it was more delightful to enjoy."

A member of a family, at whose hospitable house he was an occasional and welcome visitor, says, —

> "I often used to walk with him, and ever found him a delightful companion. I think he never failed to talk to me about religion, but it was always naturally. He was very sportive, but his mirth was never such that religious conversation was out of consonance with it."

No doubt it would have been greatly to his advantage if he had allowed himself more frequent journeys and visits, in which his mind might be removed for a time from its accustomed employments, and become quickened by contact with differing yet sympathetic spirits. But he had no faculty for relaxation.

To Mr. Loring he writes, in 1864, —

"... Through life I have had no recreation. I do not know how to *amuse* myself; and it has been one of my greatest misfortunes. I suffer from it to-day, and have all my life. By the way, were you not astonished at Chalmers' two or three hours a day of labor, and the mighty results he accomplished? Should we not all learn a leaf out of his book? I am satisfied that with us we keep the brain too long at work at a time. I think this, and too little sleep, and no recreation, lead to softening of the brain."

Almost the only thing he could not do was to amuse himself. It was only when he bade his mind rest, that it disobeyed him. Once, on his return from a journey which he had enjoyed very much, but which had been less extended than was expected, he said that, after being away from home and from his work a little while, he seemed to hear a voice say, "What doest thou here, Elijah?" and he felt that he must hasten home, and be doing something. It was strange that he did not apply to himself the lesson which he taught to others. In "Salvation by Christ" (sermon upon "A day in the life of Jesus of Nazareth") he has said, —

"The religion of Christ is merciful, and ever consistent in its demands. It requires of us all labor and self-sacrifice; but to these it affixes a limit. It never commands us to ruin our health and enfeeble our minds by unnatural exhaustion. It teaches us to obey the laws of our physical constitution, and to prepare ourselves for the labors of to-morrow by the judiciously conducted labors of to-day. . . . We sometimes meet with the industrious, self-denying servant of Christ in feeble health and with an exhausted nature, bemoaning his condition and condemning himself because he can accomplish no more, while so much yet remains to be done. To such a one we may safely present the example of the blessed Savior. When the apostles had toiled to the utmost of their strength, — although the harvest was great and the laborers few, — he did not urge upon them additional labor, nor tell them that, because there was so much to be done, they must never cease from doing. No; he tells them to turn aside and rest for a while. . . . The Savior addresses the same language to us now. When we are worn down in his service, he would have us rest, not for the sake of self-indulgence, but that we may be the better prepared for future effort."

He by no means ignored, nor under-estimated, the need of relaxation for ministers, and for all persons, although it must be confessed that he did not highly value the amount of reinvigoration, bodily, mental, or spiritual, that is gained at fashionable watering-places and European capitals. He wrote to a minister who was setting out on a pedestrian excursion to the White Hills, —

"I think highly of your 'tour to the Hebrides.' It will add greatly to the vigor of your constitution. Begin slowly, and walk only ten or fifteen miles the first day, gradually increasing the distance. It will do more for you than much more extended travel in the ordinary manner. Try and have some sort of good to do on the way. This will add interest and profit to the excursion."

And again to the same: —

"I hope that you have returned with increased health. I advise you to go on these expeditions as often as you can get company. You will gain more in every way than in a railroad car, and will confirm your health and extend and intensify your love of nature greatly. You will also see much more of mankind. I would stay at private houses as often as possible."

But we have wandered from the story of a day. At about nine he rejoined the family in the parlor. After prayers were his own devotions, and those who occupied the room above the study heard his voice last at night, as it had been the first sound in the morning. Through the greater part of his life he had worked till far into the night; but in later years, convinced of his need of more sleep, he always went to bed at ten. Unless his mind had become absorbed in some subject or event of unusual interest, he slept soundly, or if, for a moment, aroused, was soon again asleep.

The Sabbath presented features less marked than would have been the case had not the employments of each secular day been so largely spiritual. He was not legal in his spirit, and did not constrain himself, nor others, by rigid Sabbatical rules. His life was the expression of duty, modified by the spirit of Christian liberty. It was from love, it was for his pleasure, that he spent the day in exercises of devotion. He read nothing but the Scriptures, and books tending directly to spirituality. The religious newspapers and periodicals (except the Herald and Magazine) he did not read on the Sabbath. In his manner, in his conversation, as he came from his study on that day, there was a calm seriousness, not a sadness, as of one who had been looking on eternal realities.

In the house of God he longed for simplicity, for sincerity, first of all; for life, fire, zeal; for the truths of the Scriptures, urged in the spirit of the Scriptures, and enforced by the words of the Scriptures. He was habitually charitable in his judgments, and this charity seemed to grow more pervading as he advanced in years. But if there was any instance in which he approached the verge of harshness, it was in his estimate of sermons that had in them no power to save or sanctify the soul; that were made up of cold, formal, and fruitless exhibitions of doctrine, however orthodox, of brilliant rhetoric, metaphysics, political economy, or kindred material. But when the *truth* was presented with warmth, with earnestness, with an evident desire for the salvation and edification of the hearer, he was satisfied and gratified, however homely the garb. We quote again from Mr. McKenzie's Christian Visitor: —

" Coming down the aisle of my church one day, after closing the services, I met him with his hand extended;

and without letting go of my hand, he drew me to his side in a pew, and said, — 'My son' (thus he was in the habit of addressing me), — 'my son, I have been pained and grieved with your preaching here to-day. It has been evident to my mind that you have been pleased and proud over your finely-wrought and finished discourse. Those sermons were, as sermons, very creditable to your ability as a preacher, but very discreditable to you as an ambassador of Christ. There was too much learning and too little of Christ in them. Go home, my son, and burn them up, and on your knees weep over your delinquency.' All this was said with a tenderness and affection which put to silence any disposition to rebel under the stroke which my proud ambition had received. On another occasion he said, 'My son, you preached the gospel to-day, and may God bless you. You did me good. I feel that I am a poor hell-deserving sinner, but that Jesus Christ is my Savior. When a preacher makes me feel thus, I know he is proclaiming the truth, and that God is with him.'"

CHAPTER XIV.

HUMANITY. — FOREIGN MISSIONS. — HOME MISSIONS. — SLAVERY. — INDIVIDUAL EFFORT. — TEMPERANCE. — THE "SOCIAL EVIL." — EAST TENNESSEE. — THE SYRIAN CHRISTIANS. — PROVIDENCE AID SOCIETY. — BUTLER HOSPITAL FOR THE INSANE. — RHODE ISLAND HOSPITAL. — PROVIDENCE REFORM SCHOOL. — RHODE ISLAND STATE PRISON. — EMPLOYMENT OF MONEY. — PRIVATE BENEFACTIONS.

THE reader of the preceding pages does not need to be informed that, as the love of God was the controlling motive of the life we have sought to delineate, so its great aim was to manifest the fruits of that love by deeds of unselfish benevolence to man.

Dr. Wayland's private kindness, and his public labors; his patient watchfulness over the young, and his toils in the pulpit and in the pastoral office; his efforts for the enlargement and liberalization of high education, and for an increase in the numbers and in the efficiency of the ministry, — were simply the expression of his desire for the elevation and happiness of humanity.

Believing, as he did, that the gospel of Christ contains a remedy for every human woe, it was natural that he should desire to see mankind enlightened by its teachings and informed by its spirit; and hence his devotion to the cause of Christian missions. His opinions upon the true method of conducting missions are indicated in the Memoir of Judson, in his report on "the relative proportion of time that should be devoted by missionaries to teaching, translating, and other occupations, apart from preaching the gospel," presented in 1854 to the Missionary Union, and republished by the A. B. C. F. M., and in the following extracts from letters.

To Rev. Dr. Anderson, who was about to visit the Eastern missions of the American Board: —

"I have just received your letter, and answer it immediately, for I presume your time is short, and you want the points before you as soon as possible.

"The general movement of Christianity has been this. It begins among the poor. Persecution keeps it there, and makes every man a minister, or preacher, or exhorter, or propagandist. Thus it spreads, and nothing can withstand it. Soon it silences persecution, and is then ashamed at finding itself among the poor and middling classes. It aspires to take its place among the rich, wise, learned, and worldly. This leads to the casting pearls before swine; that is, a surrender of principle to expediency, which is the meaning of that much abused passage. Hence results the doctrine that a man must be learned in order to be a minister. This separating the ministry from the people leads to the distinction of clergy from laity, and ends, in its last result, in Puseyism and Romanism, and, in various forms, to the sanctity of the office, and the idea of a quasi or real priesthood. Arrived at this point, the church stands still, becomes one with the world, and dies out in formalism, until some new development breaks forth and pursues the same course. In this country, Congregationalism and Presbyterianism advocated a learned ministry. They did not increase, except by hereditary succession. The Baptists began on the other principle, and overran the country in spite of all opposition. The Methodists followed, and did the same thing. They both now are aiming at a learned ministry, and they are standing still, except in new parts of the country, where these ideas do not prevail.

"The same is true among missionaries. In this country and in India, the whole effort is to dress up Jesus Christ so that we may not be ashamed of him when we meet him in respectable society. But he will not be so introduced. He still cleaves to his old friends, the publicans and sinners; and if we will not meet him in such company, he turns away from us. I have, of course, no objection to education in the ministry; but I object to giving it a place not authorized by Jesus Christ, and making it a *sine qua non;* thus establishing a ministerial caste. I think that these ideas lie deeper than has been commonly believed. Look at the example of Jesus Christ. He took the lowest place, and so long as his disciples kept there, the cause of Christianity prospered. He put the ploughshare in the lowest stratum, and kept the point down. We raise the point, and it flies out of the ground; then it moves very easily, and the horses caper off with it; but it turns up no soil; the ground bears no fruit; and, plough over as much as we will, it is all barren as the plain of Sodom. But I did not mean to make an allegory; I only suggest this for you to think of. It concerns your mission; and were I going on such an errand, I should like to have every suggestion, even were it but of the smallest value."

To the same: —

"I rejoice that you are succeeding so well with your debt. I thought that the Jubilee would lift you over. Let us thank God and take courage.

"In reading your last Missionary Herald, I was somewhat impressed with the thought that you are relying too much on intellectual cultivation in the preparation of your native ministry. I fear you will fall into the New England error. Give the Holy Spirit some freedom of action, and see if he is not able to do something by himself, if he will."

To the same: —

"I read your Memorial Volume some time since, and intended to read it a second time before writing to you. This, however, may detain me for a week or two, and so I will not wait.

"It is throughout a noble volume. Dr. Hopkins' sermon, with which it commences, is very able, and a fitting introduction. The work accomplished, of which it gives an account, is really wonderful, and is the mere forerunner of greater things to come. It commenced when Napoleon was at the zenith of his power, and all the Continent of Europe was at his feet. Compare the two.

"It is a branch of the stone cut out of the mountain without hands — that is, if stones have *branches*.

"But the idea that you have developed is worth all the labor of fifty years, — and without that labor it could not have been consummated, — that the business of the foreign missionary is to sow the seed, establish a church, and then go on to regions beyond, thus following in the steps of the apostles. This puts a wholly new aspect on the work, and breaks up effectually the tendency to make every station a little Christian city, with translators, periodicals, presses, schools, and every element of European civilization.

"It is a delightful work to set forth thus the labors of half a century, of which you can say with Æneas, 'All which I saw, and part of which I was,' and to show at what cost of talent and labor such a work was accomplished. *Tantæ molis erat Romanam condere urbem.* You see how you put me in mind of Æneas again. I rejoice that you have been spared to do what no one but you could have done. It is the most important volume on the subject of missions that I have ever seen. God be with and bless you."

We also insert the following from Dr. Anderson, written in 1866: —

"His reliance for the conversion of the heathen world, so far as means are concerned, was upon agencies strictly spiritual. I think I may say that he had no confidence in any system of missionary operations which went upon the ground of placing much reliance upon purely secular agencies, even though the result of relying upon spiritual agencies was, that 'not many wise men after the flesh, not many mighty, not many noble, are called.' We ever agreed that the solution of the great problem, how the rich, and great, and noble, shall be reached, will be in some way consistent with a determination not to know anything, among the heathen, save Jesus Christ, and *him* crucified. And we had a common anxiety that missionaries descended from the Puritan stock should carry this principle out at all hazards. On the great practical points in the working of foreign missions, I am not aware that we differed. I speak of the *foreign* field, for I think that I was obliged to dissent from some of his later speculations on what may be called the *home* department of the foreign missionary work. I recollect saying as much to him, but am not able now to lay my hand upon the pamphlet containing these views."

We presume that, in the closing words of the above paragraph, Dr. Anderson refers to the sentiments which Dr. Wayland put forward in 1859, in a little tract, entitled "Thoughts on the Missionary Organizations of the Baptist Denomination." In this pamphlet he proposed that the existing missionary bodies, with their large and cumbrous machinery, should be laid aside, and that each association of Baptist churches should undertake, for itself, the conduct of missionary affairs, on a scale proportioned to its resources.

While, however, Dr. Wayland had definite views of the best means of promoting missions, and while he deemed it right to express them, he did not adhere to them with anything like pertinacity or pride of opinion.

To a minister he writes, —

"I have no trouble about your views of organization, &c. I do not care a fig about the question. Only let missions prosper, and I care not how it is done.

"The feelings of personal regard, which you so kindly express, I cheerfully reciprocate. I have cherished a sincere attachment to you ever since I knew you, and have rejoiced in your prosperity and usefulness. I have dissented from many of your views, and I presume you have from mine; but this is only what is likely to happen with men differently constituted. May God go with you, and grant you much of his presence and blessing."

With many laborers in the missionary field Dr. Wayland maintained an interesting correspondence. We had hoped to present some of his letters to these brethren; but, from causes which we are unable to explain, they have failed to reach us. The following letters contain passages of interest bearing on his personal feelings towards his missionary brethren.

To a minister: —

"I do not look at Mr. Vinton as you do. There were various things in his communication which I am disposed to wish had been modified. But, at the same time, I must make allowance for the feelings of a man who had been travelling for years in the pestilential jungle, laboring for souls, while we had been living at home in our ceiled houses; who had given his life, not to us, or to the committee, but to Christ and the perishing Karens; who had labored like *two* men, while others were sitting at ease. I would unloose the shoe-strings of such a man. He will have a bright crown when his Karens meet him before the throne.

"As to the question on which we differed in opinion: when I am asked whether this paper is white or black, I look at it, and must give such an answer as is consistent with truth. If a man *comes* to me, and declares, 'If you say that it is white, Mr. —— will go to New York, and therefore it will be better for the cause that you call it gray,' I reply, 'I must say what it is, and nothing else.' If I am asked whether I want Mr. —— to go to New York, I will answer that question by itself; but I will not answer one question when I am asked another. Such has always been my rule in all business transactions. I may very likely have erred; but I have found the rule to work well, to say just what I mean, and nothing else.

"In all these matters I look at the Karens, and the souls of the perishing, and the brethren who are laboring for them. We at home are doing a small work in comparison with them — some of them, at least. I think that the missions are in a bad condition. . . . If you do not think so, you ought to say so; but if this is my opinion, I am not called upon to withhold it because I cannot see things as others do. In these matters we must all exercise the right of private judgment, and act according to our individual light.

"May God overrule all to his glory and the good of souls.

"We expect too much of missionaries. We do not allow them enough relaxation in the way of revisiting their homes. We ought to bring them back statedly once in ten years, if they need it. We lose continually our best men in the very meridian of their usefulness. We judge otherwise of pastors at home. We send them abroad in pursuit of health; and we destroy our foreign pastors in the hour of our greatest need. We must make some change in this matter."

We have seen that Dr. Wayland was eminently an American. He loved his country. Its privileges awoke his gratitude, its real glories kindled his patriotic pride, and its many defections from perfect rectitude saddened him. When he was in a foreign land, the happiest hours he spent were those passed in thinking of his home and preparing for his return. To a relative who was travelling on the Continent he wrote, —

"As to this country, with all its faults, I would hardly talk with a man who should compare it with France. Our curse is, that we do not know our own blessings. *O fortunatos nimium sua si bona nôrint!* was the reflection ever in my mind when I looked upon Europe and thought of my own country."

He was very jealous for the honor of his native land, and did not concede to any foreign nation the right of moral censorship over America.

To Rev. Dr. Hoby, 1852: —

"The country is prospering, and we manage our affairs not very well, but at least as well as you. You are greatly excited about the Cardinal and Puseyism, which we do not intermeddle with. Slavery is bad, and we labor with it as well as we can; but it cannot be cured yet. We thank you for your labors in our behalf, but would excuse you if you could find anything as valuable to do at home, or in Poland, or Italy, or Hungary."

From his profound patriotism, and his religious ardor for the diffusion among all men of the gospel of Christ, sprang his zeal for home missions — a zeal that grew more animated as he advanced in life. With his later years, while he never for a moment dreamed that too much had been done for the conversion of the remote heathen, he deeply felt that the wants of our own land had been overlooked. In 1854 he remarked, in a sermon, that very many professing Christians were, apparently, more deeply interested for the heathen of distant continents, than for the ignorant, destitute, and perishing of the next street.

He did not scatter his sympathies over far-off territories, forgetting his own neighborhood. He was deeply interested in the work undertaken by state conventions, of caring for weak churches, and for localities destitute of gospel privileges.

"He used to say," remarks Dr. Caswell, "'Look over Rhode Island, and see these feeble churches. We have lived here thirty years, and they are feeble still. Something must be done to raise them up.'"

Longing to see all the inhabitants of his own country practising the precepts of Christ's gospel, and attaining to the highest happiness and elevation of which they are capable, there could be no doubt as to his estimate of American slavery.

In 1854, in his speech on the Nebraska Bill, he said, —

"Taking Christ for my example, and striving to imbibe his spirit, can I do otherwise than take to my bosom all the oppressed and down-trodden children of humanity. Jesus Christ, my Master, is not ashamed to call them brethren; and can I have any partnership in an attempt to trample them under foot? The Union itself becomes to me a thing accursed, if I must first steep it in the tears and blood of those for whom Christ died."

In 1857, in his letter to the investigating committee of the American Tract Society, he urged the duty of the society to bear its testimony, through its publications, in regard to the sinfulness of enslaving, buying and selling human beings, and the numberless sins of which slavery is the parent.

In a previous chapter we have exhibited the profound and deepening abhorrence of slavery which possessed him as he was re-writing his Moral Science.

To a minister, who wrote informing him that, in the state where he resided, every citizen was compelled, on becoming a voter, to take an oath to support the constitution and laws of the United States, and inquiring whether he could properly take that oath while determined not to obey the Fugitive Slave Law, he wrote, —

"In all such cases of conscience as that to which you refer, I think the proper direction is that of the apostle, 'Whatsoever is not of faith is sin.' That is, what we cannot do with a clear conscience, do not at all, for we greatly injure our conscience whenever we in any manner put a blind before its eyes. I did not know that voters were obliged to take any oath. I never was thus called upon. If you cannot do it with a clear conscience, you must abstain. You can express your views on the subject; you can say which party is, in your opinion, right, and which wrong, and give your reason for not voting. Consistently adhere to right, calmly and lovingly, and all men will esteem you more in the 'long run.'

"I have always declared that I would never aid to arrest a fugitive, or do a thing to return him to slavery. I would make no opposition to the government, but would patiently endure the penalty. This I have a right to do, on the principle that I must obey God rather than man. Whether this applies to the oath to obey the constitution and laws, I do not see clearly, and would advise you to consult the best judicial authority as to the meaning of the oath. Is it intended to express agreement to every particular, or, as the old Puritans had it, to the general scope and tenor? It is easy to show your love for the constitution and laws in other ways besides voting."

One of his sons having sheltered and aided a fugitive slave, and having given him a letter to Dr. Wayland, the latter wrote, —

"I gave him money, clothes, mittens, and shoes. It is a clear case of humanity, and I was happy to give him shelter. . . . I am glad you sent the poor fellow."

When slavery had gained supremacy over all departments of the government, and was aiming at conquests yet greater, he not unfrequently expressed his conviction that a crime of dimensions so vast, and of character so atrocious, God would take into his own hands, and would punish with an overthrow so marked, that none could fail to recognize the divine hand, although the particular agencies through which this result would be reached, he could not predict.

On his entrance upon active life, Dr. Wayland entertained a high estimate of the good to be achieved by organizations. But the experience of many years gradually impressed him with the belief that too much confidence is liable to be placed in combined action, to the neglect of personal, individual exertion. In speaking of the efforts for the removal of slavery, he often cited the example of that eminent and pious Friend, John Woolman, who went individually to slaveholders, setting before them the commands of God, and inducing many of them to emancipate their slaves. He was of opinion that a similar course of fidelity and religious labor, if pursued by Christian persons, would have produced the most benign results, at the smallest possible expense of human suffering.

The same remedy suggested itself to him for the evil of intemperance. If Christian men would go personally to the drunkard and to the rum-seller, and would converse with them, appealing to their consciences, and pleading with them to abandon their ruinous courses, accompanying every effort with prayer for the aid of the Holy Ghost, he believed that it could not fail to receive the divine blessing. He had often heard persons in Providence speak of one ——, a dram-seller, whose shop was notorious for the number of young men who had there been led to ruin. Dr. Wayland determined to converse with him; but his efforts were for a long time in vain. The man seemed to have an intuitive knowledge of Dr. Wayland's design, and carefully avoided him. But at last they met. Dr. Wayland conversed with him fully, kindly, plainly; plying every motive by which a moral being could be influenced. Mr. —— replied, that it was all true; that he knew how he was despised and hated by the good, and that he could but despise himself. Often, he said, he was on the point of giving up a traffic so fraught with misery. He subsequently became much changed in character, abandoned the liquor trade, and when he died, his friends had hopes of his salvation.

In 1860 Dr. Wayland writes to a minister,—

"I am much perplexed about the Maine Law question, and do not see my way clear. All our efforts thus far seem failures, and I fear we are on the wrong track. What is the use of trying to punish Irishmen for selling liquor, when mayors, judges, and the highest men in social standing make people drunk at parties? No law can be effective which does not strike all alike. The 'rummies' (I mean the poor ones) have the best of the argument. I do not know what to do. Church members are as much in the wrong as others. In such a case, what can law effect? Hence I doubt. If you, however, see your way clear, act according to your conscience, but weigh the matter well."

The "vice of great cities," and the means of staying its frightful devastations, greatly enlisted the attention of Dr. Wayland. For years he rendered all the moral encouragement, and all the pecuniary aid in his power, to a woman who had taken on herself the work of rescuing the fallen, and seemed singularly fitted by boldness and address for this service. But he had reason, subsequently, to believe that he had been deceived in her character. We do not know that he saw any light as to the means of removing this hideous stain upon our civilization.

His hand was ever ready for the relief of distress. In 1864, when a movement was made to send supplies to the destitute in East Tennessee, he was conversing with two gentlemen, one of whom expressed some doubt as to the character and worthiness of the recipients. "But," said the other, "they are starving" Dr. Wayland said, very emphatically, "That is enough. There is no need of saying any more."

He could not with indifference hear of suffering in regions however remote. In 1860, when news reached this country of the massacre of the Syrian Christians (so called) by the Druses, and of their distress, he wrote at once to R. Anderson, D. D., —

"I read your circular in part before our monthly concert. I also read a letter on the same subject from Mr. Johnson, our consul at Beyroot, which I received the day before. We appointed two gentlemen to take charge of the subject, and coöperate with other churches and associations who might become interested in the matter. Would it not be well for you in Boston to have a central committee, that we might act through you, and try and send a ship-load of provisions as soon as possible to those starving sinners? I say sinners, for there is apparently little to choose between them, only one sect has fallen among thieves, and is stripped, and wounded, and left half dead. If you have anything to suggest, please do so. It is a matter in which we must act in concert, and secure *provisions*. Money at a place where food is at famine prices, would be of small value."

A few days later he writes, —

"I wish you would use the enclosed $—— in such manner as will do the most good to the Syrian sufferers. I cannot wait for our committee."

He was increasingly impressed with the belief, which we suppose is now universal among all intelligent philanthropists, that to help the poor to help themselves, is to give them the truest relief. During the prevalence of the panic of 1857, when labor was paralyzed, and starvation was imminent, he originated the conception of the Providence Aid Society, whose main design was to supply work to the destitute by opening an office, where all needing employment and those able to furnish employment could be brought together. With this design was united the plan of districting of the city, and the efficient action of district committees, who should personally investigate and judiciously relieve all cases of want coming under their notice. Of this organization he was president from its origin to his death, and was rarely absent from the monthly meetings of the board.

His name and his labors were prominent alike in the foundation of the Butler Hospital for the Insane, and in every movement for its increased efficiency. He was for a long time a member of the board, and even during the years when he was most engrossed with labor, he never failed in the discharge of the duties imposed by this trust.

To quote from the annual report for 1865, —

"For many years he labored as a trustee of this hospital with a zeal and fidelity exceeded by no one, giving us the benefit of his clear, practical views and matured judgment. It is not for us to dwell upon his world-wide fame as a teacher and an author, a philanthropist and a Christian; but as connected with this and other institutions and societies, whose object is the relief of human suffering, we may testify to his remarkable individual exertions to promote the end sought to be attained. To do his duty was his only concern; self-sacrifice was of no account with him. The cause which he knew not he searched out, and the blessing of those that were ready to perish rested upon him."

Perhaps the noblest charity of the state, alike in the beneficence of its purposes and in the magnitude of its endowments, is the Rhode Island Hospital. In the inauguration of this enterprise, Dr. Wayland was able to render a service of extreme delicacy and of great moment. In June, 1863, when the people of Providence were intensely interested in everything which related to the proposed scheme, at a public meeting, designed to stimulate into increased activity the generous purpose of the community, a gentleman of high standing presented an offer, from a number of persons (not named), to give one hundred thousand dollars, upon various conditions, one of which was, that the interest of twenty-five thousand dollars should be devoted to the support of the chaplain of the institution, who should be, through all time, a clergyman of the Protestant Episcopal church. In case this condition was declined, the sum of seventy-five thousand dollars was offered.

The subject was referred to a committee, of which Dr. Wayland was the chairman; and to him was assigned the delicate and responsible task of drawing up the report. He accepted the appointment with sincere regret, both because he was reluctant to tax his brain with new duties, and also because he feared that his convictions would compel him to propose a course that would inflict pain on those who had been his warmest friends. He presented a report, which, while accepting the other features of the offer, recommended that the condition in question be declined, in accordance with the predominant sentiment of the community. But the recommendation was made in such terms, and the report was instinct with such a spirit, as to avoid the difficulties which had been feared, and to unite all humane and public-spirited citizens in the proposed charity. The report was adopted, the people of Rhode Island were enthusiastic in their support of this truly noble and Christian enterprise, and the gentleman by whom, as was supposed, the previous offer was made, has ever been its most munificent benefactor.

Upon the establishment of the Providence Reform School, Dr. Wayland (though never a member of the Board of Trustees) visited it every week; constantly advised with the efficient superintendent, Mr. Tallcott; for a long time knew personally each of the boys, and understood his disposition, his temptations, his history. He was always ready to address the lads. Mr. Howland, who, for ten years, had charge of providing the speakers at the Sabbath services, says, —

"I once engaged two young gentlemen to speak, and also Dr. Wayland. The day proved frightful. There was a foot of snow on the ground, and it had been, and was still, raining. The snow was all slosh. The two young gentlemen did not appear; but, punctual to the hour, there was Dr. Wayland."

He said to Mr. Tallcott, —

"Remember, the boys must always have their Thanksgiving service, as well as their dinner. I would rather go without my dinner than that they should not have some one to speak to them."

He rarely failed to address them six or eight times in the year; and (what may create a little surprise) there was no speaker, out of five or six hundred, whom the boys were more glad to hear. He did not often tell them stories; he spoke quite slowly; at times it was not easy to hear him; yet somehow he reached their hearts. When the question was asked them, "Whom do you want to have speak to you?" the two names most often uttered in reply were, Gilbert Congdon * and Dr. Wayland.

His words became proverbs. Years after, the boys who had left the school would write back to the superintendent, "As Dr. Wayland said to us once;" and would quote some remark that had become "like a nail fastened in a sure place."

Upon the day of Public Fast, observed after the murder of Abraham Lincoln, he spoke to the boys from the words, "As for our Rock, his way is perfect." "And when is anything perfect?" he asked. "Why, it is perfect when it cannot be made better. If you have done a thing perfectly you cannot improve it." Then he showed how God's way, throughout the war, had been perfect; how all our defeats had been for our good. Then he told them of Abraham Lincoln, of his boyhood and his early hardships. He showed him toiling in the flat-boat, and mauling rails. As he spoke, the boys leaned forward to listen. Then he carried Mr. Lincoln through all his life, and drew the lesson that even in this event God's

* A highly esteemed minister of the Society of Friends.

way is perfect, and that all would be for our good. He was full of the subject, and spoke for an hour and a half; but there was not one weary hearer.

A year and a half later, a gentleman, visiting the Reform School, said to one of the lads, "Do you remember Dr. Wayland?" "O, yes." "What do you remember that he ever said?" "Well, he said that if anything is perfect, you can't make it any better."

Not more than a week before Dr. Wayland's last sickness, he called at the school just at dusk, and said to Mr. Tallcott, "Is not this your evening for meeting?" Mr. Tallcott replied, "No, this is not the regular evening; but we will have the boys together in five minutes, if you will say a word to them." So they were assembled; and he spoke to them, in the September twilight, for the last time.

The reformation of convicts was an object that lay very near Dr. Wayland's heart. He was for many years president of the Prison Discipline Society. Later in life, having, as we have seen, become impressed with the need of individual effort for the successful achievement of the various objects of Christian reform, he began to labor as a Sabbath school teacher in the Rhode Island State Prison. But he soon was satisfied that the external condition of the inmates was such as to preclude any bright prospects of their moral amendment. In June, 1851, Governor Allen offered him an appointment upon the board of inspectors, to whom the care and government of the state prison and of the Providence county jail are committed. Dr. Wayland inquired if any salary attached to the office; and on hearing that the labor was entirely gratuitous, he at once accepted the appointment. The new board elected him chairman, and devolved on him, for many years, the preparation of the annual report.

Both the prison and the jail had been, from the commencement, a source of annual loss to the state. In 1846, the expense exceeded the revenue seven thousand five hundred and sixty-three dollars; in 1848, five thousand four hundred and sixty-two dollars. This outlay would not be worthy of mention had it been the price paid for the proper results, physical and moral, of imprisonment. But the prison was, probably, in all essential particulars, the worst of any in New England, perhaps in any of the northern states. The state prisoners were confined in cells erected in 1837. These cells are "constructed of solid blocks of split granite, with the external faces exposed to the cold blasts of winter, and the internal faces devoid of furring and covering. During the cold weather, the crystals of frost remain upon the interior surfaces of the cell walls, sparkling in the light, and chilling the shivering prisoners. These stone dungeons are imperfectly ventilated as well as lighted."* The air was close and almost insufferable. It was not without difficulty, at times, that visitors, unwonted to the atmosphere, could avoid violent nausea upon entering the prison. The result was a great prevalence of rheumatism, pulmonary diseases, and diarrhœa, as well as the peculiar malignity of contagious and epidemic complaints. Nor was any hospital provided for the sick.

The moral effects were even more discouraging. The number of cells being less than the number of inmates, two or more were confined together, and each corrupted his comrade. No chapel was in existence, and the efforts of the chaplain and of other benevolent persons were conducted under every disadvantage. There was no library, or other means of useful relaxation. The female convicts, from ten to twenty in number, were crowded into two or three cells, the young and erring catching contagion from the utterly depraved. And while such was the condition of the *prison*, that of the *jail* was vastly worse.

The institutions did not answer a single purpose for which they were designed. They did not reform, they

---

* From a report of the board.

did not awe; indeed, they did not even restrain and confine the convicts, as appears from the fact that in September, 1847, twelve made their escape in a single day.

The legislature, in the same month in which Dr. Wayland and his associates entered on their duties, made an appropriation to erect a new wing for the state prisoners. This building, under the direction of the board, was constructed upon the most approved plans, and in accordance with all the teachings of modern intelligence and humanity. The cells are well warmed and lighted, affording ample security, yet inflicting no needless suffering. And, while the unwholesome and every way hideous cells of the old wing cost eighteen hundred and fifty dollars each, the new cost but two hundred dollars each.

The report for 1852 states that the female convicts were all employed in useful labor, under the care of a suitable matron.

In the report for 1853 it is stated that a library of four hundred volumes had been provided, to which all the prisoners had access, with excellent results upon their character.

In 1854 the board were able to report that, for the first time since its establishment, the income of the prison had exceed its outlay by one hundred and twenty-five dollars, and that this revenue was not secured at the expense of humanity and moral reform, for the physical, mental, and moral condition of the inmates was higher than ever before.

"The health of the prisoners has been remarkably good since they were removed into the new wing. They spend most of their leisure in reading; their moral character is manifestly elevated, and a large portion of them leave the prison better prepared to become useful members of society than when they entered it."

But the condition of the jail still remained little ameliorated. The inmates had been removed into the old cells before described. Three or four were confined in a single apartment. No adequate provision was made for the constant employment of the prisoners. "A prison of this character thus becomes a very expensive nursery of vice."

While such was the condition of the male prisoner, that of the female inmates of the jail was incomparably worse. In each of three small cells, ten feet by twelve, six or eight females were confined night and day.

"The atmosphere, in spite of every effort, becomes intolerably offensive. The physician expresses his apprehension that it will generate jail fever. Is the General Assembly of Rhode Island willing any longer to perpetuate a system so utterly useless, expensive, and inhuman? The convicts, although they have done wrong, are men and women, entitled to the privileges of humanity. They have a right to a comfortable abode, pure air, and the opportunity of moral improvement. When the law sentences them to imprisonment, it does not sentence them to breathe an atmosphere which exposes them to pestilence and death. When the law sends them to a house of 'correction,' as it is termed, it surely does not mean to place them in circumstances where reformation is impossible, and where the only result of our treatment must be to render them more depraved and hopelessly vicious."

Moved by these appeals, and not uninfluenced, we may believe, by the evident self-forgetfulness and public spirit of him, who, with his associates, was devoting time, labor, and wisdom to the interests of humanity, the General Assembly made an appropriation; and in 1855 the report states that a wing, calculated to afford accommodation for thirty male and thirty female prisoners, was approaching completion. They also report that the income of the *prison* exceeded its expenses — fourteen hundred and thirty dollars. Although this revenue was more than swallowed up by the expenses of the *jail*, yet a proof was afforded that, under favorable circumstances, no reason existed why such an institution should not be self-supporting.

The reports, not confined to a bare exhibition of the internal state of the prison, offer, from time to time, important suggestions, bearing on the jurisprudence and legislation of the state. At one time the evil effect, as well as the expensiveness to the state, of very short sentences, is indicated. At another it is estimated that the amount annually paid by the county of Providence alone, for imprisonment for intoxication, if divided among the several towns of the state, would purchase for each a library worth two hundred dollars. At another time it is stated that the people of Rhode Island are taxed, in connection with the jail, five thousand seven hundred and fifty-one dollars a year to support the rum-shops of the city of Providence. In 1853 the report suggests that, —

"The interests of the prison have been injuriously affected by the too frequent exercise of the pardoning power, where no new facts in the case are elicited. If the laws are unjust, they ought to be amended. If they are just, they should be administered without respect to persons. It, however, frequently happens, that convicts who have respectable friends, or who have reserved from the avails of successful villany a sufficient amount to employ earnest counsel, are pardoned; while the friendless, and those who have surrendered all, serve out the full time of their sentence. This creates in the minds of the prisoners a feeling of injustice, and deprives the law of its moral effect on the criminal. It seems unreasonable for the state to employ its highest talent and integrity in the detection and trial of crime, and then to set aside the whole proceeding on the pleading of counsel."

In 1856 the inspectors report that the prison had earned over its expenses, two thousand and thirty-one dollars, although this balance was again swallowed up by the expenses of the jail. They also report, —

"Probably no workshop in the city, employing the same number of men, has suffered so little from illness as the state prison. The moral character of prisoners is, so far as we can discover, improving. . . . Some of those whose term has expired are now at work in the city, and have secured the confidence and respect of their employers. . . . The library is diligently and extensively read. The fees for the admission of visitors enable us to make large additions to it annually. . . . The prison has, during the past year, been lighted with gas, in order to afford the inmates better facilities for mental improvement. The inspectors are happy to report that the state prison has now become what the General Assembly has always intended to make it — a valuable means of reformation. Men who have been seduced into habits of vice have here the opportunity of acquiring the means of self-support, a taste for intellectual improvement, and a knowledge of their duty from the Word of God."

The report urges the total removal of the old prison, and the erection in its place of a wing, on the plan of those already constructed.

The chaplain * reports, in 1856, that the completion of the new chapel afforded greatly increased means for the religious instruction of the prisoners, and that "in no year has the improvement in the physical, mental, and moral condition of the inmates been more decided and cheering." The completion of the new wing also afforded room for the establishment of a hospital.

The report for 1857 states that the prison had earned twelve hundred and fifty-six dollars over its expenses, and that the annual deficit in the jail accounts had been lessened. With this report was transmitted a catalogue of eight hundred and fourteen volumes, composing the library.

In 1859 the inspectors report that the earnings of the prison over its expenses had more than balanced the expenses of the jail, and had left six hundred and thirty-five dollars returned to the state treasury from the two establishments. "The state prison and jail have, therefore, for

* Rev. William Douglass, to whom we are greatly indebted for much valuable information with reference to Dr. Wayland's labors in behalf of the prison.

the first time, paid their own expenses and exhibited a balance in favor of the state. For this result the Board of Inspectors have earnestly labored, and they congratulate the Assembly on its final accomplishment." The volumes in the library amounted, at this time, to nearly a thousand.

The report just alluded to is the last, we believe, prepared by Dr. Wayland, although he remained for several subsequent years a member of the board.

The report for 1860 exhibits a revenue from the prison of twenty-eight hundred and seventeen dollars, and (after deducting a loss of two hundred and thirty-four dollars for the jail) a profit to the state of twenty-five hundred and eighty-three dollars. The improvement in the character of the prisoners still continued.

For 1862 the board, for the first time, reported that the prison and the jail had *each* earned more than its expenses. The same fact is stated in the reports for the two following years.

It is not, probably, too much to assert, that the prison became as well managed, as healthful, as favorable to moral reform, as any similar institution in America. It is proper to add, that in efforts for these results the whole board faithfully coöperated. Rewarded only by a sense of good done to mankind, they did not withhold any sacrifice of time or labor. Their attendance at the meetings was regular, and their regard for the interests of the institution was, in many cases, more exact than they would have paid to their own.

But we apprehend that we do not err in saying, that of all these movements Dr. Wayland was the informing and animating spirit. His name and his character assured the public, and especially the legislature, that no private interest was to be advanced; and his unwearied activity inspired all his associates. In his labors he fixed his attention upon three objects. He desired to promote, within proper bounds, the *comfort* of the prisoners. He carefully watched the character of their accommodations and of their provisions. When complaint was made of the beef served out to them, he examined it, ate of it, was satisfied that it was not suitable, and caused it to be changed. He sought to *economize* the resources of the state, — with what success has already been shown. And he desired to attain, as the great end, the *diminution of crime*. In reaching this result, he was of opinion that the chief agency is the production of a change in the moral character of the criminal. We are thus led to remark another aspect of his labors.

His relation to the prisoners was not merely official. He stood to them not alone as inspector to convicts, but as man to his brother man; or, rather, shall we not say, as the disciple of Christ to sinning, suffering, immortal beings. His labors for the spiritual good of the prisoners were unceasing. He conversed with them personally in their cells; he frequently preached to them on the Sabbath; and always he was present at the more familiar exercise of the Sabbath school, of which he was superintendent, in addition to teaching a class. "It was truly wonderful," one gentleman says, who was associated with him as a teacher,* "to see him standing among them, and to see them talking as freely, as familiarly, as if he were their friend from childhood." The marvellous power of illustration, the faculty for simplifying difficult truths, the knowledge of the Word of God, that had held scholars in rapt attention, were now put into requisition to draw to Christ these outcasts from society. "I have never," said a convict, "believed that there was anything in religion; but when I see Dr. Wayland come here to talk to us, I know that religion must be real." Nor was it, on his part, a matter of duty and of constraint. He loved to be there. During a year or more previous to his pastoral labors in the First Church, he not only attended the Sunday school,

* Professor Chace.

but remained during the morning service, and listened, with interest and edification, to the practical, evangelical sermons of his former pupil, Mr. Douglass, the chaplain. Often he said to Mr. Douglass, "I never enjoyed religious worship more than in this place and with this congregation;" and once he remarked, "If the Savior were to visit the city of Providence, I do not know any place where he would be more likely to be found than here." At another time, in speaking of his Bible class, he said, "I love to present the gospel to these poor fellows in all its precious promises. How adapted it is to meet the wants of just such men!"

These labors were not ineffectual. On more than one occasion there were indications of religious interest. During the fall of 1856, several of the inmates seemed deeply impressed, and many appeared changed in heart.

He writes to his son, —

"November 17, 1856.

"I spent the morning and afternoon of yesterday at the prison. Instead of the Bible class before preaching, we had a conference meeting, and invited the prisoners to speak. Five arose and gave quite interesting accounts of their religious hope, and several more would have spoken if there had been time. I asked one to pray, and he prayed with much fervor, appropriateness, and simplicity. I think that as many as seven or eight give us reason to hope for them, and others are deeply anxious. Some of them speak of a joy in religion that is wholly inexpressible. Their manifestations of gratitude to those who have labored to be useful to them are very touching. I went over in the afternoon and had an individual conversation with most of them. It was a very edifying occasion. I do not know how it is, but some how or other, all my instincts lead me to labor among the poor and forsaken. I enjoy worship vastly more among these poor prisoners than among the rich, and well dressed, and intelligent. That prison chapel is much more pleasing to me than the —— high steeple, or any of our quartette choir congregations. It seems to me vastly more like the true worship of the Master."

It was probably at the meeting referred to in the above letter, that a lad arose, — Pat Cassidy by name, — who had been a pickpocket in New York, had come to Rhode Island to rob, and had been arrested and found guilty of a larceny in Woonsocket. After speaking of his past life, he said, —

"A week or two ago, I was sick, and afraid I should die. Mr. Douglass came, and asked me if I was prepared to die. I asked him how that was going to be. He taught me this prayer: 'God, be merciful to me a sinner.' He made me say it over and over, till I had it by heart. Well, as I said that prayer, I thought of that '*me* a sinner.' I felt worse and worse. I walked up and down my cell, feeling as if the floor would split and let me into hell entirely. And I tell yez there is a hell. And so I walked with the sweat dripping off of me, till, at last, I remembered the words I heard Dr. Wayland say here: 'The blood of Christ Jesus, his Son, cleanseth us from all sin;' and as soon as I thought of that, says I [clapping his hands], 'Pat, my son, that is for you.' And then in a minute don't you think but I was ready to fly?"

Pat continued to give every proof of being a Christian. After serving out his time, he went to Fall River, and joined the Second Baptist Church. He was afterwards employed on board a vessel sailing to New Orleans. In that city he caught the yellow fever and died; and in the opinion of a pious man, the master of the vessel, who was with him, he died in hope.

During the same period of religious interest, W. H., who had been sentenced for life for murder committed in a state of intoxication, gave evidence of being converted. Some years later (having been in prison fifteen years), he was pardoned, and has ever since maintained an irreproachable character. We mention these as examples. Some persons, of course, there were, in whom Dr. Wayland and others found themselves deceived. It is impossible to say whether they were self-deluded; whether they really meant well, but were afterwards led astray; or whether they were intentional deceivers.

Dr. Wayland's solicitude did not cease when those who had been inmates of the prison were no longer under his official care. On their departure, he counselled them, tried to secure employment for them, and, in one instance, when a released prisoner thought that, with a little capital, he could perfect an invention which he had devised, Dr. Wayland loaned him fifty dollars, which, we believe, still remains as a permanent investment.

And they felt a pride in their relation to him, in being Dr. Wayland's pupils, that went far to restore the self-respect which imprisonment is so apt to obliterate, and without which reform or high character is impossible. A gentleman, who was a fellow-teacher, relates, that once, in the south part of Rhode Island, he saw a number of men at work in an oat-field, one of whom said to him, "How do you do, professor? How is the doctor?" The gentleman seeming not at once to recognize him, he said, "I used to see you at the institution, and I used to be in the doctor's class." Another gentleman relates a similar incident as happening to him in the interior of Massachusetts. Their pride and their fondness for "the doctor" seemed to overmaster the reluctance with which they would naturally recall the circumstances under which they knew him.

The view which we have given would be defective and erroneous, if we did not add that in his sympathies and benevolent efforts there was nothing of weakness or maudlin tenderness; there was no "coddling" of the prisoners, nor — during the latter part of his experience — any want of understanding of their character. He knew them to be depraved, designing. He was convinced, as he once said, that the word of a convict is utterly worthless when he sees the least possibility of securing a release by any representations which he can make. He realized fully how unspeakably difficult is the work of reforming criminals.

Yet, though often painfully disappointed by the inherent wickedness of those whom he had believed to be reformed, he was never disheartened. If not as hopeful, he was still as unwearied, as ever. Partial or complete failure did not paralyze his efforts, for he knew that a deed done for God, and from love to Christ, must bear some fruit. "I do not know what will be the result," he once said, when commencing a very arduous undertaking; "but I know that if I do my duty, God will be glorified." Ingratitude did not chill his humanity, for it was not inspired by any desire for gratitude. Kindled by no human motive, it could by no human power be quenched. It was the love of Christ that constrained him. The same unwearied tenderness that had been shown towards him, a sinner, by one who loved him and gave himself for him, he gladly exercised towards his fellow-sinners. Whatever the result of these efforts on earth, he knew that nothing could rob him of the heavenly reward promised in those unspeakably divine words, "I was in prison and ye visited me," — words which were often music in his thoughts, as he went, laden with years and with growing infirmity, from his home to the prison; as he entered the iron door; as he sat down beside murderers, and forgers, and burglars, and told "the poor fellows" of the blood that cleanseth from all sin.

He felt a peculiar pleasure in applying the gospel to the hearts of these men, because he was sure that this was just what they needed; that this could save them, and this alone; and also because he felt that the gospel gains new trophies and testimonies of its power by the renovation of such hearts.

We have thus far referred mainly to the amount of time and labor bestowed by Dr. Wayland upon the numerous benevolent enterprises in behalf of which his feelings were enlisted. But he was quite as prompt to expend money in aid of every deserving charity as to offer advice, or to express sympathy. He never urged upon others a liberality which he did not enforce by his own example.

Indeed, it would be impossible to give a just idea of his character, without alluding to his pecuniary contributions in answer to the private or public calls of humanity. He regarded almsgiving as a duty, placed by the divine Teacher on a level with the practice of prayer and a holy life. And how he should secure the means of discharging this duty, and of cultivating the graces which flow from it, often occupied his thoughts. Inheriting nothing from his parents save their prayers, he could gain the means of benevolence only by the exercise of industry and economy.

He desired, in the first place, to keep out of debt. His experience at Andover, his weeks of dependence, burned into him a hatred and horror of indebtedness that ever remained. He often quoted, as expressive of his view of the use of money, the lines of Burns: —

> "Not for to hide it in a hedge,
> Not for a train attendant,
> But for the glorious privilege
> Of being independent."

"One of the first elements of freedom," he once said, "is to be out of debt." And in writing to a former pupil, just entering in life, "I am glad you see the day-star of competence. It tells of yet better things, if anything can be better."

He once said that when he began his life in Boston, he expended up to the limit of his income. But one of his deacons asked him, after a year or two, "Are you saving anything?" On his replying that he was not, the deacon said, "You ought every year to lay up something. Now begin at once. I want you to lend me some money, and to lend me some every year." Acting on this suggestion, he laid up something (though often very little) every year. One result of this wise frugality was, that he was able to say, "I never had a bill presented to me twice, nor have I ever had a note discounted."

Next to being independent, his desire was to be able to respond to the claims of benevolence. When he was twenty-one years old, it will be remembered that he rejoiced in the prospect of his tutorship, because it would enable him to have something for charity. And in 1856 he wrote, "I must work in order to have something to give away. I have been losing by bad investments."

A gentleman, always active in every scheme of philanthropy that appeals to the citizens of Providence, has said, "I never liked to go to Dr. Wayland in regard to any charitable object, for he always gave more than I felt that he ought." In 1863 the committee charged with soliciting donations for the Rhode Island Hospital were agreed that Dr. Wayland ought not to be called on, for they felt that he was not able to give anything. But meeting a member of the committee, he said, "Why have you not called on me?" His friend replied, "We did not feel that it was right to ask you to contribute." Dr. Wayland said, "I could not sleep if this thing were going on and I had done nothing towards it;" and he put down his name for a sum that in proportion to his means was munificent. The gentleman with whom he held the conversation was afterwards reminded by other members of the committee that they had agreed not to ask Dr. Wayland for anything. He replied, "What could I do? I could not help myself. He *would do it*."

In 1862–3, owing to the advance in prices and the diminished sale of his books, he found that he was in danger of being without the means of benevolence; and, in order to have something for charity, he gave up housekeeping, and all the pleasures associated with his home, and boarded for several months. Later, during the war, he heard a friend speak of the expensiveness of tea, and the good that might be done with the cost of this article. He at once resolved to forego this, one of his few luxuries, and for several months continued to do so.

It was about this time that he received a letter from a brother in the ministry, not personally known to him, who wrote expostulating with him on his inconsistency in inculcating the duty of Christian self-denial while living in luxury. He read the letter with thoughtful attention, seeing in it the sincere utterance of a conscientious man, and feeling only the kindest sentiments towards the writer. But probably Dr. Wayland did not see, and certainly those about him could not discover, any particular in which he could live with more plainness, with less self-indulgence.

He had a religious horror of waste. He once expressed the opinion that, in the millennium, people would so conduct their cooking, and all their household arrangements, as to secure perfect economy. All these things, which would have been petty if their end had been selfish accumulation, were ennobled by the object which he had in view. It was by economy only that he was enabled to practise benevolence.

He was never wealthy. Those who thought otherwise were deceived by the largeness of his donations. During many years he gave away more than half of his entire income. After his salary as president ceased, the amount of his contributions was necessarily diminished. With his later years he inclined to bestow his benefactions without the intervention of a society, " seeking out the cause that he knew not," and enhancing the value of the gift by the sympathy which accompanied it.

It would be unjust did we fail to add, that, in all his plans of benevolence, from his marriage in 1838, his wife coöperated with a largeness of heart and an openness of hand akin to his own. During twenty-seven years of a life united by the holiest ties, neither cherished a desire for the relief of woe, or for the promotion of the welfare of mankind, that did not find in the other a full and absolute sympathy.

CHAPTER XV.

THE REVISED MORAL SCIENCE. — THE CUSHING INSTITUTE. — THE WARREN ASSOCIATION. — SICKNESS AND DEATH. — MEETING OF THE GRADUATES. — FUNERAL. — THE PUBLIC. — PROFESSOR CHACE'S ADDRESS.

THE chief labor of Dr. Wayland, after the publication of his Memoir of Chalmers, was the revision of his Moral Science. He urged forward this work with an earnestness that was, perhaps, intensified by the remembrance of the repeated interruptions that had already prevented its completion — an earnestness that probably led him again to transcend the limits of his endurance.

The proof-sheets of this volume were corrected during the summer of 1865, and the work was issued from the press in October.

In 1854, Thomas P. Cushing, Esq., of Boston, a native of Ashburnham, Worcester County, Mass., a brother-in-law of Dr. Wayland, had died, providing in his will for the establishment of an academy of high order in his native town. Dr. Wayland was named as an executor, and subsequently was, by the act of incorporation, made one of the trustees of the "Cushing Institute." The first meeting for the permanent organization of this educational enterprise was to be held at Ashburnham, on Wednesday, the 6th of September, 1865.

Although much enfeebled by the almost unparalleled heat of the past summer, and by the literary labor to which we have just alluded, Dr. Wayland could not neglect this opportunity of testifying his unabated interest in the cause of popular education. Accordingly, leaving his home on the 5th of September, and spending one night in Fitchburg, he reached Ashburnham at the time appointed for the meeting. He was elected president of the Board of Trustees, and, at the request of his associates, presented, in brief, his views as to the course of studies that should be pursued in the Institute.

"He mentioned particularly reading, spelling, penmanship, music, grammar, rhetoric, geography, arithmetic, geometry, algebra, trigonometry, natural philosophy, botany, physiology, agriculture, drawing, book-keeping, intellectual and moral philosophy, political economy, and the science of government. In this plan neither ancient nor modern languages found a place.

"The scholars were to be carefully instructed in the use of their mother tongue. He would have no classes preparing for college, on the ground that an arrangement of that kind might foster distinctions, excite jealousies, and produce an unhappy effect on those students who should confine themselves to English studies. Besides, he had observed that in schools where the classics are taught, they receive undue honor and attention. On this point he spoke at length and with great earnestness. He believed that the Cushing Institute would better subserve its design by giving instruction in the English branches only." *

At the conclusion of the meeting of the trustees, Dr. Wayland returned to Fitchburg, and on the following day proceeded to Providence. We are favored with a letter from Lewis H. Bradford, Esq., of Fitchburg, from which we quote: —

"The evening previous to the meeting at Ashburnham, having heard that Dr. Wayland was at the Fitchburg Hotel, I called upon him, with one of the trustees. We found him intensely interested in the proposed institution. He

* For this statement of Dr. Wayland's views, as expressed to the trustees, we are indebted to Rev. A. P. Marvin, of Winchendon, Mass., who was present at the meeting, and made careful minutes of the remarks of the chairman.

remarked that the light which it might shed upon this part of the country was of incalculable importance.

"On the evening of the following day, he attended the prayer meeting of the Baptist church in Fitchburg. In the course of a brief address, he exhorted us most affectionately to be faithful followers of the Lord Jesus, and then united with us in prayer. No one but myself knew the name of the speaker, but all felt the power of his presence and the weight of his counsels.

"I gave him my arm at the door of the church, and as we walked to the hotel, he said, 'Brother Bradford, we do not pray enough; we lack faith in God.' Arrived at the hotel, he kindly insisted that I should go to his room, where he conversed with me at some length with regard to the future of the Institute. One idea which he expressed I shall never forget — that its object should be to make *men* and *women*, rather than *graduates;* of the latter, he said, we had an abundance.

"I took this opportunity to thank him, in behalf of our Baptist church, for his generous contribution towards the erection of our first place of worship."

Dr. Wayland writes to his sister, on the 16th of September, 1865, —

"There has been a long time of silence, and I presume that I am in fault. The truth is, that I have been, for the past four or five weeks, daily receiving proof-sheets, and have been obliged to read them carefully. Work of this kind consumes a great deal of time. When this was finished, I made a visit to Ashburnham — quite a journey for me. But it is now all over, and I am at rest. And yet, I hardly know why, — perhaps because travelling, or the hot weather, has had an unfavorable effect upon me, — I have felt dizzy and 'powerful weak' since my return. I hope to be revived by the rain and cool weather, which may now be reasonably expected. During the whole summer we have been but moderately well. I have been the best of the three, and from this you may judge of the average."

On Wednesday and Thursday (September 13 and 14) the "Warren Association" met, with the "Central Baptist Church," in Providence. Dr. Wayland manifested a peculiar interest in this meeting, and was present at all of its sessions, excepting those held in the evening. He was appointed chairman of the committee on the "state of religion in the churches," but requested his friend, Rev. W. L. McKenzie (a member of the committee), to prepare the report. Towards the close of the morning session on Thursday, the regular business of the association having been completed, the question arose whether the body should adjourn until its next annual meeting, or should spend the afternoon in a conference upon the facts presented in the report just named. Rev. Dr. Lincoln, chairman of the committee of arrangements, said to Dr. Wayland, "Will you address the association, if we decide to hold an afternoon session?" Assent to this proposition having been secured, there was no objection to a temporary adjournment.

During the intermission, Dr. Wayland seemed to look forward with profound interest to the afternoon meeting. As his own home was at a considerable distance from the church, he dined with a friend. His meal was hastily finished, and saying to his host, "I must not fail to be at the afternoon meeting in season," he hurried away. He was in his seat among the very first, before the meeting was called to order.

When the introductory services were concluded, he arose and addressed the congregation.

"The sentiments and emotions expressed by this servant of God, 'this prophet of our captivity' (as one has styled him), were a most solemn reiteration of what, for a few years previous, he had been proclaiming through the press, and uttering in private. . . . In his public addresses, in the pulpit, in the prayer and conference-room, in his personal interviews with numerous visitors in the retirement of his study, in books, tracts, and letters, everywhere and in every way, he had been sounding an alarm; faithfully reproving and warning, earnestly inviting and *beseeching* the churches and the ministry to awake and cry mightily unto God to pour forth his Spirit, and revive his sinking cause." *

His words were earnest, affectionate, instinct with truthfulness, and profoundly impressive. They could hardly have been more so, had he and his brethren been aware that he was soon to put off this tabernacle, and that they all, among whom he had gone preaching the kingdom of God, should see his face no more.

Dr. Wayland was followed by Rev. Dr. Swain, of the Congregational church, who gave some account of the state of religion in his denomination, inviting his brethren to contend earnestly for the common faith of evangelical Christianity. Addresses were also made by other ministers and by laymen. The entire service produced a deep and quickening effect upon the minds of all who were present, and, we are warranted in believing, made itself felt in a higher spirituality, in a more absorbing zeal, and in more fruitful labors during the succeeding year.

For some months previous to the time of which we write, Dr. Wayland had seemed conscious of a growing sense of weariness. It was with increasing effort that he performed even the slightest labor. He had written to his son in August, "We are living by main strength;" and, still later, "We are only middling. . . . I work in the garden three or four hours a day; but this is all. I crawl about, accomplishing very little." Yet, except as he felt the depression natural to this enforced inactivity, he was cheerful, and probably looked forward to several years of labor in the service of his Master.

On Friday, the 22d of September, he found himself exceedingly weak. He took his accustomed walk in the afternoon, with a relative who was visiting the family, but seemed unusually silent. After tea he went to his chamber much earlier than was his habit. On Saturday, for the first time in many years, he did not leave his bed.

* Rev. W. L. McKenzie, in the Christian Visitor.

His debility was extreme. He had occasion to sign his name, but the signature bore little resemblance to his ordinary writing. His physician was summoned. He prescribed entire rest, and some simple remedies. With an intimate Christian friend, who sat by his bedside for an hour on Sunday evening, Dr. Wayland conversed freely and fully. He said,—

"I feel that my race is nearly run. I have, indeed, tried to do my duty. I cannot accuse myself of having neglected any known obligation. Yet all this avails nothing. I place no dependence on anything but the righteousness and death of Jesus Christ. I have never enjoyed the raptures of faith vouchsafed to many Christians. I do not undervalue these feelings, but it has not pleased God to bestow them upon me. I have, however, a confident hope that I am accepted in the Beloved."

Monday was a bright September day; and in the course of the forenoon, while he was alone, he arose, dressed himself, and went into his garden. Did he know that it was for the last time? and did he desire to bid farewell to the cherished objects of his care? or was he rather testing his remaining strength? It was not without considerable difficulty that he returned to the house, and regained his room.

On Tuesday morning, when his breakfast was brought to him, Mrs. Wayland observed that he used only his left hand. She said, "Shall I not feed you?" and he consented. Alarmed at this acknowledgment of weakness, she called Dr. Miller in consultation; but he did not recommend any remedies in addition to those already prescribed. At about ten o'clock, Mrs. Wayland left the room to write a telegram. Returning, she found her husband lying across the bed, motionless, helpless. Apparently he had attempted to rise, possibly hoping to repeat the experiment of the previous day; or, perhaps, wishing to see of how much effort he was capable. The fatal blow had fallen! He was placed in a more natural position, and lay unconscious except when aroused, his eyes closed, his right side paralyzed. His oldest son arrived in the evening, and said to him, "Do you know me, father?" He responded by a look of affectionate intelligence, and distinctly articulated, "Yes," but immediately relapsed into unconsciousness. All hope was gone. The disease was steadily drawing nearer and nearer to the sources of life; it was only a question of time.

On Thursday, his two sisters (now, with him, the sole surviving children) arrived; and on Friday morning his second son, summoned by the sad tidings from his home in Michigan, took his father's hand. But it returned no answering pressure, nor did eye or voice give token of recognition. On Saturday afternoon, September 30, 1865, at twenty minutes before six, his wife, his three sons, his sisters, and the wife of one of his sons, stood by his bedside. It was apparent that a change was at hand. His daughter, seeing that the end was near, gently laid her hand upon his cheek. He opened his eyes with an expression of entire consciousness, — the same, exactly, that his children had so often seen on his face in the study, as he looked up from his Bible, — and of perfect intelligence, but an intelligence not of this world. Then he closed them, and all was over.

Throughout all the week, when any one, known to be a friend of the family, was seen upon the street, he was constantly met with the inquiry, "How is the doctor to-day? Is there any hope?" On the morning of Sunday, the tolling of the bell of the First Baptist Church from eight to nine o'clock smote heavily on a thousand hearts, telling them that the servant of God and the friend of man was no more on earth. In the prayers offered in all the sanctuaries of the city, the bereavement was noticed. When Mr. Douglass said to the convicts in the state prison, assembled in the chapel, "You will never see your friend Dr. Wayland again; he is dead," he was interrupted by their sobs.

Monday's issue of the Providence Journal contained an obituary article from the pen of Professor James B. Angell,* the fidelity and gracefulness of which could not be surpassed. On the same day, the Baptist ministers of Boston and New York, at their accustomed meetings, passed resolutions commemorating the event. On Tuesday afternoon the graduates of the college met at Manning Hall. Hon. H. B. Anthony was called to the chair. A series of resolutions was read by Professor Chace. A silence of several minutes ensued, broken at last by Chief Justice Bradley. He was followed by A. Payne, Esq., E. H. Hazard, Esq., President Sears, Rev. Dr. Caswell, and Rev. Dr. Lincoln. Dr. Caswell, overcome by an emotion unspeakably more eloquent than words, was unable to complete his remarks.

Meanwhile the deceased lay, resting at last, within his chamber, the windows of which looked forth over the garden, down the slope, towards the gleaming river. But he saw now a brighter river, trod greener fields, beheld a more beautiful paradise. No painful traces of sickness and infirmity were visible. All was calm, majestic repose. To borrow his own language, "Death was a conquered foe, and had been able to erect no trophy over the mortal tabernacle that had been the scene of conflict."

On Wednesday, at half past nine o'clock, after prayer had been offered with the family, the body was removed to the First Baptist Church. It was placed in front of the heavily-draped pulpit, and for an hour all who desired passed in order, and looked for the last time upon those well-remembered features. The corporation and Faculty of the University, the delegates chosen by the Baptist ministers of Boston, gentlemen of eminence in literature, in science, in political station, citizens of Rhode Island, and residents of remote states, joined in the sad procession. But profounder and more significant was

* Now president of the University of Vermont.

the emotion manifested by the young disciple whom he had guided, the aged saint whom he had consoled, the poor whose sufferings he had relieved, and the members of the long down-trodden race who had enjoyed his earliest and almost his latest Christian labors.

Rev. Dr. Caldwell, pastor of the church, read passages of Scripture and offered prayer; Rev. Dr. Caswell made an address most appropriate and comforting; and Rev. Dr. Swaim closed the services with prayer. The remains were then borne to the "North Burying Ground." In this ancient cemetery are the graves of many of the friends with whom he had loved to labor for the welfare of mankind; of Nicholas Brown, and Professor Goddard, and Moses B. Ives, and of others honored in the history of Rhode Island for their private worth and public services. There, on a knoll which receives the last rays of the setting sun, in a spot selected by himself, where were resting the remains of his early-lost wife, and of his infant daughter, he was buried.

For many weeks and months the ground had been parched with drought. During the dry season Dr. Wayland had prayed daily, at the family altar, for two things: for showers to refresh the thirsty soil, and for an outpouring of the Spirit of God. As he was laid in the grave, the rain fell in torrents — a promise of spiritual blessings, of answers to prayer yet to be realized.

On the following Sabbath, commemorative sermons were preached from many pulpits in Providence, Boston, New York, and in other parts of the country. These discourses were delivered, not alone by clergymen of his own denomination; professors of faiths widely differing from his paid a tribute of reverence to a great soul and a noble life.

A committee, appointed by the graduates of Brown University, requested Professor George I. Chace, of the class of 1830, to deliver an address commemorative of "the virtues and services of Francis Wayland." On Tuesday, September 4, 1866, the alumni of the college assembled in the First Baptist Church. After prayer by Rev. Dr. Fisher, of the class of 1847, the following ode, composed by Hon. Thomas Durfee, of the class of 1846, was sung: —

Early to him the Spirit came,
  His soul with love and light to fill,
And touched with consecrating flame
  His mighty mind and lordly will.

It called him to a noble task —
  To teach the Fair, the Good, the True:
With pious heart he did but ask
  To do what God would have him do.

From near and far his pupils flocked,
  Drawn by report that told how well
His keen analysis unlocked
  The wisdom hid in learning's shell.

Year after year, and day by day,
  O'er them he watched, for them he wrought,
To lead them in the wisest way,
  To teach them that which best were taught.

Yet for themselves he bade them think,
  Regarding reason more than rule,
And freshly from experience drink
  The truths untaught by book or school.

And as they clomb the path he showed,
  Before them, luminous and pure,
His genius, ever towering, glowed
  To guide and keep their feet secure.

Meanwhile, with tireless tongue or pen,
  He toiled to spread the gospel light,
And kindle in the hearts of men
  The love of freedom and of right.

No caste or color, clime or creed,
  The fervor of his zeal allayed;
He strove to realize in deed
  The life of love for which he prayed.

The convict, in his lonely cell,
  The slave by cruel fetters bound,
The heathen, with his fetich fell,
  In him a benefactor found.

For his belief was no mere word,
  Which, uttered, dies upon the lip;
But faith, co-working with the Lord,
  In meek and loving fellowship.

He sleeps in death: its darkness hides
  The grandeur of his form and face:
The lesson of his life abides,
  A blessing to the human race.

Professor Chace encountered an unavoidable embarrassment; for those to whom he spoke had known so well the life and character which were to form the theme of his discourse that he could hardly hope to equal the demands of their recollections, or of their conceptions. Yet such were the keenness of his analysis, the justness of his portraiture, the heartiness of his appreciation, and the felicity of his diction, that the most enthusiastic were satisfied, and the coldest were kindled into sympathy.

THE END.

APPENDIX.

THE following list of the published writings and addresses of Dr. Wayland, although necessarily imperfect, will perhaps be of some value for purposes of reference: —

1823. Discourse on the Moral Dignity of the Missionary Enterprise.
1825. Discourse on the Duties of an American Citizen.
1826. Discourse on the Death of the Ex-President.
1828. Report on System of Public Schools in Providence.
1830. Murray Street Discourse — Certain Triumphs of the Redeemer.
1830. Discourse before the American Sunday School Union at Philadelphia, on Encouragements to Religious Effort.
1830. Inaugural Address before the American Institute of Instruction.
1831. Moral Efficacy of the Doctrine of the Atonement — Sermon preached at the Installation of Rev. William Hague (Boston).
1831. Phi Beta Kappa Oration (Brown University) — Philosophy of Analogy.
1831. Address before the Providence Temperance Society.
1832. Sermon at the Ordination of Rev. John S. Maginnis (Portland) — Objections to the Doctrine of Christ crucified, considered.
1832. Sermon at the Installation of Rev. William R. Williams (New York).
1832. Sermon on the Abuse of the Imagination.
1832. Sermon before the Howard Benevolent Society, on Motives to Beneficence.

1832. Volume entitled "Wayland's Discourses," comprising most of the public addresses above mentioned.

1834. Missionary Sermon on the Moral Conditions of Success in the Propagation of the Gospel.

1835. Discourse at the Dedication of Manning Hall, on the Dependence of Science upon Revealed Religion.

1835. Elements of Moral Science.

1836. Elements of Moral Science, abridged.

1837. Elements of Political Economy.

1837. Elements of Political Economy, abridged.

1837. Two Discourses on the Moral Law of Accumulation.

1838. A Discourse at the Opening of the Providence Athenæum.

1838. Limitations of Human Responsibility.

1840. Introduction and Notes to the Pursuit of Knowledge under Difficulties.

1841. Address before the Rhode Island Society for the Promotion of Domestic Industry.

1841. Discourse on the Death of Nicholas Brown.

1842. Discourse on the Affairs of Rhode Island.

1842. Thanksgiving Discourse on the Occasion of the Close of the Rhode Island Rebellion.

1842. Discourse on the Claims of Whalemen (New Bedford).

1842. Volume entitled "Thoughts on the Present Collegiate System in the United States."

1843. Article in Bibliotheca Sacra (1st series), on the Doctrine of Expediency.

1844. Articles on the Debts of the States, in North American Review and Christian Review.

1845. Article on the Life of Dr. Arnold, in North American Review.

1845. Domestic Slavery considered as a Scriptural Institution — Discussion with Rev. R. Fuller, D. D.

1846. Discourse on the Death of Professor William G. Goddard, LL. D.

1846. Address at the Dedication of a School-house in Pawtucket, Rhode Island.

1847. Three Discourses on the Duty of Obedience to the Civil Magistrate.

1847. Introduction to Recollections of Real Life in England.

1847. Article on Prison Discipline, in the North American Review.

1848. Memoir of Miss Harriet Ware.

1850. Report to the Corporation of Brown University.

1850. University Sermons.

1851. Address before the Rhode Island Society for the Promotion of Domestic Industry.

1852. Address before a Meeting of the Citizens of Providence, on Occasion of the Death of Hon. Daniel Webster.

1853. Memoir of the Life and Labors of Rev. A. Judson, D. D.

1853. Sermon on the Apostolic Ministry (Rochester).

1854. Address before the American Institute of Instruction.

1854. Address at Union College, on the Education demanded by the People of the United States.

1854. Report to the American Baptist Missionary Union, on the Relative Proportion of Time that should be devoted by Missionaries to Teaching, Translating, and other Occupations, apart from preaching the Gospel.

1854. Address before a Meeting of the Citizens of Providence, on Occasion of the Passage of the Nebraska Bill.

1854. Elements of Intellectual Philosophy.

1856. Notes on the Principles and Practices of the Baptist Churches.

1856. Address before a Meeting of Citizens of Providence, on Occasion of the Assault upon Hon. Charles Sumner.

1857. Letter to the Investigating Committee of the American Tract Society (New York).

1857. Discourse on the Death of Rev. J. N. Granger, D. D.

1857. Discourse on the Death of Moses B. Ives, Esq.

1857. Two Discourses on the Present Crisis.

1858. Sermons to the Churches.

1858. Salvation by Christ.

1858. Revised Edition of Sabbath Hymn and Tune Book, for the Use of the Baptist Churches.

1860. Address at a Meeting auxiliary to the American Tract Society (Boston).

1861. Introduction to the Life of Trust.

1861. Tract, on Prayer for the Country.

1862. Tract, entitled "How to be Saved."

1863. Letters on the Ministry of the Gospel.

1864. Memoir of the Christian Labors of Thomas Chalmers, D. D., LL. D.

1865. Article entitled "John Foster on the Duration of Future Punishment," in the American Presbyterian and Theological Review.

1865. Article on Choice of Companions, in Hours at Home.

1865. Article on the Ministry of Brainerd, in the American Presbyterian and Theological Review.

1865. Address to the Citizens of Providence on the Assassination of Abraham Lincoln.

1865. Revised Edition of Elements of Moral Science.

In addition to the foregoing were various contributions to the Baptist Magazine, the Macedonian, the Christian Watchman, the Christian Reflector, the Examiner, the Christian Review, the Providence Journal, and the Michigan Christian Herald.

INDEX.

Waiting for the Verdict. By Mrs. REBECCA HARDING DAVIS, author of "Margaret Howth," "Life Among the Iron Mills," &c., &c. One vol., octavo, illustrated, bound in cloth. Price, $2.00.

This is a story of unusual power and thrilling interest.

"It is not only the most elaborate work of its author, but it is one of the most powerful works of fiction by any American writer."—*New York Times.*

The Life and Letters of Rev. Geo. W. Bethune, D.D. By Rev. ABRAHAM R. VAN NEST, D.D. One vol., large 12mo., illustrated by an elegant steel-plate Likeness of Dr. Bethune. Price, $2.00.

This is one of the most charming biographies ever written. As a genial and jovial friend, as an enthusiastic sportsman, as a thorough theologian, as one of the most eloquent and gifted divines of his day, Dr. Bethune took a firm hold of the hearts of all with whom he came in contact.

Dr. Bethune's Theology, or EXPOSITORY LECTURES ON THE HEIDELBERG CATECHISM. By GEO. W. BETHUNE, D.D. Two vols., crown octavo (Riverside edition), on tinted paper. Price, cloth, $4.50; half calf, or morocco, extra, $8.50.

This was the great life work of the late Dr. Bethune, and will remain a monument of his thorough scholarship, the classical purity and beauty of his style, and above all, his deep and abiding piety.

"When the Rev. Dr. Bethune, whose memory is yet green and fragrant in the Church, was about to leave this country, he committed his manuscripts to a few friends, giving them discretionary power with regard to their publication. Among them was the great work of his life; in his opinion *the* work, and that from which he hoped the most usefulness while he lived, and after he was dead, if it should then be given to the press. This work was his course of lectures on the Catechism of the Church in which he was a burning and shining light.—*New York Observer.*

The Life and Labors of Francis Wayland, D.D., L.L.D. Late President of Brown University; by his sons, Hon. Francis Wayland, and Rev. H. L. Wayland. Two vols., 12mo., illustrated by two steel-plate Likenesses of Dr. Wayland. Price, $4.00.

This is a most interesting memoir of one of those noble specimens of a man, who now and then appear and direct, and give tone to the thoughts of their generation. The volumes are enriched by Dr. Wayland's correspondence with most of the leading men of his day.

DR. WAYLAND'S WORKS.

Principles and Practices of Baptists. By Francis Wayland, D.D. 1 vol., 12mo., cloth. Price, $1.50.

"We hope the book will find its way into every family in every Baptist church in the land, and should be glad to know it was generally circulated in the families of other churches."
Christian Chronicle.

A Memoir of the Life and Labors of the Rev. Adoniram Judson, D.D. By Francis Wayland, D.D. Illustrated with a fine Portrait of Dr. Judson. Two vols. in one, 12mo. Price, $2.50.

The Elements of Intellectual Philosophy. By Francis Wayland, D.D. One vol., 12mo. Price, $1.75.

Sermons to the Churches. By Francis Wayland, D.D. One vol., 12mo. Price, $1.00.

"Dr. Wayland is a clear thinker, and a strong and elegant writer. His Sermons are models worthy of study."—*Christian Intelligencer.*

The Life and Letters of Mrs. Emily C. Judson (Fanny Forrester), third wife of the Rev. Adoniram Judson, D.D., Missionary to Burmah. By A. C. Kendrick, Professor of Greek in the University of Rochester. With a steel-plate Portrait of Mrs. Judson. One vol., 12mo. Price, $1.75.

The Sexton's Tale, and other Poems. By Theodore Tilton, Editor of the New York Independent. Illustrated by an ornamental title-page and elegant tail-pieces for each Poem, printed on tinted paper, and bound with beveled boards and fancy cloth. One vol., 16mo. Price, $1.50.

This is the first collected edition of Mr. Tilton's poems, many of them as sweet as any thing in our language.

The Autobiography of Elder Jacob Knapp, the great Revivalist. One vol., large 12mo., with steel-plate Likeness of the Author. Price, $2.00

In this book the author gives an account of the many won derful scenes through which he has passed, more interesting and remarkable than any tales of fiction.

A new Enlarged Edition of Mrs. Putnam's Receipt Book, and Young Housekeeper's Assistant. A chapter on Carving has been added, and a very large number of new receipts, with special reference to economy in cooking. One vol., 12mo. Price, $1.50.

A Complete Manual of English Literature. By Thomas B. Shaw, Author of "Shaw's Outlines of English Literature." Edited, with Notes and Illustrations, by William Smith, LL.D., author of "Smith's Bible and Classical Dictionaries," with a Sketch of American Literature, by Henry T. Tuckerman. One vol., large 12mo. Price, $2.00.

www.ingramcontent.com/pod-product-compliance
Lightning Source LLC
LaVergne TN
LVHW020126110826
845151LV00001B/289

* 9 7 8 1 4 2 5 5 4 1 6 5 1 *